Praise for

If Mama Were Here: *Living Without Mama*

"I would hope that if there are people who are dealing with terrible problems right now and feel that they will never get over their sorrow, that they will consider reading this book. Even if you wish to read an inspiring story, this may very well be the book for you."

— Andrew Gugurich, Marquette Mining Journal

"*If Mama Were Here* brought tears to my eyes and hope to my heart. Donna Jean's haunting memories of her childhood will serve as an inspiration to her readers. Her warm family memories after the death of her mother poignantly demonstrate the depth of family love and commitment. Life was not easy but Donna Jean's irresistible optimism can serve as a benchmark for everyone."

— Ruth Ann Ritter, English/Literature Teacher

"I laughed, I cried as I fell in love with Donna Jean."

— Sue Hansen, Nurse

"What I expected when reading this book was a moving grief-walk, opening into a new life filled with hope and joy. What I didn't expect were the unusually vivid characters that distinguish the book. Even days later, I found myself in a quiet room with them, learning lessons, sharing life stories. This journey, a walk with faith, hope and love, is well-worth the time."

— Norma J. Kulas, Author

"This book would be very helpful for anyone who lost a loved one. It is a touching tribute to Donna Jean's family. Because most of the story is told through her yes as the seven year old it feels as though the reader is going through this journey with her. Now in her adulthood she found a way to heal through life's hurts."

— Families First, Traverse City, Mich.

"Your life story is as rich as that of the Walton's!"

— Jim Miller, Funeral Home Coordinator

Previous book:
If Mama Were Here: Living Without Mama

Book three of the trilogy, coming soon:
Donna Jean's Journey

Faded Genes

Memories of a Motherless Daughter

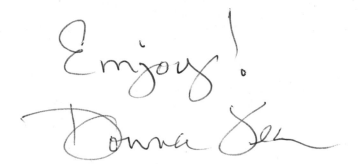

Emjoy!
Donna Jea

DONNA JEAN POMEROY

St. Jacques Publications
9515 EE.25 Road
Rapid River, MI 49878

Copyright © 2007 Donna Jean Pomeroy

PICKIN' TIME
Words and Music by JOHNNY CASH
© 1958 (Renewed) CHAPPELL & CO., INC.
All Rights Reserved Used by permission of ALFRED PUBLISHING CO., INC.

JEST 'FORE CHRISTMAS
Words and Music by EUGENE FIELD
1850 - 1895
Public Domain

Cover design & interior formatting, Greg Kretovic

Back cover photo, Portrait's Plus Studio, Dan White photographer

Manufactured in the United States of America
Library of Congress Catalog Number
Txu1-201-791

ISBN 978-0-9703177-3-5

This book is dedicated to all
children who have grown up motherless.

Acknowledgments
CR

Kathy Rood White has always been there for me. She encouraged me to tell my story and helped me separate wheat from the chaff.

Others that I'd like to thank for their contributions in reading, editing or rereading my manuscript are Sue Hansen, Gayle Nelson, Diane Pomeroy, Jacqueline Jacques, DeeDee Farrell, Tara Segerstrom, Judy Lauria, Ruth Ann Ritter, Christine Groleau, and to my niece, Leah Kretovic, who went the extra mile for me.

Forward

CR

If I were to use a psychological thermometer to measure my self-esteem over the years, I'd tell you that at this point in my life my temperature has hit an all-time high. It's consistent, ranging between 70 and 80 degrees on any given day. I'd relate it to the temperature of Hawaii, with its occasional rise or fall of a few degrees. If my temperature regarding my self-confidence was at zero in my first book, the period of my life that I'm about to share would read forty below! It's not easy sharing this information, but in doing so maybe someone else will experience healing. I hope that my life of turmoil, and the process of working it through, will give others hope that they, too, can achieve healing of hurtful memories. The result of all the hard work is self-esteem and self-worth.

If you're suffering emotionally right now and think that life isn't going the way it should, don't say as I did for so many years, "This must be *God's will!*" Get help for your problems because, although suffering is part of our world, it's not God's will for anyone to suffer needlessly.

I tell my story, not to entertain but to educate people, not just about growing up in a large, poor family, but also what life was like without my mother's love and protection and how my father dealt with his immense responsibilities. So if you're interested, hop on board. We're headed to Siberia!

One
CR

The land where I was raised is like a good marriage, where Father Sky and Mother Earth come together in harmony, where summer mornings greet you with the kiss of friendship and the nights with the twinkling of starlight. Winters of snow and Jack Frost are not only anticipated, but also welcomed. Natural disasters are unheard of in this part of the world; there are no hurricanes, no tsunamis, no earthquakes, no volcanoes, no floods. It's as if the Great Lakes serve as armor against nature's foes.

My grandfather's family came here from St. Pierre, Canada in the late 1800s and settled on the Garden Peninsula, the southernmost tip of the Upper Peninsula of Michigan. A true paradise of beauty, the place lives up to its name. It's where blackberries and raspberries hang from their vines and blueberries are in full supply. The smell of apple blossoms and wild roses freshen the air. Seagulls caw with laughter and whippoorwills sing children to sleep at night. Yet, many times the only sound is silence sweeping over the meadows, climbing the maples, birch and pines. Generation after generation has reaped a rich harvest from this land of good and plenty. Included among them are great catches of salmon, whitefish and perch.

But I've heard it said, "Nothing lasts," and "Every good thing must end," as it did in Garden. I was there, my family and me, in a home of tranquility, love and happiness. But within a few hours we found ourselves living in a barren land, an unfamiliar territory. In 1960 our family was dealt a major disaster. A flood came, but it was a flood of tears. Weeds flourished, the weeds of doubt and fear. And drought came, a long drought of poverty.

In 1938 my parents Rose Marie LaMarche and John Anthony Jacques married. Following their wedding there was no question in Dad's heart and mind where the two would settle down. It had to be Garden! Outside of town he built a three-room house on property that his grandfather once owned. This was the land of milk and honey to Dad and where they'd raise a family. And a large family they had. Year after year another child came, first four boys, then six girls. I, Donna Jean, was lucky number seven. Soon my mother's stomach was again expanding. Number eleven was on the way! This time, not only would there be a new addition to the family, but to the house as well. The added space included a bathroom (although it didn't have any of the furnishings), a utility room, a large kitchen and two bedrooms.

Dad worked long and hard as a lumberjack, returning each day in time for supper, then picking up his saw once again to go to his second job to cut stove wood until after dark. On the weekends he sold the wood to the townspeople. Despite all his efforts as provider, many of our basic needs were not met, like keeping us in shoes and decent clothing. "I'm not going to let these hard times suck the blood out of me," Dad said one morning at the breakfast table. "We'll make a bigger garden this year and I can buy a couple extra pigs. And ol'

Betsy, she's still giving plenty of milk." Mom patted his hand, smiled and nodded. Dad believed a family could live off the fat of the land, as he so often reminded us whenever we were (reluctantly) sent to a new berry patch or to pick another harvest from the garden.

Although my mother's workdays were never ending, she never complained. All that seemed to matter to her was that we had a roof over our heads, food in our mouths, clothes on our backs, and that we prayed together daily. She canned more than five hundred quarts of fruits and vegetables each year, and along with the slaughter of pigs, cows, chickens and deer, it seemed the Jacques's family story would end like a fairytale with, "Happily ever after." Unfortunately, 1960 would not be just another chapter in our book, but a completely different story.

My mother had been bedridden for months. This pregnancy was harder than the previous ones, due to an in-grown goiter that kept her from getting the oxygen she needed. Each day claimed more and more of her energy until she was no longer able to take on her usual responsibilities. The days were long for my siblings and me without her up and about. Her duties were divided between us, but since we six girls were under the age of nine, there were very few jobs we could accomplish. As the last days of the year came and went, we tried to be patient while looking forward to her getting back on her feet after the baby was born.

"This year's been tough," Dad said. "'59 is going out like a lion, so '60 is bound to come in like a lamb." But by no means did the new year come in gently. Just nine days into it, my mother died while giving birth to our baby brother Jude. On that day a beast of a burden was brutally dropped upon my dad's shoulders. Tears from us, his children, fell daily, like chilling fall rains. I suspected my dad, too, had plenty of sorrow, but he never showed it with tears. He had little time for himself. There was too much to be done around the house, not to mention his chores that had been neglected lately. One day I accompanied him into the cellar to check out the supply of canned foods. We separated the empty jars from the full ones. My mother had been unable to do her usual canning, so only sixty-two quarts of food stood full on the shelves.

"The noose seems to tighten more and more every day," he said as we climbed out of the cellar. I didn't know what that saying meant, but for some reason I thought he was hoping to find the shelves miraculously supplied. Actually, I did too. I figured it was the least God could do to help us out, considering He'd taken our mother from us.

Daytime was met with new beginnings, but nighttime brought the sorrow again. Someone was always crying, including me, but when dad would ask why, I'd say I had a stomachache. I decided he had enough problems trying to cheer up Monica, Anna, Catherine, Sarah and Luke without adding my name to the list. I felt if one more tear fell it would be enough to drown us all, especially after overhearing my dad talking with my Uncle Ernie one day.

"Night after night I lie awake for hours wondering how I'm going to manage to go to work and care for my kids, too."

"No doubt, it's going to be rough sailing," my uncle responded as my dad continued on.

"To make matters worse, I've been denied Aid for Dependent Children. Social Services said that ADC is designed for *women* raising their children alone."

"That's not right!" my uncle declared. "I'd give them a piece of my mind!"

"Oh, I already gave them a piece of it when they suggested finding homes for Jude and the girls. I'll be damned if that's ever going to happen."

Hearing their conversation made me realize I had to try very hard to be a good girl. I needed to do whatever I could to help Dad out so that my sisters and I would never end up in someone else's home.

Three giant steps backward followed every step forward. Like termites in wood, poverty infested our lives more than ever. At first Dad kept us oblivious to his struggles, but within months they became apparent in his actions. He began eating Tums and Rolaids as if they were his primary diet.

"I wish they wouldn't send these letters out right before Christmas," he said one day after reading the mail. He refolded the letter and placed it up in the cupboard. Later, Sarah got it down and read it.

"It's a tax bill," she said to the rest of us. We didn't know what a tax bill meant, but that night at the supper table my dad said that we needed to tighten our belts or we'd find ourselves on the back of a slow-moving train, like a bunch of hobos. From that night onward, Dad spent more time kneeling in prayer beside his bed. From the living room we could hear his foot hitting the floor, which meant our giddiness and laughter was distracting him.

Although I was only seven and a half, I sensed my dad had big troubles, especially when he admitted that it would be impossible for him to raise our newborn brother. Aunt Geraldine and Uncle Roy had taken Jude home from the hospital soon after my mother's death and had been caring for him ever since. One day I overheard my dad talking with my grandmother and aunt. Aunt Geretha said she'd take Jude and give him back to us when he was potty trained, as Dad requested. But Grandma spoke up, "Geri, you lost a two-year-old and that was devastating for you. Giving up a child once you've had him a couple years won't be any easier. Plus, Rosie told me more than once that if she could have a baby for anyone, she'd have one for Geraldine. [My aunt and uncle had one child but it died after three days.] So Johnny, I think the best place for your little boy is with Rosie's brother, Roy, and his wife."

"As long as they know I'm not giving him away. But if they're willing to care for him until he's potty trained, maybe Jude will fare best there."

"Like I said, that's your best bet," Grandma reassured him again.

"Well, I'll talk it over with my boys and see what they think."

About a week later as I lay in bed unable to sleep, I heard Dad telling my brothers what he was thinking of doing in regards to Jude. The boys agreed. I couldn't believe my dad was really going to give our baby brother away. I wanted to run to the kitchen and scream at him. I wanted to tell him we girls could take care of Jude, but I knew he'd say we were too young, too little. Since my mother's death we were always being told we were too little for this or too little for that, except when it came time to do dishes, wash and iron clothes, or scrub the floor. So instead of telling Dad anything, I pulled the blankets over my head, turned onto my stomach and silently cried to my mother about not being able to keep our brother. I made a promise to myself that night that I'd never have a baby, so I wouldn't die and the baby wouldn't have to be given away.

The following night Dad told my sisters and me that he was going to let Uncle Roy and Aunt Geraldine raise Jude until he was potty trained. It brought tears to Dad's eyes when Anna, who was only four, asked if Jude was still going to be our brother. "Of course," Dad answered. "He'll always be your brother. He'll always be a Jacques. And we'll visit him and they'll bring him to see us, too." Two more months passed, however, before Dad shared his decision with our aunt and uncle. It was on a Sunday when he took us to visit Jude. On the way to their house, we girls were driving John and Dad crazy. We were arguing about who was going to hold our brother first. The car was barely stopped and we were stepping from it, each trying to get to the door first. "All right!" Dad hollered. "*I'm* in command here! So listen to me." He rang the doorbell as he looked down at us. "Don't go throwing your coats all around when you get in there. And don't be asking to hold the baby."

"Well, well," Uncle Roy said as he opened the door. "What a surprise!" Despite my dad's warning, my sisters and I tried getting through the door at the same time, while Uncle Roy tried his best to

stop each of us so he could get his usual hugs and kisses. We went flying past him and into the dining room where the crib was.

"Well Jude, lookie here," Aunt Geraldine said as she pulled the
strings of Jude's gown together and tied them. "Your big sisters have
come to see you."

"Can I hold him?" Sarah asked excitedly that morning.

"No," Catherine shouted. "You got to hold him first last time."

"I get to," I said, with my arms outstretched to snatch him from
my aunt.

"No way, I'm the next oldest," Bernadette crabbed as Anna and
Monica busily climbed onto a side of the crib.

"Get to the couch, all of you, or we'll leave right now," Dad ordered as he walked over to the crib. He picked Jude up, cradled him in
his arms and smiled as he looked at our brother.

"Listen, John," Aunt Geraldine said. "It's almost noon. I'll get
some lunch ready so we can all have a bite to eat. The baby's all
yours." Dad nodded, then held Jude up so we could all see him. "Well,
the little chap has really grown," he said, chuckling. We girls stood
from the couch and followed Dad's eyes hoping to be the one called
to hold Jude. But his eyes went to the door where John was standing.
"Would you like to hold your little brother?" John still hadn't taken off
his coat or boots. He shrugged his shoulders and tipped his head.

"Do you think Ma would want me to? She was really mad at me
for not hauling water for her."

"Get over here," Dad said. "And let bygones be bygones." John
slipped off his coat and boots and left them on the floor by the door.
Dad didn't say a thing.

"We'd get in trouble for dropping our coats to the floor," we whispered among ourselves, each drooling for our chance to hold the pre-
cious bundle.

That day we stayed longer than usual. Both before and again after
lunch everyone had a chance to spoil Jude. When Dad took him again,

7

Aunt Geraldine and Uncle Roy called us kids into the kitchen and let us eat our fill of sugar cookies and milk. It wasn't until Monica insisted on going home that we returned to the living room. "It's time to get going anyway," Dad said as he pulled Anna's little finger away from Jude's eye.

Everyone hurried to the car but me. I wanted to see if my dad was *really* going to give our baby brother away. I stayed in the entrance and peeked through the cracked-open door. I heard him tell my aunt and uncle what he expected. Then with trembling hands, he placed Jude into Uncle Roy's arms. I ran to the car crying which prompted John to ask what was wrong.

"I have a tummy ache," I said.

"Well it's your own fault! You shouldn't have pigged out on all those cookies," he said, as Dad came walking to the car.

On the way home my dad didn't talk, or sing, or hum like he usually did. He didn't tell stories or nursery rhymes, or tease us girls about boys or John about a girl. Most surprising of all, he didn't even smoke his pipe!

Two
ભ

Every day of that first year after my mother's death was January ninth for me. Awakening each morning to the reality of her death was more frightening than the nightmares of my sleep. Day after day I hoped and prayed and listened for the doorknob of the house to turn by her hand. As days passed, she became like Bigfoot to me. I wanted to spot her, capture her, and bring her home. I wanted to take her to school for *Show and Tell* to prove to the world (and myself) that she really did exist. It wasn't until the first Christmas after her death that I finally realized that no matter how long or how far I looked for her, nor how loud I screamed or cried, my mother would never be coming home, not to me, not to my ten siblings, not to my father. And as the cold days of that second winter gave way to the dog days of yet another summer, I realized my life would never be the same as it had been when I was seven.

Sometimes before the light of each new day the eerie sound of silence would awaken me. Morning after morning I would lie in bed and wait for my mother's humming to the tune of a Kitty Wells or Patsy Cline song and for the wonderful aroma of her baking powder biscuits or cinnamon rolls to waft through the air. When it didn't happen I wanted to cry and stay in bed forever. I hadn't planned to, but one time during the night I got up and went into the kitchen. Standing there on the cold linoleum floor, I imagined my pregnant mother rolling out dough for cinnamon rolls. I could see her smear butter over the dough, sprinkle it with cinnamon and sugar, roll it up, cut it into pieces and then place the rolls onto the brown sugar-coated pans. I took a chair, closed my eyes and sniffed until the smell of baked goodies filled my senses. "See, she's real!" I told myself, and returned to bed. My mother seemed to follow me that night, and like so many times in the past, she tucked me into bed and kissed me good night. Then she read Bible stories until I was sound asleep.

Most mornings, however, the sound that would awaken me was that of the poker hitting the grate within the stove as my dad shook the ashes to the bottom tray. Other times it was the banging of pots and pans or Dad complaining because he couldn't find a clean dish in the kitchen. "Well," he'd say, "they went and stacked the damn dishes again!" or "Son of a bitch, they've ate the last of the bread! Guess I'll be going without lunch again today."

Dad's anger was foreign to me. He'd always been a joyful person from morning to night, a playful person, a big tease. His anger made me question whether being motherless was truly God's will, like I'd heard so many relatives and friends say. If it was God's will, I didn't like the way He was doing things. I wanted to hate God, to scream at Him, to scold Him for doing sloppy work the way my schoolteacher had scolded me for doing sloppy work. However, fear of God's revenge always won out. It kept me from verbalizing what I was thinking. I was afraid He'd punish me by sending another disaster upon us, not plagues of frogs or grasshoppers like He'd done to the people of the Bible, but taking my dad home to heaven, like He'd taken my mother, leaving us orphans. Just the thought of such a calamity brought me to tears. I didn't want to listen once again to well-intentioned people saying the things they'd said about my mother, like how she was in a better place, or that she was at peace, or especially that she'd finished her work here on earth. None of the remarks made sense; in my eyes my mother had a lot of work to do that my dad, brothers, sisters and I were now half-heartedly doing.

With our once-pleasant home in disarray and fearing my dad could also die, my mind started playing tricks on me. People and the words they spoke seemed farther away than I knew them to be. An item as mundane as a chair or plate appeared much smaller than it was and colors looked dull. Sometimes I felt as if I couldn't move, catatonic-like, yet other times I felt I was floating. Every task I did was completed in slow motion. Getting out of bed and ready for school each day became my biggest challenge. Icy cold water splashed onto my face each morning temporarily took away the sorrow. It melted the despair and helped me come alive. In some peculiar sort of way, the cold water gave me the courage needed to fight the demons of death — my mother's death, the worry of my father dying and of my wanting to die, to die and go where my mother was, be it heaven above or the earth below. The shock of the water took me out of self-pity and into the awareness that it wasn't just me who had lost a mother, but my siblings, too, and that my dad had lost his wife. I had to live, if not for my sake, for the sake of my little sisters. They needed me. That was the one thing I knew for sure those days.

I recall a time on a hot June morning, about a year and a half after my mother died. My five sisters and I sat beneath a pine so we would be sheltered from the boiling sun. Sarah, the oldest of us six girls, was now eleven; Bernadette, ten; Catherine, seven; Anna, almost six; Monica, nearly three; and I, Donna Jean, was soon to be nine. We were all but babies a year and a half earlier, far from maturity, yet our tree of life had been shaken, forcing not only my sisters and me into an existence beyond our years, but had also lightning bolted my teenaged brothers into parenting roles. Under the pine on that June morning, my sisters and I had our first real conversation about our dead mother. Anna said she couldn't remember what our mother looked like. To her surprise, some of my other sisters had also forgotten the face of our dear mother. Catherine asked why there weren't any pictures of our mother hanging on the walls. Bernadette wondered if anyone else was still missing our mother like she was. But most amazing was when little Monica asked, "Is Mama gone to da store?"

"No," Sarah said, picking Monica up and placing her on her lap. "Mama's in heaven."

"Why did she go there?" Anna asked.

"Because she died. Heaven is where dead people go," Bernadette explained.

"I heard someone say a baby killed her!" I said, wondering how that could be.

"Not *a* baby! *The* baby!" Sarah shot back. "Baby Jude."

"Then I'm never going to the hospital to get a baby out of my tummy. I don't want my baby to kill me. I don't want to die!"

Never before had we sisters listened to each other with such interest or been in such total agreement on issues. Never before was it that we weren't able to answer the many questions we each had. Dad had never forbidden us to talk about our mother, but instinctively we decided never to talk about her in his presence. That day while nestled atop piles of brown pine needles and some pestering ants, we vowed never to tell Dad that we'd talked about our mother and vowed never to ask him for the answers to our many questions. Together we promised to take care of each other and ourselves by doing the things our mother used to do.

That year Matthew, the oldest of the boys, turned twenty-one, finished his tour with Uncle Sam and came back home. Along with working in the woods with Dad, he started collecting old cars to start an auto salvage business. Mark had gotten a hardship discharge out of the Marines the year before and came home to help raise us girls. However, he soon fell in love and got married. Luke started smoking, drinking and driving cars really fast, quit school at sixteen and left for Chicago. At thirteen, John, who hated babysitting his little sisters and doing the farm chores by himself, escaped his duties whenever possible by joining the school's basketball team.

As for us girls, Monica lost her baby fat and Anna got little blue eyeglasses. Catherine learned to fix things, even the "unbreakable" things we broke. Bernadette became the disciplinarian, giving us the gumption to start our chores each day. Sarah got her first "monthly" and became negotiator when my sisters and I fought. And I became the instigator. Being dominated by the right side of my brain, much too often I threw logic out the window and favored my creative side, like the sunny June morning as we sat beneath the pine.

After our conversation about our mother ended, I convinced my sisters that one sure way to help Dad would be to burn grass. He'd done it every year and I'd noticed he hadn't burnt any since the spring before our mother died. It hadn't rained for weeks, so the field of green grass and clover behind the house resembled a clearing of tumbleweeds.

"I have an idea," I said to my sisters. "There isn't any wind today, so why don't we burn grass for Dad?"

"No," Sarah said without hesitation, "not without Dad and the boys here."

"But the grass has turned brown and it's all snarled up."

"So what?" Bernadette replied. My other sisters didn't say a word one way or the other, that is, until I said, "Well I heard where there's a tumbleweed, there's a snake!"

"SNAKE!" they shouted.

"And poisonous," I said. Just the thought of a snake slyly sneaking up the pathway and taking up residence on our front lawn, or worse, crawling in through a door we carelessly left open, was enough to convince even my older sisters that we had to get ready for the blaze. I'd observed Dad preparing for burning grass in the past, so I followed suit.

"Matches?"

"Got 'em."

"Shovels?"

"Got 'em."

"Water?"

"We got some," Anna said as she and Monica came toward me each carrying a lard pail of water.

"We need more than that!" I laughed.

"We can't carry anything bigger," Anna complained.

"Forget it. Bernadette and I can get more later." I turned to my other sisters. We were finally ready.

"Catherine, light the match!" I said as we huddled together on the ground on that hot, humid day drinking from the lard pails as we watched and waited through nearly a full box of (useless) matches. Finally, STRIKE! A small flame ignited the first clump of tangled grass. It was amazing to see the fire spread like icing on hot cinnamon rolls. We began running to the positions we'd determined ahead of time; our places to stand to make sure the fire wouldn't burn beyond. To our surprise the fire beat us to our spots and was rapidly spreading toward Matthew's junkyard and to the forest beyond — the forest Dad was so proud of owning.

Crackling and the occasional pop of a glass bottle was all we heard during those first few minutes. We gathered back to where the match was lit. No one screamed. No one knew what to do. But the scalding summer day proved to be a blessing. My dad and brothers found it too hot in the woods to work that day, so they came home early. When they saw what was happening, they drove through bushes and shrubs to get between the fire and the junkyard. Quickly they jumped from the car, grabbed the mats from the floorboard and began beating the fire. I looked at Anna and Monica who were standing behind me holding the empty pails. Catherine, Sarah and Bernadette were stepping on leftover spots of fire.

By the time the fire was out, my dad and brothers were drenched with sweat. My throat was parched. I tried to swallow, unsure if it was from the smoke or the thought of the trouble I was soon to be in. I knew the only way my sisters would share the blame of this event would be if I were dying. And I surely wasn't dying, so I grabbed Monica and Anna's hands and ran with them to the house. The dishes were still stacked from breakfast, so I hurried to the sink to wash them. One way of getting on Dad's good side was if he were to see me doing something useful. Yet, when he came in the house, I put my hands over my ears. I didn't want to hear him shouting, but he didn't say a word until later that night. As I crossed the kitchen on my way to the bedroom he said, "I thought I could trust you when I'm away. Lately, the littler ones behave better than you. Don't you have more sense in that head of yours to know that you can't be playing with matches?" He gave my hair a tug and told me to get moving. He followed. After the six of us climbed into our beds, he told us what had happened to the little Saxon twins, how they burnt up in a car they'd been playing in. John walked in on the tail end of the conversation.

"See what I mean, Dad?" he asked. "These girls are nothing but troublemakers, but you always blame me for everything bad that happens around here." Dad didn't reply.

"We were just trying to help," I said.

"Maybe so," Dad replied, but again warned us about playing with matches and added that we were never to play around Matthew's junkyard, not even when he was home.

That night I had a nightmare of my sisters and I locked in an old car while flames of fire rushed toward us. We desperately tried to break a window to get out of the car, but our arms were so heavy that we could barely lift them. Our screams for help went unheard. The fire kept coming closer. I looked into the eyes of my sisters. They were blackened, sunken deep within their heads. Together in unison they asked, "Why did you light a match, Donna Jean?" Night after night the dream came to haunt me. Many nights I'd lie awake in tears, afraid of what could've happened the day of the fire.

As time went by, the apple blossoms turned to little green apples. The Guernsey calved. Dad towed his old '49 Chevy to the junkyard and bought another used car — a long yellow '53 Cadillac. Yet, two things didn't change. I was still mad at myself for burning grass and I kept having the same nightmare. Time and time again my sisters asked what the nightmares were about, but I was too ashamed to tell them. Finally, after waking early one morning in total panic, I told them why I sometimes screamed during the night. Having to tell them about us burning up in an old car was scary. I started to cry, afraid that confessing my dream would cause it to come true.

"Quit thinking about it," Bernadette said that morning. "After Dad and the boys leave for work, we'll do something fun to get it off your mind."

"Hey," Catherine said, "it's not going to be too hot today. Why don't we lay in the sun this afternoon to get a tan?"

"Great idea," Bernadette exclaimed, "as long as all our chores are done."

We didn't want anyone to see us lying outside, so we push-mowed a spot in the back yard, raked it and placed a blanket down. Then we hurried into the house to find skimpy clothes to put on. Monica found a bathing suit that we'd gotten in a box of hand-me-downs. It was much too small for her, but she wore it anyway. I tied a knot in the bikini top Anna had on and pinned the bottoms so they'd stay up on her. On the way outside, Bernadette grabbed a stick of margarine from

16

the refrigerator. "What the heck is the oleo for?" Sarah asked when Bernadette threw it on the blanket.

"To put on our skin. It works like suntan lotion. Mama once told me that when she was a teenager, she and her best friend Catherine rubbed margarine on their skin before laying in the sun and it helped their skin get nice and brown."

"Pass it over," Anna said. "If Mama used it, I want to, too."

"Oleo! That's weird," Catherine said as it slid down her knee like a kid on a slide.

While the margarine was passed back and forth and back and forth, we rubbed every bit of exposed skin so we could get the best tan ever. On the blanket we shared secrets and told each other's fortunes and wondered what lake Dad would take us to for a picnic that weekend. At one point we were so bored that we took bobby pins and put them up our noses and then circled them round and round to see who could make themselves sneeze first. Later, with our family's only needle and thread, a couple of us managed to sew our first initial under the skin of the palm of our hand, while the others played a game we made up called *Don't you smile, don't you laugh.* Over and over one would tickle the face of another, trying to get the person to smile or laugh. If they did, that person had to get a different person to do the same. We lost all track of time and when Dad and the boys arrived home they found us snoozing in the sun on that first day of summer.

"Well, well," Dad said. "Are these my chief cooks and bottle washers sleeping as snug as bugs in a rug?"

"They look more like tomatoes to me," John said.

"Very *red* tomatoes!" Luke laughed.

We stretched and yawned and oohed and ahhed our way to our feet. "You look like a bunch of chicks hatching," Dad added.

The sun and margarine had scorched each and every one of our white bodies. Anna's bikini top had slipped up on one side and the sun had scorched her boob. We were in so much pain that my dad had to stay home to care for us the following two days. He forced water down our throats, re-cooled wash cloths, washed the sheets and blankets so they were free from sand and cracker crumbs, and even turned on the television (which was unusual during the day) so we could keep our minds off of our burns. Since our brothers had taken the car to work, Dad had to walk the two and a half miles (roundtrip) to the store for groceries. For the evening meal, he opened cans of pork and beans, and made potato salad and lime Kool-Aid. The next day he gave us cornflakes for breakfast and made bologna sandwiches for lunch and supper.

On the third day, the pampering came to an end. The sun was just waking when Dad hollered for us to get out of our sacks. "We're leaving for the woods. Make sure you get your jobs done and don't get into mischief!"

The pain from our burns had started to ease. It had been fun having our dad at home, not only for waiting on us, but just to have him home mothering us.

Three
♋

As a child I dreaded the holidays without my mother. I was much too young to realize that getting through them after the loss of a loved one is a struggle for most people. I thought it was something of my own creation. The first big event following her death was my first communion, which took place on Mother's Day. In my seven-year-old mind, I believed it was the day that she was going to quit playing "hiding games" and come back to all of us. When it didn't happen, each holiday that followed seemed harder than the previous. Without my mother everything was completely different, from not having her in the kitchen to bake her usual Christmas cookies, date bars and banana bread, or cooking the turkey or ham. At Easter she'd been that "tricky rabbit," hiding our baskets of goodies where we couldn't find them, like in the oven.

It was also my mother who'd made sure we had washed up properly before getting dressed. She'd check behind our ears, under our necks, elbows and feet before allowing us to put on our fancy clothes, clean white socks and polished shoes. She was the one who knew how to put our hair into rag curls before bedtime and how to carefully take them out the following morning before combing the hair around her finger so the long curls would sweep down our backs. It was she who kept our hats out of reach so we wouldn't wreck them or get them dirty so they would be presentable to wear to church, since it was customary for all female Catholics to have their heads covered before entering the sacred building. Since her death, most of us had outgrown our hats and would have to search the house for a scarf. Sometimes in a last-minute effort to find something suitable to wear, a couple of us would be forced to grab doilies from beneath knick-knacks.

Waiting for that first year of big events and holidays to be over proved to take longer than it had been waiting for my seventh birthday to arrive. Everything, I thought, would be better once the holidays were over. But by the second year the memories of my mother continued to remind me of what we were missing. To add to my misery, I became fearful that my dad would remarry. The last thing I wanted was a different mother! My sisters and I had talked about such a possibility and we'd all agreed to never let that happen.

"Can I go to the store with you?" I asked Dad as he finished the list of items we needed to complete our picnic lunch for the upcoming Fourth of July.

"Get out to the car and duck down so the others don't see you. I don't want the whole troop tagging along," he said.

A couple minutes later when we entered Cal's store, Dad and I went to the meat counter, located in the back. A lady was waiting there for Cal to help her. She smiled when she saw us and started talking to my dad. After a few minutes passed, Dad told me to go pick out one of the watermelons from the big crate at the front of the store. While I was up front it dawned on me that the woman was probably Dad's girlfriend and that he'd gotten rid of me so he could be alone with her.

"Oh, Honey," Dad said, as he talked with the lady. I took a deep breath and slapped my hand over my mouth. "Oh no! I don't want a new mother!" I grabbed a watermelon from the big wooden crate and hurried back to spy on them. From the aisle of canned foods I could see Dad's honey clearly. She was a tiny lady with skin nearly as white as milk, but with brown spots over it. Her long fingernails were painted bright red and she wore a big, shiny ring on her pinky finger. Her eyes were shaped like spoons without handles. Her hair was puffy and reddish brown. Her heart-shaped lips had fire-red lipstick on them and some gold covered the edges of her two front teeth. Around her neck was a red silk scarf and under it were large, ivory pearls. The red, white and blue top she was wearing was tucked into the white pedal pushers she wore buttoned under her sagging boobs. Quietly I walked toward them listening to every word they were saying.

"Did you get everything you need?" Dad asked when he saw me. I didn't answer.

"Did Mama like watermelon?" I asked slamming the melon into his gut and giving his honey a dirty look.

"Hey, watch what you're doing," he complained, grabbing it and continuing to talk to the lady.

"Ooh," I said puffing my lips together and squinting my brown eyes toward her as I turned to go back to the front of the store. Later when Cal added up the cost of all the items the lady was buying, she reached into her huge beaded purse and took out a wad of money to pay Cal. He put her groceries into bags and said he'd carry them to her car. "Good," I said to myself, because I didn't want my dad talking to his girlfriend any longer. I didn't want him to marry her. I didn't want a new mother.

"Oh, I can get that for Honey," Dad said, grabbing a bag in each arm, leaving her to carry a carton of Viceroys and a smaller bag containing cat food.

"I'll carry this one," I said as I grabbed the bag out of her hand and followed them. No way was I going to let them be together alone.

Dad put the groceries in the back seat of her car. I whipped the bag I was carrying next to his. "Hey," he said, giving me a dirty look. "Watch what you're doing!" He closed the door. She took his hand into hers and thanked him for carrying out her groceries.

"How you doing, sweetie?" she asked looking into his eyes.

"I'm okay," he said. "But it helps knowing people care." He opened her door and held it as she got in. Again she thanked him, said good-bye and left. Dad and I went back into the store. He signed the black book for our stuff and we left. Panicky thoughts ran through my mind all the way home. When we got there I asked my dad if he liked the lady he was talking to. "Oh sure," he said, "she's a real sweetie."

"Ooh," I snarled. "That's exactly what she called him! I have to tell my sisters."

Dad got out of the car and went to get the mail. I hurried into the house and gathered my sisters into our bedroom. "I have something bad to tell you." They listened intently. "Dad has a girlfriend! Pretty soon we're going to have a stepmother."

"How do you know?" Sarah asked.

"I just met her at the store."

"Is she pretty?" Anna asked while looking down at the doll she was holding by the hands and swinging back and forth.

"What do we care if she's *pretty* or not?" I said, sarcastically.

"Don't we want a new mother?" she continued.

"I just want our own mother back," Catherine said.

"How do you know she's Dad's girlfriend?" Bernadette asked.

"Because I heard them talking. He was saying, 'Honey this,' and 'Honey that.' And she called him sweetie!"

"If she comes to live with us, I'll trip her when she walks past me and put the frogs and toads I catch under her pillow," Catherine exclaimed.

"Mama didn't have a stepmother after her mother died, so we shouldn't have to have one either," I said.

"Well I'm certainly not going to listen to her if she tries to tell me what to do," Bernadette said.

"Do you think she'll do that?" I asked.

"She might try," Sarah interjected. "Cinderella's stepmother bossed her around."

"Yeah," Catherine said, "and look what happened to Hansel and Gretel. Their stepmother was planning to eat them!" With that thought we all started bawling our hearts out.

"Mama!" I cried, "Please come home!" That plea brought Dad dashing into the room.

"What is so terribly wrong?" he asked, only to be bombarded by opinions from every direction.

"We don't want you to marry your girlfriend. I don't want a new mommy. I won't ever listen to what she tells me to do. I'll put pepper in her coffee or chase her with a snake! I'm going to run away from home." But worst of all was, "I hate you, I hate you, I hate you," I yelled as I went running out of the bedroom. Dad caught me by the arm and pulled me back into the room.

"What's all this nonsense about? Who told you I have a girl-friend?" My sisters all looked at me.

"Well, I heard you talking to your *Honey* when we were at the store." Dad let out a big laugh. "Leave it to you, Donna Jean. That old lady isn't my girlfriend. Her name is Honey Brown. Everybody calls her Honey!" He laughed again as he smacked the top of my head with the mail. "Now enough of this nonsense! Scram out of here, all of you, and get your jobs done or there'll be no pop and chips tonight!"

Four
CR

During those first couple years following the death of my mother, I talked to her a lot. Though she was dead, conversing with her seemed as natural as eating or sleeping. At first the conversations were all the time, but later they became only at difficult periods of my life. Nevertheless, during the first few months following her death I bombarded her with question after question. "Why, oh why, did you choose to live with God and the angels? Don't you care about us anymore? Are you like God up in heaven? Do you know everything? Can you see everything? Are you mad at me for being mad at you?"

I would wait for a word, a sound or a sign that she was still with me. I desperately wanted to see her. I was sick of just the memories. They'd become useless. Even the best of them couldn't do the things she'd once done, like wipe Anna's snotty nose, help Sarah sew a button back on Catherine's coat, stop Monica from crying or help me iron my dress for school. Yet day after day and month after month came with still no sign from her, so I begged God to wipe away all memory of her. Weeks passed until I awoke one morning to the realization that it had happened! I could no longer visualize her, not her face or her smile, not her hands or her feet, nor could I remember the feel of her touch. I panicked.

"Something's wrong with Donna Jean," Sarah hollered as she went running for Dad.

"What's the matter now?" he asked as he picked my limp body from the bed.

"I'll get a cold cloth," Sarah exclaimed.

Dad sat at the edge of the bed and laid me across his lap. He patted the cool cloth over my face. I looked up at him. "I miss Mama," I cried.

"Come on, straighten up," he said. "You have a bus to catch this morning, and I've got to get to work."

"Is Mama okay?"

"Yes, yes, she's okay."

"Does she still know me?"

"Of course, she does. When a person goes to heaven they know everything." He stood me up on the floor and gave my butt a pat. "Now get moving." As he left the room he looked back at me, then closed the sheet that hung as a makeshift door. I was still afraid I'd never see my mother again. I knew for sure it wouldn't be in this life, but I feared it might be never. "What if I sin and don't go to heaven? Is God really real? Is there truly a place called heaven? If so, how did Mama get from her grave to that place?" I asked myself as we waited for the bus.

"Come on, *Honey*," Sarah said, "It'll be okay." Her words were medicine for my soul that day. My tears stopped as fast as they had started. I began laughing.

"I'm not *Honey*," I told her, laughing even more.

Still, night after night I begged God to let my mother come back home, promising that I'd never misbehave again. I'd do all the housework without being asked, I'd go to confession every week, even when I didn't want to, and I'd never sass Dad again. The list went on and on and on. But nothing I promised was good enough. God never gave back my mother, so I decided to blame it all on her. I told myself that if she didn't care about us anymore, I wasn't going to care about her either. So the nightly dialogues with her came to an end. Instead, I'd pick a spot on the wall, ceiling, picture, light switch or wherever, and stare at it until my eyes welled with tears. Over and over each night, I'd practice this weird behavior. Thank goodness for school. It gave me something else to think about, although school also was a place of inner conflict for me.

"Dad! Did you hear me?" I asked one morning. "I want to take piano lessons from Mrs. Lyons."

"Oh, boy," he said, taking my hands. He held them out. "You do have piano hands. Look at these long fingers."

"Can I have the money then, to take lessons?"

"Not this year. But we'll see what next year brings."

At that moment, I wanted to hit my dad. I wanted to push him, pinch him or yank out gobs of his jet-black hair. I was tired of hearing, "Maybe next year, next month or next week." For once I wanted him to say, "Sure you can. Here's the money." But he never had money to spare, not for hot lunch, clothing, toiletries or doctor and dentist visits. Even getting our pictures taken at school each year proved disappointing. We had very few pictures of ourselves, so naturally we were excited the day our pictures arrived at school. Like so many other kids, my siblings and I would run off the bus, pictures in hand, excited about showing Dad how they turned out, even if they were hideous — closed eyes, big frown, open mouth, messed hair — it didn't matter, we wanted Dad to buy our pictures so we could trade them for pictures of our friends. Two weeks later when he still couldn't come up with the money, we'd reluctantly return them.

One year I asked my schoolteacher what they did with the pictures that nobody bought. She said they burned them. I cringed. "If only we could have ours," I thought. So I asked her if I could take mine home since they were just going to be burnt. She told me that if she didn't receive the money, they had to be returned. I couldn't understand *burning* them. The thought of our bodies being tossed into a fire left me feeling scared and hopeless, like I didn't belong in school, or the world for that matter. I wondered if anyone cared if we existed.

"Dad," I asked one day, "Are we different than other people?"

"Only if you think we are," he responded. He must have known what I was referring to — being poor and not feeling equal to the other kids. He took the deck of cards from the top of the refrigerator. "Get over here, everyone. You may as well all listen to what I'm going to say." I was confused. What was Dad going to tell us with a deck of cards? Was he going to take time to play games when he never had before? We gathered around the table and he told us a story from a song by Tex Ritter called *Deck of Cards*. It was about a soldier boy who was caught with a deck of cards in church. He was brought before a judge who promised to punish him more than he'd punished anyone before because he thought the soldier was just playing cards in church. The boy explained that he was using the deck as a prayer book because he was too poor to afford a Bible. He told how each card helped him recall his faith. The Ace reminded him that there is but one God, God Almighty; the Deuce that the Bible is divided into two parts, the old and new testaments; the three of the Trinity, the Father, Son and the Holy Ghost; the ten, the ten commandments; the Jack of Spades, the devil, and so on and so forth. The judge was so impressed with the soldier's wisdom that he was not punished after all, but admired.

I'm not sure why the story affected me so much, but for some reason it made me feel like I was somebody, and not necessarily poor. For sometime afterwards, I didn't care so much if I had a microscope, camera or other neat things like many other kids had. Playing with the same old deck of cards, playing the same old games such as *Five-Hundred Rummy*, *Thirty-One*, *Concentration* and *Solitary* seemed much more special.

When we played cards we always had to wait on Anna; her turn always took twice as long because she couldn't see very well and had to hold each card up to her face. One day she brought a note home from school telling Dad that she must see an eye doctor. A couple weeks later her problems were solved when she got a pair of little blue glasses. My sisters and I were happy that she could see better, but jealous of her little blue glasses. Although we couldn't see anything with them on, and Anna couldn't see anything without them, we forced her to share them. We took turns wearing them around the house for five to ten minutes at a time, until our eyes crossed and we began bumping into things and knocking them over. We gave them up only after our eyes burned so badly that we didn't want anything more to do with them.

One day we younger girls were taking turns wearing Anna's glasses in Luke's car, pretending to be going to town, when I spotted an unusual deck of cards in the glove compartment. "Hurry, Catherine!" I pleaded. "Give Anna her glasses. Look at the naked ladies on this big deck of cards. Let's take them into the house to show Sarah and Bernadette."

"Where did you get these cards?" Sarah giggled.

"Oh, no! Naked ladies!" Bernadette exclaimed, as we gathered together.

"Them are boobies, right?" Monica asked, pointing to the breast of one of the women.

"I have some of them on my tummy, too," Anna remarked as she lifted her blouse.

"We all do, even boys," I told her.

"Only girls' boobs get big," Catherine added.

"Sarah's are starting to," I said.

"Show us, Sarah," Catherine said, getting ready to lift Sarah's shirt.

"No!" she yelled, slapping Catherine's hands away.

"Shush," Bernadette said. "Don't be yelling."

"Hide them. Hurry. Dad's coming!" Catherine whispered as Dad came into our bedroom to see what the commotion was about. We tried to hide the cards behind our backs but a few fell to the floor. He picked them up and looked to see what we were all fascinated with. He shook his head from side to side, then put a hand out for the rest. "Where the hell did you get this trash?"

"Luke's car," Monica spoke up. Dad took the cards and threw them into the stove. "No filth is coming into this home!" he said.

Dad must have talked to Luke about the cards because we never again saw pictures of nude women. But it didn't mean the boys were fair when playing cards. They played as if we girls were a group of rough and tough gamblers. One game was *Knuckles*! Of course being older, wiser, smarter and stronger, they won every game. The winner got to take the deck and slap the edge of it across each loser's knuckles, a strike for each card remaining in the player's hands. Sometimes our hands would bleed. We'd go crying and screaming to Dad. He had nerves of steel for most things, but he hated to see us hurting. Time after time he reprimanded the boys for playing *Knuckles* with us, but when we kept going back for more, he declared that he wasn't going to protect us any longer if we were foolish enough to keep playing the game.

"Out of here," he scolded Anna and me one day when we once again went crying with blood coming from the top of our hands. He was trying to snooze and when we continued to cry, he got mad and stomped out of the room and into the kitchen. He lifted John and Luke from their chairs. "Outside," he demanded. "School may have been canceled but it doesn't mean I can't put you both to work."

"We can't buzz wood in an ice storm," Luke said, chuckling.

"Out! Or you'll get the blacksnake (his belt) across your rear-end!" They hurried outside, laughing as they went.

Things were peaceful for a while. Dad checked on the bread dough he'd made and my sisters and I went back to playing cards. Before long we heard a loud noise and ran to the window to see Luke driving up in an old car from Matthew's junkyard. John jumped out and ran to the house. He opened the door and hollered, "What do you think, Dad? Luke got a junker started."

"I heard," he said. "It sounds worse than the last one he got going." John closed the door. Again we ran to the window. As Luke revved the engine, the car backfired. "I don't know what they think they're going to do with that old car," Dad said.

John climbed back in and they took off down the road. We waited and watched, but when they didn't return we decided to help Dad shape the bread dough into buns and loaves of bread, and then watched as he rolled out a big ball of dough for cinnamon rolls. He was sprinkling it with the cinnamon sugar mixture when we heard the boys coming back. With nothing better to do, we ran to the window again. We watched as Luke drove the car right past the house, then hit the brakes. The car went slipping and sliding and then into the ditch. The engine stopped. We screamed! Dad came running. Luke got out of the car. Dad opened the door and was about to say something, but Luke's friend Orlie and John pulled up in Orlie's Jeep. Orlie hooked a big chain onto Luke's car and pulled it back onto the road. After Orlie unhooked the chain, Luke sped off. Soon he came roaring back. As before, he hit the brakes, went slipping and sliding, made three or four half circles, before ending up in the ditch for the second time. Within minutes he came speeding for the third time, once again hitting the brakes, but this time the car rolled over, right on its top, in the middle of the road. We held our breath as we waited to see if Luke was okay.

When he climbed out of the car, a big smile was on his face. "Alright!" he hollered, with his fist clenched and raising his arms high. "Did you see that Dad? I just rolled the son of a bitch over!"

Dad was disgusted. "Stop the nonsense!" he hollered as the guys tried to figure out a way to get the car turned over.

"Dammit! Park that car! Stop before someone gets hurt!" he blasted from the front porch. Then stepping back into the house, he whipped his package of Plowboy tobacco clear across the living room. "Those boys aren't going to be satisfied until it's too late. One of them will end up dead before it's all said and done." Again he yelled to them, but still they wouldn't quit. Dad slammed the door, picked up his Plowboy and went to the kitchen to put the bread into the oven. While it was baking, Monty, another friend of Luke's, came by with some other guys and they helped turn the car back over. Then Monty joined the demolition. Both his and Luke's cars zigzagged this way and that as they tried to roll their cars over.

One time they slammed into each other. When Luke climbed out of his car he could barely stand. That's when Dad went to the bottom kitchen cupboard, the one next to the refrigerator, and took a swig of his Kesslers. The next swig came after Monty ran to the house for a rag to wrap around his forehead to stop the bleeding above his eye. Then, when Luke kept making donuts in the middle of the road, Dad went to the kitchen again for more of his whiskey. This time he poured himself a glassful. When the two cars sideswiped, Bernadette, Catherine, Anna, Monica and I clapped at Luke and Monty's brilliant stunts, but not Sarah. Sarah watched between fingers clapped over her eyes. When she couldn't see Luke getting out of the smashed car, she yelled.

"Make them stop, Dad! Make them stop!" But by this time Dad thought the "demolition derby" was pretty amazing, too. However, the following Saturday was a whole different story. When Dad found out that John and Luke had invited a bunch of boys to come over to watch car stunts, he was furious. When the kids showed up, he wouldn't let the car stunts take place.

"Don't you boys have anything better to do, like chores or school-work?" Dad asked the town kids in a very stern manner.

"Since when do you care so much about schoolwork?" Luke asked sarcastically.

"Since this morning!" Dad shot back. "So clear out of here, all of you."

After they'd left, Luke about flew into the house. "Don't think I'm only going to work around here and never have any fun. When my birthday rolls around, I'm quitting school!"

"You're not just going to be sitting around here," Dad said.

"Hell, no!" he said. "I'm heading for Chicago. I'm getting out of this place!"

Matthew had moved to Chicago shortly after the grass fire inci-dent and was living with Aunt Lucille. He and Luke had been sending letters back and forth. My mother's cousin Lizzy owned several apart-ments, so they planned to rent from her. Luke and Monty had been to Chicago several times during November and December, hauling Christmas trees there to sell.

Sticking to his plans, Luke quit school eight days before his six-teenth birthday and began packing the few bits of clothing he owned. "Do you have that map I gave you?" Dad asked, as Luke put his few belongings into his car.

"I don't need a map. I can get there now with my eyes closed." But Dad insisted he take it and continued to question him to be sure he knew which roads to take.

"Things aren't going to be any better in the city. You've been mak-ing *good money* with me in the woods."

"For God's sake, Dad, things in Chicago could never be any worse than here! I'm going there to make some *real* money! Then I'll get some of the things we need around here. Plus the girls deserve more, like *hot* running water and a gas stove for the kitchen instead of this *antique* wood burner. Decent furniture wouldn't be such a bad idea either."

Five

ca

Despite another major blizzard, Luke left for Chicago that winter day in another old car he'd fixed up. It was the first day of February, 1962. As the snow circled the '56 Chevy, he revved the engine, drove slowly out of the driveway and onto the road. I listened to the sound of his horn beeping until it faded. He was probably halfway to Chicago when Mark and his wife, Sandy, came from Escanaba to pick up Monica like they did every Sunday afternoon during the school year. My grandmother had watched both her and Anna for a while after my mother died so that Dad could work, but when Grandma came down with pneumonia and ended up in the hospital, Dad told her to go back home. By the following September, Anna started school, but Monica was still too young.

Whenever Monica had to leave with Mark and Sandy, I hated it because she would cry and tighten her grip around the neck of the person holding her. "Why don't you want to go back with Mark?" my dad asked one time when she started to cry. Through tears and sniffles she told us it was because Sandy would drink Pepsi and give her Kool-Aid. So Dad dug deep into his pants pockets and came out with a dime, nickel and a couple pennies and gave it to her so she could buy herself a pop, too.

"Monica," I said before she left, "In just five more months you get to come home for good. It'll be summer vacation, and then next school year you'll be in kindergarten."

"Fer always and always, I will get ta stay at home?"

"Yes, for always," I said, as I walked her to the car. I smiled because for a change she wasn't crying, kicking or screaming.

"Uh-oh," Anna said later that evening when she noticed Monica's raggedy blanket with the nylon trim.

"You bigger girls should always make sure that your little sister has her blanket when she leaves because it takes the place of her mother's cheek. There'll be trouble for her, and Mark too, at her bedtime," Dad told us.

I wanted to tell Monica before she left that the following week that Dad was picking her up on Tuesday night so she could come to my class's Valentine's party. But I knew she'd think it was the coming Tuesday and would cry when Dad didn't show up, so I said nothing. My teacher had said we could ask someone from home to join us. Sarah and Bernadette wanted to make our younger sisters look pretty for Valentine's Day, so they asked Dad if they could perm their unruly straight hair. They'd come up with the idea after seeing a Toni commercial on television. At first Dad said they couldn't put "that crap" in their hair, but when Sarah told him that Mama would probably perm their hair if she were still alive, he changed his mind.

"If I give you money for perms, you'll all have to make your Valentines for school," he said. Everyone agreed. So after school on Friday, Dad took us to Manistique. While we were there, we visited with Jude. It had been Christmastime since we'd seen him. We'd made him a special Valentine and were anxious to give it to him. "Remember now," Dad reminded, "you're not running in there like a herd of cattle." So like angels we walked from the car to the door, but once again, when Uncle Roy opened the door, in we charged, all fighting to see Jude first. Later when we were on our way to the D.M.C. store, Dad said he was ashamed of us for the way we behaved. We lowered our heads and made eye contact at each other while pointing fingers. Despite our behavior, Dad kept his promise about buying the perms. He also bought crayons and colored construction paper for making our Valentines, and to our delight he'd bought two bags of hot, salty peanuts, which we devoured in minutes.

"Their hair is so thin and straight, but the perms will make it look thick like the girl's hair in the Toni commercial," Sarah said bright and early Saturday morning as she and Bernadette read the directions for the process to perm Anna and Monica's hair. I watched in amazement as my beautician sisters took bony-looking curlers and tiny pieces of tissue paper and wrapped strands of hair over them. When all their hair was rolled, they carefully read the directions again, put on the plastic gloves and then mixed up the solution. It smelled terrible. We could hardly breathe as they squirted the foamy solution onto the curlers. The processing time wasn't even up and Monica and Anna were screaming. The solution was burning their eyes and the top of their heads, too.

"Wash that crap off of them!" Dad demanded as he came in from outside carrying an armload of wood.

It was a good thing they stopped the perms when they did because when they removed the rollers both heads of hair looked like piles of spit curls. Catherine and I started laughing because our little sisters had old lady hairdos. Bernadette and Sarah hurried and washed out the perm solution, but the curls were already snug to their heads. To make matters worse, a few hours later Anna tried brushing the curls out, causing her hair to look like a mound of insulation atop her head. I lifted her up to see herself in the mirror. She screamed and began to cry. "Donna Jean, look at my hair!" I took her by the hand and we ran to the living room to show Dad.

"What the hell did you do to these little ones?" he asked my older sisters, looking as if he was going to cry. "They had beautiful angel-like hair until the two of you got your hands on it. I should never have let you talk me into such foolishness." Sarah and Bernadette's chins dropped.

Later that night Dad had an idea. He took his Brylcream from the bathroom cabinet and put some of it on his hands and worked it into Anna's hair. The little curls came back but it looked better than it had.

"I still don't like it," she said as she knelt upon the dresser to look at herself once again. "But it's better than fuzzies."

The following night Dad sat with us at the kitchen table between our little Brillo-head sisters to help us think of special sayings for the Valentines we'd give to our friends.

You know I
"Carrot"
About you Valentine.

Won't you
"Peas"
Be my Valentine?

We drew the carrot or peas or whatever symbol Dad gave to the card, colored it in and then added the chosen words. When we finished, they looked beautiful.

On the day of our party, we got to walk around the room passing out our cards, placing them on each other's desk. Most of the kids had theirs in envelopes. I didn't, but I didn't care because *everyone* would get to see them. Unfortunately, some boys thought my Valentines were stupid and they threw the ones I'd given to them in the wastebasket. I started crying. Mrs. Knuth scolded them. "I think her Valentines are wonderful! A gift from the heart!" Although she complimented me, I was still embarrassed. It suddenly dawned on me that some of my classmates probably thought my cards were dumb looking, like the way I thought my little sisters' perms looked dumb.

A few months later, Mr. PanCarry, one of the schoolteachers, took us girls and Mark for a ride in his convertible to pick wildflowers. Monica had Mama's brown and tan striped purse filled with Valentines that the rest of us had gotten at school. As we rode with the top down all our hair blew in the wind, except for my two little sisters'. Their hair sat still. "Stop the car," Bernadette yelled. "I see some pretty flowers." After picking them she hopped back in and slipped the flowers into Anna and Monica's hair. Mark and Mr. PanCarry turned around to see.

"Lady Slippers!" Mr. PanCarry exclaimed. "You're not supposed to pick them. They're a protected species." Bernadette looked at him and wrinkled her brow. "But I'll never tell, if you don't," he said.

"No, I won't tell," Bernadette answered, not understanding what he was implying. So the flowers stayed, adding a bit of beauty to a frightful mess.

As the summer months continued to pass, little by little Bernadette cut the permed ends off of Anna's and Monica's hair. By the start of school, only the ends of their hair were still damaged. By Christmas, the perm was completely gone. As we helped them dress for midnight Mass, they looked beautiful. Monica had little green barrettes in her hair to match her paisley dress and Anna had red ones in hers to match the red and navy plaid skirt and white blouse we'd ordered for them out of the Sears catalog.

"Now, there're my little girls," Dad said, when we paraded them into the kitchen for everyone to see.

Six
☙

Another spring was in the air, yet snow was falling as we readied ourselves for school. It was March 26, 1963, Sarah's thirteenth birthday. Dad usually made big pancakes, the size of a plate, but as I recall, that morning he made thirteen small ones. He called them silver dollar pancakes as he stacked them onto the only unbroken china plate left from a gift of dishes he and my mother had received on their wedding day. He stuck the three candles I'd found in the junk drawer on top of them. "Everyone to the table," he hollered. I can still picture Dad placing that plate of pancakes in front of Sarah and singing *Happy Birthday* to her. Of course, we all joined in. After finishing the song, Sarah blew out the candles with one breath, which caused a huge smile to plaster across her face. We may have been little, but we all knew what blowing out the candles in a single breath signified: whatever she'd wished for, it would come true. But if her wish were for a happy birthday, blowing out the candles at once would prove to be nothing more than hogwash.

"Make sure you turn off these lights before you get on the bus," Dad scolded, as he got ready to leave for work. He'd been mad at us time and time again for causing the electric bill to go sky high.

"Hey, Dad," Sarah said. "Don't forget! You said I could have a party on my thirteenth birthday, and today's the day."

"I told you last night, there'll be no party here tonight. There's not a thing in this house!" He left, slamming the door behind him. Sarah ran and opened it.

"You promised!" she hollered. "Plus, I've already invited my friends to come after school."

"Well, you better un-invite them," he hollered back. Sarah let out a scream, slammed the door and then ran to get her shoes. Returning to the kitchen, she sat with a foot up on the chair using her fingers as a shoehorn to get her shoes on. "They're coming. I don't care what he says!"

On the way to school Monica and Anna were worried that Sarah would get in trouble from Dad if she brought her friends home. I wasn't worried about Dad getting mad; I knew he'd only stay mad for a little while. I was worried because there really wasn't anything in the house to put on a birthday party. All day at school I prayed that Sarah would change her mind and tell her friends they wouldn't be able to come over after all. Any lame excuse would do — she'd disobeyed Dad so he'd changed his mind; we were getting unexpected company, like aunts and uncles; or even that she felt she was getting a relapse of the flu. But on the way home five extra girls were on our bus — Bonnie, Paula, Suzanne, Amber and Janie, all Sarah's friends. They were laughing and talking loudly, Sarah not so much. When our stop came, I wanted to stay on the bus so I wouldn't have to face the embarrassment with Sarah.

As usual, Dad wasn't home from work, so the fire in the wood stove was out. To our amazement, the oil burner in the dining room was also out, obviously out of oil. The house was so cold that whenever Sarah's friends talked a burst of smoke-like air puffed from their mouths. Her friends thought it was hilarious. They watched each other's breath in amazement, but not Sarah. She looked like she was about to cry. I felt trapped in a sense of hopelessness, unable to do anything to help, until I heard Anna ask if she should go chop kindling to start the fire. "I'll go," I said.

"Me, too," Catherine added, slipping out the door behind me. John hadn't returned home after school. He was the one in charge of starting the fire, but Dad had let him stay for track practice and had told us older girls to start it when we came home. Our usual jobs were dishes, both before and after supper, helping Dad make the evening meal, and sometimes doing a load of laundry. But by the looks of the countertop we evidently hadn't been doing our jobs. Dirty clothes were piled high on the utility room floor. Other wash was clean and dry but still hanging from makeshift clotheslines strung across the living room. Not one of us had even taken the time to make a bed before leaving for school. We knew Dad would be thoroughly disgusted with it all when he arrived home. The fact was he'd been frustrated with the whole bunch of us lately for not helping him out more. Doing schoolwork before housework was not his idea of putting priorities in order.

Catherine and I split kindling wood and carried it into the house. Bernadette placed the pieces on top of the wrinkled paper that she'd put in the bottom of the stove. After opening the draft, she lit a match to the paper and blew on it, waiting for the kindling to ignite into a sure flame. Sarah's friends watched in fascination as the fire began to crackle and spread. As smoke began to roll within the stove, Bernadette closed the door, grabbed a few more pieces of the kindling and proceeded into the kitchen to light the kitchen stove. We needed it hot to cook whatever we could manage to muster-up for supper. Catherine and I went to haul in some hardwood. Returning with our arms filled,

Bernadette grabbed two small chunks for each of the fires. Then she turned to us and raised her shoulders and whispered, "All we have is rice, beans, pig lard, powdered eggs, cocoa and stuff to bake with."

"We can make biscuits," I suggested.

"Good idea," she said. "I know we have the stuff for that."

As Bernadette, Catherine and I busied ourselves in the kitchen, Sarah and her friends stood watching as we sifted flour, greased the tins and rolled and cut out the biscuits.

"Where's your cake?" Suzanne asked.

"I don't have one," Sarah answered. "Since Mama died we don't have cake on our birthdays. Dad will buy me ice cream though."

"Where do we put your presents?" Paula asked as she looked around for the designated place.

"Yes, where should we?" Janie echoed. "I'm sick of toting this around."

Sarah shrugged her shoulders. "I'm not sure where to put them. I've never had a party before."

"Never?" Bonnie asked in amazement as she slipped off her shoes.

"If you take off yer shoes, yer toes are gonna get cold," Monica said.

Bonnie giggled. "I like the way your little sister talks," she said, as she slid her feet back into her shoes and then asked Monica if she could hold her. Monica raised her arms and Bonnie lifted her from the floor.

"Why, you're as light as a feather. I always wanted a little sister." Everyone started laughing and taking turns lifting Monica, and then Anna, too. Later they tried lifting Catherine and me but they couldn't even budge us.

"I'm thirsty," Suzanne said, meandering toward the sink. "Where are the glasses?"

"Up here," Anna said, pushing a chair to the cupboard so she could reach them. "Here's one."

"Oops, this is cracked. Can I have a different one?" Anna reached for another. "This one is chipped. Just let me get my own," she said opening the cupboard doors all the way.

"Oh my gosh!" Paula exclaimed. "I thought we were the only ones that had to use pint jars for glasses."

"Pint jars," the other girls said, running to get one.

"This is great," Janie exclaimed. "I wish we could use jars at our house. Then I wouldn't have to fill my glass as often." But as the water poured out of the faucet and into the jars, one by one they commented about the odor of it. None of us said a word.

"What's that weird smell coming from the water?" Paula asked.

"Whatever it is, I can see spots of it floating on the top," Bonnie said.

We all knew to keep our mouths shut. Dad had warned us that if we talked too much about the things that went wrong at home we kids could become wards of the state. "Important people" would come and take us to live with other families. So we kept quiet until Monica said, "Dat yucky stuff is fuel oil. John spilled it on da ground, right by da well." The girls gathered around her. I had never heard Monica speak so clearly as that day when she informed Sarah's friends about the "big oil spill." She explained how John had to walk to the store with an upside-down hood from an old car as a makeshift sleigh. Monica told how he had to pull the five-gallon can of fuel oil home on the sleigh because it was too heavy for him to carry. She looked sad when she explained that John had cried because he hated when he had to go all the way to the store pulling the hood. She even went so far as to tell them about the fight John and Dad had had earlier on the morning of the spill and that John said he'd look dumb pulling the big hood down the road. He didn't want anybody to see him. Dad told him just to ignore everyone.

Monica continued the story, telling how John wasn't tall enough to reach up to the fuel oil tank, so he'd stood on a chunk of wood to pour the oil in. Dad had told him the job had to be done before he got home from work. She told how, as John was pouring the oil into the tank, he'd slipped off the wood and the can of oil went flying and spilled all over the ground. Anna topped off the story when she opened the door and showed everyone exactly where the spill had taken place. Sarah stood behind her friends with her hand over her mouth, shaking her head back and forth. Every now and then, when her friends weren't looking, she'd put up her fist and shake it toward Monica and Anna, who'd become tour guide. The rest of us knew they were definitely in trouble with Sarah, but we giggled among ourselves because we were in awe at how accurately our youngest sister had told the whole ordeal. To the best of our recollections, she'd never once even mentioned the oil spill before, not to John, not to Dad, not to any of us.

"So did the oil seep through the ground and into the water?" Suzanne asked.

"Right into our well," Anna exclaimed pointing to the pump just feet from the oil tank. Sarah turned her two little sisters away from the door. "Get lost you brats!" she exclaimed.

"I'm hungry," Paula said. "Are we having sloppy joes and potato chips?" I grabbed Sarah's hand and squeezed it. She looked at me with tears in her eyes. There wasn't a three-layer birthday cake like Bernadette said her friend Colleen had had. There wasn't a cake shaped into a large heart like Catherine's friend Susan once had. And there weren't any cupcakes with colored sprinkles on them like my friend Anne had at her birthday party. There weren't any sloppy joes cooking on the stove, no potato chips in a fancy bowl, no pickles laid perfectly on a little silver platter nor colored mints in a pretty candy dish.

"What games are we going to play?" Janie asked. Before anyone had time to answer, Amber asked for a quart jar and some clothespins. Bernadette ran to get some. Amber pulled out a kitchen chair, set the jar on the floor in front of the back of it, and asked, "Who wants to go first?"

"I do," Catherine yelled, throwing up her hand. She knelt on the chair and put her arms over the back of it. Amber handed her the six clothespins. One by one Catherine tried dropping them into the jar. "I got two in," she was saying as Dad walked into the house. Though Sarah had warned him, he was surprised to see the girls, and disgusted because the fires in both stoves were now nearly out again.

"I've told you girls time and time again that you have to almost close the draft once you get the fire going or the wood will burn like paper," Dad snarled. Sarah's face and neck blotched out in red spots, especially when Dad announced to the girls that he'd be taking them home.

Dad hadn't brought home ice cream either, like Sarah thought he would. I knew the only way that would have happened was if it were a payday for him. At the store a couple days earlier, I'd overheard Cal tell Dad that he couldn't charge on his slip anymore until he'd paid on his bill. Still, I thought Dad would at least bring home Kool-Aid. But the only thing he'd come into the house with was his Husqvarna chainsaw and his big long file. He set his saw by the wood stove as usual so the heat from the fire would keep the oil in the motor from freezing.

Dad seemed to be trying to figure out which girls belonged to which families of the community, then he said, "I hate to do this girls, but you can come some other time when the weather is nicer. I'm wet to my waist and I want to get out of these clothes, so if you get in my car, I'll take you home." The girls ran for their coats. None of them said a word.

"I hate you, I hate you, I hate you," Sarah screamed when Dad got back. He didn't correct her for saying those mean words. She ran to the bedroom and sobbed her heart out. When supper was ready she wouldn't get up to eat. After Anna and Bernadette cleared the table, I told her she had to get up because it was her turn to wash the dishes.

"Get out of here!" she yelled. "It's my birthday! I don't have to do a thing on my birthday!" I ran to tell Dad what she'd said. He was trying to light the oil burner.

Most days Dad kept the oil burner at the lowest position to save on oil, which sometimes caused it to go out. The house never felt warm. This day certainly wasn't the first time the oil burner had run out of fuel. Several other mornings, evenings, and even during the night, we'd wake up freezing. Whenever it went completely out, the cold seemed unbearable, especially since blankets were in short supply. We'd take the coats from the racks and shake the rugs from the floor and put them on top of the blankets. We girls referred to our house as a house of all seasons during the wintertime. The utility room felt like the hottest day of summer. Spring breezes seemed to always be passing through the kitchen, and the bathroom felt like a brisk fall morning. The bedrooms were usually invaded by winter winds that blew in through the cracks around the windows — the windows that many times were painted by Jack Frost. Most mornings over the course of a winter, we'd awaken to see our breath forming into tiny ghost shapes dancing above us. Everything was cold, but stepping on the linoleum floor always made me gasp. We rarely had pajamas to wear, and it was just as well, since sleeping in our clothes kept us warmer. Each morning after Dad stoked the fire, the warmth wouldn't reach the kitchen for more than an hour. The bedrooms wouldn't feel relief for another hour or so after that. By then we'd be on the bus on our way to school.

Whenever I stayed overnight at friends' houses, their houses were so different. They were warm and cozy, and they had tons of extra blankets and quilts. I wondered why it couldn't be that way at our house. At Candy's it was so hot we didn't even have to cover at night. The warmth of the house and all the blankets they had weren't the only things that made me envious. Her dresser drawers were full of socks and leotards, t-shirts and underwear, slacks and sweaters, and anything else one might need. Many times I wondered if she'd consider giving me a pair of her socks so I wouldn't have to wear ones with holes in them, but I didn't have the courage to ask her.

"Dad! Sarah won't get off the bed to do her dishes," I hollered.

"What the hell are you trying to do, get me burnt? Don't go screaming when I'm working with fire!"

"Well, Sarah won't get up to do her dishes. She said that it's her birthday, so she doesn't have to do a thing!"

"She's right," he said. "She can have the night off. You other girls can do them for her." We started whining and complaining as if Dad were sending us out in the dark to pull parsnips from under the snow.

"I'm not doing dishes on my birthday, then!" Bernadette announced.

"Me, either!" I said. Statements soon followed from the rest of my sisters claiming the same birthday privilege.

"No, you won't have to do a damn thing," Dad said closing the door of the oil burner and mumbling that he'd better clean the burners before trying to start it again.

So from Sarah's birthday onward, none of us ever had to do any work on our birthday.

Seven
CR

Luke came home from Chicago two weeks after Sarah's birthday. He had written to say he'd be visiting for a few days. When we heard a car horn continuously beeping, we ran outside because we knew it had to be him. He drove up in a turquoise and white '58 Ford hardtop convertible. Despite the drizzling rain, he insisted on going right to our mother's grave. At the cemetery he opened the trunk of his car and took out a big urn filled with real flowers which he set it next to our mother's headstone. "It's only mid-April," Dad said, "and way too early to put live flowers on the grave. We could still get snow, and for sure frost."

"I heard on the radio it's supposed to be nice weather through the weekend. What it does after that, I don't care." Dad clasped his hands behind himself, as he looked the flowers over, admiring the urn and the arrangement of roses in colors of yellow, red and white. "These are nice," he said to Luke as we knelt around our mother's grave to pray. As we did, Luke started to cry. Monica, although she was only four and a half, stood up and put her arms around his neck. "You don't hafta cry," she said. "Mama's up in heaven! Way up in da sky." Luke laughed, then cried, and laughed and cried until his laughing and crying meshed together until we weren't sure what he was doing. As soon as the rest of us would start to laugh, too, he'd start to cry. Dad continued praying, then said, "We have to get back. I have pies in the oven."

On the way home, Luke stopped at the store and bought a gallon of ice cream, along with chips and pop. We stayed up past our bedtimes that night, eating the goodies and enjoying each other's company. I heard Dad, Luke and John talking into the wee hours of the morning about the latest deaths in the community, the houses and barns that were being built, planting of the garden and the things Luke was going to buy for our house with Matthew's financial help. Late the next afternoon, Luke took us girls shopping in Escanaba. Together we picked out a new couch, chair, end tables, coffee table and lamps. Luke was anxious to get them home, but the manager of the store said they wouldn't be delivered for a couple days. "That's okay," Luke told him, "as long as they're there before I leave to go back to Chicago."

Luke had also bought a console stereo but insisted on taking it home with us. He helped the man carry it to the car. They put it on the back seat. It took up every inch of space so Anna and Monica rode in the front with Luke, Bernadette and Sarah, and Catherine lay up on top of the stereo. I sat on the back floorboard. Luke popped a top off a beer and drank it down, and then popped another and another on our way home. He wanted to get home fast so he could play the stereo. Every sharp corner he maneuvered, my sisters in the front would scream because he kept going onto the shoulder of loose gravel. When we went around the sharp Valentine corner, he was going so fast that Catherine flew off the counsel and into the front with the rest. I was glad I couldn't see a thing and relieved when we finally got home. The

49

last time he'd driven that fast with us in the car was when he was still living at home. We had been on a back road when he'd seen some deer up ahead in the road. "Hold on tight, and everything will be all right," he'd said as he stepped down on the gas pedal. The next morning we'd had venison steak for breakfast.

Luke opened his car door before he'd come to a complete stop in the driveway. After getting out of the car, he did his usual happy gesture. He clenched his fists, raised them high with force, then hollered, "Dad, get out here! We're home!" Both Dad and John came and helped Luke carry the stereo into the dining room. It was beautiful but looked out of place next to the beat-up furniture. The sound that came from it, however, was fascinating. Until midnight, we listened to songs and to an occasional newscast. A few days later, Luke went to see Jude. While in Manistique he bought some records and returned home in the nick of time for the arrival of the new furniture. It was beautiful and made our house look cozy. Together we relaxed on the new couch and chair while we listened to Buck Owens and Merle Haggard. It was the first time in nearly three years I felt at home.

Luke returned the first of May. After having worked a lot of overtime at his job, he had earned enough money to put in a septic system and sink, stool and tub in the bathroom, along with cold running water. He was happy with the work he, Dad and John had done, but he was mad at Dad. He had sent him two hundred dollars to buy a gas range to replace the wood-burning stove in the kitchen. Unfortunately, Dad used the money for other things we needed. Instead of a new range, he spent twenty-five dollars on a used broken-down one that he was so sure he'd be able to fix, but had been unable to.

"Dammit, Dad," Luke cursed both when he first got home and again before leaving to go back to Chicago "Why didn't you spend the money on what you were supposed to? Now I'm going to have to go into town and try to charge a range."

"No, no," Dad said. "We don't need that right now. This old Monarch works fine." Luke didn't say another word. A few days later, a new kitchen range was delivered to our house. My sisters and I loved it. For a time we didn't even mind cooking. Before long, however, we again ran out of bottled gas, the second time since getting the range. It was the week before Memorial Day. I was home sick from school when Dad came running into the bedroom.

"The gas company is here! Get to the door and tell the man your dad's not home but he wants you to leave the gas, because we're out."

"My clothes are all wrinkled. I don't want to answer the door," I said. "Plus, you're here, why can't *you* tell him?" I asked, still half asleep and troubled by his insistence.

"If you don't get out there *right now*, we're not going to have anything to eat for the holiday," he said. Suddenly the knock came on the door.

"Why can't you go?" I asked again.

"Because I don't have the money to pay him, and he won't leave gas if I don't pay!"

Slipping out from under the covers, I headed to the door. I looked back at Dad. He lay on the bed and pulled the blanket over his head. I couldn't understand why he did such a thing. He peeked out and gestured for me to get going. By the time I got to the back door, the knocking had turned to banging. I opened the door. My head dropped to my chest. "Your Dad home?" he asked. I forced my eyes up. The guy was young and cute, and although I was only ten and a half, I felt him look me up and down. I hadn't felt good for days. I was sure I looked like a big sticky marshmallow that had been rolled in dirt.

"I'm supposed to drop off a tank of gas." Again he asked if my dad was home. At that moment I had to do something I was told never to do. I had to lie! I cocked my head and raised my shoulders a bit. "Ah, I don't think so."

"You mean you don't know?"

"No, I mean, I don't know where he's at right now."

"He ordered bottled gas. Does he still want it?" This is easy, I thought. "Yes, I remember he said, 'If the gas man comes when I'm not around, make sure he leaves a tank.'"

"Did he leave the money for it?"

"I don't think so."

"Then I'll have to come back another day." He began to turn around. "Oh, dear Lord, what should I do?" I thought.

"No! You can't leave. My dad said to be sure you leave gas because we're out." I could feel my hands trembling more and more with every second that passed, with every lie I told.

"Well, if I leave the gas without getting paid, I'll get in trouble with my boss, because your dad already owes for the first tank."

"Please," I said. "I'll get in trouble if you don't leave it. Memorial Day is just a couple days away and we need to use the oven." He gave a big sigh. "What a day," he sighed, and then he left. I tip-toed to the kitchen window and stood off to the side, waiting, watching, listening, hoping to see the man come around the corner of the house pulling a dolly with a tank of gas on it. My heart raced within my chest. It seemed like forever before I finally saw him. "Thank you, Lord," I said, stepping further away from the window. I stayed there waiting for the man to return after he'd hooked up the tank. He startled me when he again banged on the door.

"Sign this, please," he said, handing me a receipt book when I opened the door. I could hardly steady my hands enough to put my signature on it. Usually I was proud of my penmanship, but my signature looked more like chicken scratching. Shaking more than ever, I handed back the receipt book. He ripped the yellow copy from it and gave it to me. "Have a nice Memorial Day," he said.

I was dumbfounded by his kindness, so much so that I said nothing. Not "You, too," or "Thank you." Nothing!

Relieved when he finally drove away, I made a beeline to the bedroom. "You can come out of hiding!" I said sarcastically. Dad didn't say a word. I lifted the blanket from his face. "He's gone!" Dad got up from the bed.

"Don't go yelling like that! He's liable to come back and find me here. Then there goes the gas! And when Luke comes home he'll be mad again!"

Eight
ଓ

Maybe it was being pushed into adult roles or just my sisters and I being adventurous out of boredom, but the month of June during the year before my eleventh birthday brought with it mischievousness. While Dad and John were at work in the woods, Matthew's junkyard of old cars became a major source of exploration, despite Dad's warnings about the dangers of being in or around them. What first intrigued us about the junkyard were all the beautiful flowers that were in blossom around the old cars. The Indian paintbrush, daisy, wild pink roses, and even the dandelions were irresistible. It was Sarah who first peered into an old Studebaker and immediately summoned us to the scene.

"Everyone, hurry," she said. "I just spied a teddy bear on the back seat of this old car." We all peered in through the windows to see the abandoned creature.

"Kin I have it?" Monica asked.

"Dad said we're not allowed to get in the old cars," Sarah told her. "But he didn't say we couldn't open a door to grab out a teddy bear," Bernadette said as she grabbed the handle and pushed in the button to open the door. Within seconds we were all in the car watching as Monica covered the teddy bear's face with kisses. Soon we were exploring the other dozen or so cars to see if they held treasures, too. Catherine found a pair of Mickey Mouse sunglasses, Sarah found an old shoe, Anna found a doll's head and together we collected pennies, dimes, nickels, two quarters and a Kennedy half dollar, enough to buy us each an ice cream bar, plus penny candies at the store.

Another day while exploring the inside of an old Chrysler we found the ashtray full of cigarette butts. We couldn't resist trying to smoke a real cigarette. We'd made plenty of fake ones in the past by rolling flour up in small pieces of paper, but every now and then one of us would choke on a mouthful of the flour after inhaling instead of exhaling. We learned quickly that we could also choke on the inhalation of a real cigarette. We'd sit in the old, broken-down trucks and cars, lighting cigarette butts and taking deep drags from them. Bernadette was the first to inhale and then exhale. She blew smoke rings, like we learned to do with the early morning air of a freezing morning. "Was that hard to do?" I asked her.

"Not really," she said.

"I'm next to try," Catherine exclaimed. I lit the match and she puffed to get the Marlboro lit. "Ooh, my eyes burn," she said, swishing away the smoke.

Sarah was next to try and then I took a big drag from the Viceroy I'd lit. I began choking so I handed the cigarette to Catherine. I coughed and coughed and became dizzy. After getting my balance back, I took another drag. Each day I got better at holding in the smoke until I wanted to let it go. Little by little I puffed out just enough to make either small or big rings.

From the cigarette excursions we continued on to bigger and better things. Some of the cars had push button starters, and every now and then one of them would actually start. So with the car running we'd pretend we were going places like shopping, to the movies or to visit Grandma in Escanaba. But that only lasted so long before boredom again set in. Soon one of us was pushing down on the clutch while another tried to put the car in gear. After a lot of practice, we four older girls could shift from first into second, then third, but only Bernadette could figure out how to get it into reverse. The Mercury was our favorite. It was an automatic, like Mark's car. Whenever we got it started, we'd rock it back and forth and back and forth until even that got boring.

It was on a Friday, after pretending to be driving a car to Manistique, Escanaba, Chicago and even Alaska that we decided to take the old clunker into the field and through the woods on the rutted road that led to the cow pasture. Bernadette drove first. At the end of the woods she turned around in the hayfield. Then I took over, followed by Catherine and Sarah. We giggled until we cried as the car bounced along, time and time again leaving the road long enough to smash down brush or sideswipe a stump in the way. We could hardly believe that driving was so easy. As days passed, we became pros at pushing in the clutch while shifting, then giving the car gas, and braking only when we had to. No longer did we dread doing our daily chores. They were done in haste so we'd have more time to drive.

One day Dad and John left for work in an old car that John had gotten started because Dad's car was low on gas. Later that morning we tried without any luck to get one of the junkyard cars started, so we walked back home and hopped into Dad's car. Bernadette started it up and backed it out of the driveway. She drove down the road in front of the house until we came to the field road that led to the woods. Then we took turns driving. Since Anna and Monica were still little, we only let them steer while standing next to the driver. Letting them think they were driving guaranteed that there wouldn't be any tattletales. When Sarah was driving, we were mad because she was going so slowly. We hollered at her to speed up. Finally, with hands clenched on the wheel, the car roared. Her eyes grew big. "Yippee," we hollered. But unfortunately she forgot about the big bump and didn't slow down. We went flying to the ceiling. Catherine hit her head against the windshield and ended up with a large goose egg. Still we giggled and laughed until we came to a stop. The car had stalled. Sarah tried pushing the start button again and again, but the only sound it made was a clicking noise. "Now look what you made me do!" she snarled.

"How did we make you do it?" I asked.

"You guys are the ones who wanted me to go faster."

Catherine, Bernadette and I hurried out of the car. "Pull the lever," Bernadette said. The three of us stood on the bumper and lifted the car hood. "Hurry," she said, using her head to help brace the weight of the hood. "Lift the metal stick to hold it up."

Catherine grabbed it and secured it into place. "Now, what do we have here?" she asked. She and Bernadette looked the engine over as if they were well-trained mechanics like Luke. "Here's what's wrong," Catherine said, holding up a cable. "This is exactly what happened to Luke's battery. I watched him fix his so I know how to put this cable-thing back on." Bernadette jumped down from the bumper. "I'll find a rock to pound it on tight," she said.

It wasn't long before she hollered to Sarah, "Try starting it." And sure enough, Dad's car was running once again.

"Whew! That was a close call," I said.

"Push over," Bernadette told Sarah as she butted her out of the driver's seat. The rest of us climbed back in. Driving away, we could hear a sound. "Oh, no! What's that tick, tick, tick sound?" Catherine questioned. Bernadette stopped the car and put it in neutral. She popped the hood and once again we got out. Again the mechanics looked to see what was wrong.

"It's the fan! It's bent," Catherine shouted from under the hood of the running car. "We need a stick or something to bend it out." Catherine and Bernadette looked at me.

"You've just been standing around and watching. Run to the house and get an ax so we can chop down a little tree to use to straighten the fan. And hurry! Dad and the boys will be home soon," Bernadette said.

The big heavy axe kept nicking my legs, leaving little bloody spots over them as I was running back, so I began to walk. "Hurry," they hollered.

"I can't. My legs hurt, and so does my chest." Whenever I ran too much or too fast, snakelike pains crawled up my chest and into my throat and then I'd have a hard time breathing, like I did whenever we smoked the cigarette butts or when Dad smoked his pipe.

"Hurry, before we run out of gas," Bernadette scolded. When I finally got there, she took the axe, and she and Catherine took turns chopping the limbs off a little tree. Then they chopped it at the bottom until it fell to the ground.

"Remember how mad Dad was when cousin Mike tried chopping down one of the trees?" I said. "Dad is going to throw a fit when he sees what you've done."

"Do you have a better idea?" Bernadette asked as she grabbed the tree and lowered it under the hood next to the radiator. After some pushing and yanking against the fan the ticking sound stopped. "Shush," Bernadette pleaded when we left for home. "I have to make sure it's fixed." We were as quiet as mice until we reached the main road. "We did it!" she hollered.

"Yeah!" Catherine shouted.

When we rode into the driveway, I got out of the car to direct Bernadette back to the big rocks I'd placed on the ground in front of the tires before we moved the car. "Whoa!" I hollered. Everyone jumped out and rushed into the house. When inside, Sarah made us promise not to tell anyone about taking the car. She made us spit on the palm of our hands and say, "I won't tell anyone about taking Dad's car for at least a hundred years. If I do, it means I'm glad Mama died."

We had barely completed the ritual when Dad and John arrived home. Our eyes twisted back and forth toward each other as we waited for their grand entrance into the house. I crossed my fingers, hoping they wouldn't detect that the car had been moved. It was frightening to think what Dad would do to us if he ever found out that we'd driven his car all around the back yard and into the woods.

"What the heck?" John said, when none of us blabbered about this and that, like we usually did before they'd even got into the house. "Did the cats *finally* get their tongues?"

"We're just tired," Sarah exclaimed.

"Whew!" Catherine said, once they'd left the kitchen.

"That was close," Anna added.

"Did you see Dad when he came in? He looked back toward his car. I think he knows we took it, so I'm going to tell him what we did. Maybe then we won't get in as much trouble," I said.

"Don't you dare!" my older sisters whispered, as Bernadette twisted a pinch into my arm.

"Remember," Sarah reminded, "You promised not to tell! If you do, it means you're glad Mama died!" It was at that moment I realized I would never tell. None of us would ever tell. Our secret would definitely be taken to the grave.

Nine
CR

Tired of a fast-paced life, Matthew quit working in the city and came home to stay. He'd saved money while working in Chicago to buy more old cars to get his auto salvage business up and running, so Luke brought him home that Fourth of July. My sisters and I thought our fun for the summer was over. We knew there'd be no way we could continue to drive the old cars with Matthew around. In reality, Catherine's and my fun was yet to begin. Days later, only minutes before Luke was leaving to go back to Chicago, he decided to take Catherine and me with him. The two of us were ecstatic as we threw the few pieces of our summer belongings into paper bags. In no time we were ready and on our way.

After driving for hours, we finally stopped for food and gas. It was so hot that Luke put the top down on his convertible. As we continued on our journey, we sang a lot of songs with Luke, like "Kaw-Liga",

"Move It On Over" and "Little Jimmy Brown." It was while on the expressway that Luke asked me what I wanted for my eleventh birthday.

"It's not for two months yet," I said.

"I can still ask, can't I? I was thinking you could pick out a dress for school. I'll be taking you back home a couple days before it starts." I looked at Catherine and smiled.

"Can I pick out something, too?" she asked. "You forgot my birthday."

"Oh, no!" he said, brushing the top of her head as the wind blew her hair every which way and she struggled to keep it out of her eyes. I'd somehow managed to put on my scarf — Mama's black scarf. Whenever I wore it, I felt grown up. With the summer sun beating down upon me, I pretended to be Elizabeth Taylor. Yes, I was a movie star, riding in a convertible on my way to the big city to find the love of my life. I watched with amazement the cars that sped by until a super long black one passed us. "Was that a car?" I asked.

"That, my dear sisters, was a limo! You'll be seeing a lot of them in the city."

"That's the kind of car Dad should have," Catherine told us.

"Then we wouldn't have to be squished, right?" I said.

"Right."

We'd never seen so many cars and trucks going so fast and we'd never realized that people had to pay to ride on certain roads until Luke stopped to pay the fees at the tollbooths along the way. As darkness fell, the neon lights of the city were amazing. We tried to read as many as we could. Finally, when we could no longer stay awake, I propped my head against the door and Catherine's fell upon my shoulder. The next thing we knew, Luke was trying to wake us up. "Hey, you two. We're at my apartment, 4030 West Monroe Street." I nudged Catherine. Luke pressed the button to put his retractable top back up. As it climbed up over us, we grabbed our bags from the backseat. In the dimly lit street, we climbed the staircase to his apartment. The air was hot and stuffy. My skin felt sticky. When he opened the door to his apartment, a wave of even hotter air poured out over us.

Luke's apartment was much different from what I'd expected. It was small and smelled of gas, as if a pilot light on the kitchen range had gone out, which sometimes happened with our new range at home. "Thirsty?" he asked, as he set his suitcase by his bedroom door. Although our eyes were barely open we both admitted we were. I saw a glass on the counter and began filling it with tap water. Luke laughed. "You're not going to want to drink this water. It never gets cold; it's city water! Here," he said opening the refrigerator and grabbing out a bottle of juice, "have some of this." I drank it down and snitched a Tootsie Roll from a nearby candy dish. "Tonight, I'll sleep on the couch. You two can take my bedroom but tomorrow we'll have to figure out different sleeping arrangements."

In no time at all we were in bed, but I couldn't sleep. I could hardly breathe. In the stillness of the hot city night I anticipated the fun we'd have over the summer. Hours passed before I finally drifted off. Yet at the crack of dawn Catherine and I were ready to explore Chicago. Luke reluctantly got up that Sunday morning and took us a couple houses down the block to our cousin Lizzy's, where my Aunt Celia lived, too. They were old ladies to us, but were probably fifty-five, first cousins to each other, both of them widowed with children grown and gone. Aunt Celia was thrilled to see us. She smothered us with hugs and kisses. After all, we were her youngest sister's little girls. Lizzy owned several houses in the area, including the house across the street that her daughter, son-in-law and their children lived in. She had another unmarried daughter, JoAnne, who lived a few miles away and a son, Donald who lived just miles away with his beautiful wife Delores and their four children. They were cousins that Catherine and I were anxious to get to know and play with.

Lizzy started to make us breakfast when she realized she only had a couple of eggs, so she asked me to go to the store for some. "Where's the store?" I asked. She took me to the living room window.

"Cross the street, then go to the end of the block," she said as she pointed in the direction of the store. "See that sign sticking out from the side of that building?" I nodded. "Well, that's the store. Tell the man you've come to buy a dozen eggs and he'll get them for you."

"Okay," I said as Lizzy dug into her purse for money. Taking the dollar I slipped it down into my sock.

"Smart girl," she said. "Now you won't lose it."

Joyously I skipped across the street and down the sidewalk looking at the houses and singing "Mockingbird Hill." The houses astonished me; they looked exactly alike and seemed only an arm's width apart. As I neared the store, I noticed one of its big windows boarded up, like Dad had boarded our bedroom window after John had accidentally broken it with his baseball. None of the sights, as striking as they were, slowed me down. I continued to skip and sing right through the open door of the little corner store and up to the counter where someone was standing reading a newspaper. Peeking out from behind it, a man was surprised to see me standing there. More surprised was I to see him.

"Well, hi dare, little whait girl. Wat kin I do fer ya today?" he graciously asked. I couldn't move. I couldn't speak. I'd never seen a black man. (I'd heard my dad talk about black people, and it was never good, although to the best of my recollection, he'd never been in contact with anyone of the black race.) I wanted to run, but couldn't move. I had turned to a pillar of salt, like Lot's wife from the Bible. The man looked into my eyes. My heart thumped within my chest. For a split second I wondered if he was going to do something bad to me.

"Jest like me," he said. "Yer hair's curly, jest like mine. Feel," he said taking my hand and rubbing it across the top of his head. Then he brushed his hand across the top of mine. I said nothing. He leaned on the countertop and took my hands in his. "What kin I do fer ya?" he

63

asked again.

"Ee... ee... eg... egg," I managed. The one word coming out as if it was a compound sentence.

"Eggs? Is that what you want?" I took a breath, relieved that I didn't have to try and get the word out again.

"Lizbeth send you? Lizbeth Lavallie?"

He knows Lizzy — Lizzy knows him! I told myself, remembering that Lizzy had told me about him. My shoulders relaxed.

"Nice lady. Lizbeth's a very nice lady." I nodded, slightly smiled and relaxed even more as he turned and walked to the back of the store. I scouted the area close to me. There were medicines, newspapers, and all kinds of candy, like bags of lemon drops hanging from little hooks. My mouth puckered. I saw Sugar Babies, Hershey Bars and Three Musketeers, some of my favorites.

"Dat be twenty-nine cents," the man said, reaching for the dollar bill I held out to him. He counted back the change and I put it into the bag. "Thank you," I said and headed for the door.

"Little whait girl with the curly hair. Grab a piece of dat penny candy on yer way out."

"Me?" I gestured, pointing my finger to my chest, although there was no one else around.

"Yessa Ma'am." I looked at all the one-cent candy.

"Gee, thanks, Mister," I said, grabbing a Black Jack and then skipping out the doorway.

"He was nice," I told myself out loud as I stuck the bag with the eggs under my arm so I could unwrap my candy. "Dad's wrong! Negro people are nice!" I said, over and over and over again. When I got back to Lizzy's, I told everyone all about the nice Negro man. "Oh he's an angel," Lizzy said as she cracked the eggs into a pan.

Later that day Catherine and I helped Luke clean his apartment. Catherine found strange looking bugs in a paper bag. She screamed and threw the bag. Luke laughed. "Those are just a couple cockroaches

— city bugs. They won't hurt you." When I opened the cupboard door below the sink to get the dish soap and saw bugs with zillions of legs crawling around, I threw the bottle of Joy clear across the floor and we bolted from the room. "Just little ol' centipedes," Luke said, laughing until he almost cried. Catherine and I decided we'd much rather put up with country bugs. "Oh, I'll kill them with some Raid," Luke said.

"Raid!" Catherine and I yelled simultaneously, like in the television commercial. Luke sprayed a couple times a week but no matter how clean we kept his apartment, centipedes and cockroaches found their way into our surroundings. Then one morning while Catherine and I were watching Mickey Mouse, a real mouse darted across the floor. Luke came running out of his bedroom pulling up his pants as he came toward us to see what was wrong. "Aaah...ah...a...mouse!" we screamed from the couch as we pointed in the direction it had run.

"Get it, Luke!" I cried.

"A little, helpless mouse. That's what all this commotion is about?" He laughed so hard that he had to wipe the tears from his eyes. We wanted him to take us home, then and there. "No, I'm not taking you home. It's not just a hop, skip and a jump! You're here until September." Catherine and I got mad and ran to our cousin Betty Jane's.

Each day of the week, plus nearly every Saturday, Luke worked from three in the afternoon to eleven at night at a factory called Danly's, where they made presses for the automobile industry. Oftentimes when he was gone, I sat on the porch next door with June. She was a slim Irish woman with carrot-red hair, milky-white skin and turquoise blue eyes. Her husband was black. Some of their children were brown, some white and some black. She and I became friends, even though I wasn't even half her age. We often played a game that I'd made up called, *Exactly Alike*. It was a game like in newspapers where you'd have to find the differences in the "almost identical" photos. We'd look at the houses across the street and see what we could find, like someone sitting on a porch at one house or a towel hung over a makeshift clothesline at another. Other times I'd help June turn the jump ropes so her kids could play doubles, sometimes taking my turn as well. At some point, she always treated everyone to Cool-Pops.

But it was at Betty Jane and John's where we spent most of our time. There were always kids around and we liked that. Sometimes Donald and Delores would come over with their kids. Although Dean was only six years old and Danny just three, I had fun trying to get them to hit or catch a ball. I also liked carrying them around. Danny looked like my brother Jude and was almost the exact same age. Whenever I'd go to their house with Luke, I'd play house with them. Delores liked it when I did. She said it gave her time to get things done around the house. A couple times when Donald, Delores and their kids came over to Betty Jane's, there were enough kids to play school. I loved being the teacher.

When at Betty Jane's, we had fun playing with their two girls. We'd stay there each day until around nine before going back to Luke's for bedtime. Catherine and I took turns sleeping on a makeshift bed of blankets on the floor near the sofa. It was always so stifling that each night I'd set up the ironing board in front of us and place Luke's little fan on top of it. The little bit of air was a far cry from the late night breezes that blew in through our bedroom windows in Upper Michigan, but it cooled us enough to help us drift off to sleep. Catherine would sleep right through Luke coming home and stealing his fan back. Within minutes, I'd be like a sucker fish on the shore, gasping for air. As the nights dragged on, fears of the dreadful city bugs crawling around me would force me to cover my head, leaving me drenched with sweat.

Visiting with Aunt Celia on the weekends was a blessing. Lizzy's house was air-conditioned! Every Saturday Aunt Celia would give me a sewing lesson. On Sundays we'd go to church with her. I loved going to St. Mel's. It was a big church; ten times the size of ours back home. One Saturday afternoon she surprised us when she said we'd be going to the earliest Mass the next day. Afterwards she was taking us into the Loop of Chicago so we could see the tallest building in the world: the Prudential Building. Despite our excitement, we managed to sleep throughout the night in the coolness of the air-conditioned house. We slept so soundly that Auntie had to wake us the next morning so we'd have time to get ready for our special day.

"Okay, girls," she said after we'd eaten a quick breakfast. "I have another surprise for you."

"Do we get to take a tub bath?" Catherine asked, excitedly.

"Oh, you can take a bath here whenever you want. Although I was going to suggest you do that this morning. When you're through, I'll show you the other surprise."

Thus far we'd been enjoying the fact that Luke's apartment had a shower. We thought of it as a bath in the rain. It was much better than at home where we had to warm water to take just a shallow bath. Hopping into the warm bubble bath with the scent of roses was a thrill. We found we were almost too big to be in the tub together, yet we played like five-year-olds, piling suds on our heads to form hairdos, and making beards, boobs and whatnot with the bubbles. We hated getting out from the warmth of the water, but when Aunt Celia suggested we "move right along," we quickly washed and with towels around our half-dried bodies, we hurried to our aunt's bedroom.

Lying on her bed was two of the most beautiful dresses I'd ever seen. The blue one, the biggest one, I knew was mine. It was of soft cotton with a huge collar trimmed with lace that fell halfway down the bodice. The skirt of the dress was layered. Each layer was finished with white lace. Beneath the dress was a light blue cancan. The smaller dress was the same style, but red. At first I was ecstatic, but at second glance I realized Catherine would soon be screaming. Sure enough, her shrill was so terrifying I thought our aunt was going to have a heart attack. When it dawned on Catherine that the red dress was hers, she went running from the room, clutching the towel to her naked body as she went. "What is so terrible?" Aunt Celia asked, following Catherine into the living room where she had parked behind a chair.

Since our mother's death, Catherine hated wearing red. She had worn a red dress to our mother's funeral and since then wouldn't wear anything red. She wouldn't even use a red crayon.

"She hates the color red," I told Auntie. "She even cries when we chase her around the house with one of my dad's red hankies."

"Oh, my Lord," Aunt Celia said, putting her hand over her mouth and slowly turning her head from side to side. "You poor girls have surely been through a lot, haven't you?"

"Catherine hates church now, too. When we go to our church, she gets sick and has to go out to the car. At first Sarah, Bernadette and I thought she was faking it so she wouldn't have to listen to the priest talk, but one Sunday Sarah followed her out, and sure enough, Catherine was throwing up. My Dad thinks it's because Mama's funeral was at church."

My aunt cried as I told the story. "Come here, you two," she said. Catherine crawled out from behind the chair. Auntie draped her arms around us. "Your mother would be so proud of her little girls. What would you say if I told you that I think you should wear what you planned on wearing today?"

"Yeah," Catherine said. "I brought my orange school dress."

"I brought my yellow one."

"The color orange doesn't bother you?" Aunt Celia asked Catherine.

"Nope," she replied.

"Well, then, let's go get that orange dress on you."

When we were putting on our socks I noticed that I had brought orange ones and Catherine had taken white ones. I started laughing. "Whoa, Catherine. We have to exchange socks because mine match your dress and yours match mine." But she wouldn't trade, even when I tried to pull them from her.

"Just put on the ones you have," Auntie said. "Catherine had a hard enough morning. Let's not make her mad again. Plus, we have to hurry if we're going to make it to seven-thirty Mass so we can catch the nine fifteen train to the Loop."

The El ride was fascinating as we observed the sights and watched people get on or off at the stops. At times, I felt petrified. It seemed like we'd fall from the tracks as the El maneuvered high above ground, navigating corners and coming close to buildings. Catherine and I held on, occasionally letting out a scream. Getting closer to the downtown area was startling. The height of the buildings kept us in awe. I felt relieved when we got off the El and headed for the Prudential Building. The closer we got to it the farther back I had to tilt my head. The building looked as if it could be a highway to heaven. "Aunt Celia!" I exclaimed with excitement, "Mama saw these tall buildings, too, when she came to Chicago for Bernice's wedding (Aunt Celia's daughter). She told us all about them, how the tall buildings looked liked they were touching the sky. And now we're here, standing right where Mama was!" Catherine's mouth fell open. She came and grabbed my hands. I held on tight as we leaned back as far as we could and looked up to the sky as we circled round and round.

"Hey, you two, you're getting your auntie dizzy. Get in front of that marker over there," she said, while motioning us to the spot where she wanted us to stand. "I want to take your picture."

"I'm going to tell Mama all about this when we get home," Catherine boasted. I hurried and covered her mouth and cocked an eyebrow at her.

"What's the matter with that?" she asked as she ripped my hand from her face.

"Remember, Mama's dead!" I whispered irritably in her ear.

"Oops," she said, raising her brow, while covering her mouth.

"Oh dear," Aunt Celia said looking at the two of us. Tears welled up in her eyes. "Shall we go to the top?"

"Yippee," we said in unison.

"To the top then, it shall be!" She grabbed our hands and we headed for the door.

Stepping out of the elevator that had carried us to the top, we gaped in disbelief. Every wall was glass. We went running toward them. "Oh, my," Auntie said. "Don't get too close to the edge."

"But we want to see really good," Catherine exclaimed, as we got as close to the windows as possible. Aunt Celia remained further back. For miles and miles we could see smoke stacks, trains, the lakeshore and rivers, streets and expressways with cars and trucks that resembled toys. The people walking to and fro looked like they belonged in dollhouses. "Come see the plane!" Catherine hollered.

"This is enough for me," Auntie said. "Let's go back down and see some of the other sights of the city."

The elevator shook and creaked once again as it carried us back down the forty floors. I was glad to reach the bottom. We walked in haste to the other famous buildings. The Natural History Museum was my favorite. It was exciting seeing the first people that had lived and real stuffed animals, plus fossils and bones of every kind imaginable. Afterwards we walked to the park and ate the lunch Aunt Celia had packed for us. We shared our cheese and crackers with the pigeons, threw our apple cores into Lake Michigan, ate and then licked the wrappers of our half-melted Milky Way bars, but saved our Starks and Twinkies for the trip back home. Although the El had moved too fast for us on the way down to the Loop, it seemed to crawl on the return trip. We'd made a lifetime of wonderful memories and were anxious to share them with our cousins.

Ten
Q℞

Thunder rolled and lightning lit the sky as we headed for home that Labor Day weekend. I was glad to be on our way. I'd had a lot of fun over the summer but missed my dad and the others a lot. Monica was starting kindergarten on my eleventh birthday and Luke had given Catherine and me money to buy each of our sisters something to wear for the first day of school. We couldn't wait to show them what we'd picked out.

"How much longer 'til we get to Michigan?" I asked.

"For gosh sake," Luke complained. "We aren't even on the expressway yet. You're not going to be asking me that every five minutes, are you?" I shook my head from side to side.

"Let's play the clapping game," Catherine suggested.

"Let's not and say you did," Luke interrupted. "Count cars like you did on the way to Chicago, or do something else that's quiet."

"Great idea," I said. So we counted the hundreds of cars until that, too, drove our brother nuts. Next we read the signs, narrowing it to those that hovered the highest over the buildings. Yet, time still crawled. No sooner had we gotten out of the fast pace of the city than Luke suddenly hit the brakes and pulled into a Piggly-Wiggly parking lot. "Come on! We're going in here to get you some tablets and pencils before you drive me nuts."

"Why are you so crabby?" I asked.

"I've only been working ten hours a day, seven days a week. That's why!"

Along with the drawing and coloring supplies, Luke allowed us to each get a dollar's worth of goodies. We were embarrassed when he told the clerk that we were driving him nuts, jumping around like rabbits shitting razor blades! Catherine and I looked at each other and crinkled our faces. Back in the car, Luke cranked up the radio and we sang along to songs as we drew and colored pictures of cars and trucks, farms with silos, and schools with kids on merry-go-rounds. Then Catherine wrote a story about a little girl who didn't have any hair and I wrote about a humongous, shining star that covered the entire sky.

"Luke," Catherine said, when we once again returned to the car following a bathroom stop. "When we get home, want to play *Catch the Rabbits* with us?"

"What kind of game is that?"

"We let the rabbits out of their pen after dark and then try to catch them," I spoke up.

"It's going to be late when we get home."

"So what? We *always* catch them late at night," she said.

"Lightening bugs, too," I added.

"Why don't you two quit asking silly questions and take naps instead? The time will go by faster."

"I've been trying," I said, tossing and turning about.

Somewhere in Wisconsin we managed to fall asleep. Luke woke us when we were just miles from home, minutes from Dad and our sisters and brothers. My tummy tickled at the thought of seeing them. They were watching for us and opened the door as we turned into the driveway. They came running. We hurried from the car. Soon all six of us were gripped arm over arm in a circle and jumping up and down.

"I can't believe we're finally home," Catherine exclaimed.

"I thought you'd never get here," Sarah added.

"Ahhh!" I screamed as we took off for the house. "Wait 'til you see what we bought you guys," I blurted.

"Get back here," Luke scolded. "I don't think the rest of these bags are all mine." We quickly ran back to the car and grabbed our belongings. "Hi, Dad," Catherine and I said in passing as his hand brushed over the top of our heads while continuing to talk with Luke. Again, we took off for the house and tossed our bags on the utility floor and ran to the bedroom with the surprises for our sisters.

"Oh, wow," Anna and Monica exclaimed when they saw their beautiful dresses and socks. "I love this jumper and blouse" Bernadette exclaimed. "And I love my skirt and blouse," Sarah said. Soon all six of us were modeling our garments for Dad and the boys. Dad beamed.

"Did you two behave yourselves over the summer?" The two of us nodded and took off with our sisters again. That night the six of us gathered together on one bed, sharing secrets and talking about the fun and stupid things we'd done over the summer. Morning came and we managed to clean house, make cookies and jump rope for more than an hour before the first fight broke out.

"I figured all this getting along was too good to be true. I'm not going to put up with another year of bickering all the time, or I'll be forced to send you all off to reform school," Dad said. His agitated and disgusted state of mind astonished me. And for him to say he'd send us off to reform school scared me, although I had no idea what reform school was. Usually he took our fighting and arguments in stride, saying nothing more than a quote from the Bible and leaving it at that. "Turn the other cheek," "Forgive seventy times, seven times," and "Blessed are the peacemakers," were his favorites. It seemed he knew a quote for every circumstance of our lives. When he didn't have money to give us, the quote was, "It's harder for a rich man to enter into heaven, than for a camel to pass through the eye of a needle." Of course, I took the "eye of a needle" as a sewing needle, not as a small opening of a King's fortress, so the quote, temporarily at least, made me feel proud to be poor. Whenever we became unappreciative and focused on what we didn't have, Dad reminded us to be thankful for what we did have.

Like Dad, I couldn't wait for the first day of school to begin, but for a different reason. Seeing my friends and telling them about my summer in Chicago was going to be nearly as thrilling as the actual trip. But to my surprise, the night before school started, Dad informed John, Sarah, Bernadette and me that we'd have to take turns staying home from school throughout the year so that someone would be available for Monica when she arrived home at noon after her half day of kindergarten.

"You must be joking," John said.

"I want to get perfect attendance this year," Sarah added.

"Don't expect me to," Bernadette interjected. "I didn't even get to do anything fun over the summer. All I did was can vegetables, berries and applesauce."

"But I didn't get to see my friends for a long time," I blurted.

Regardless of each one's legitimate gripes, before Dad left for work the next morning he reminded us that someone had to stay home. One by one we all ran out to the bus, each climbing aboard. Each afternoon when we returned, Monica informed us how scared she'd been. The first day was because Dad's big pig had gotten out of the pen and had chased her. "I thought da big pig was gonna gobble me up," she cried. The second day when we got home, we couldn't find her right away. We looked throughout the house, and then outside, too, calling her name over and over and over. John finally found her in the outdoor toilet sleeping on the floor. When he asked why she went out there, she said, "Da big grader was going down the road and it was making a big noise! I thought it was gonna chop down our house."

That night Catherine and Anna tattled on us older ones for not taking turns staying home. Dad was furious. "That's probably why she wet the bed these last two nights! I can't be working all day, coming home to make supper, besides doing other things and then be up half the night, too!" The next morning he demanded to know before he left for work which one of us would be staying. We all started yelling "Not me! Not me!" Again, Dad got mad. "Do you want me to keep food on the table, or not?"

John said he had to be in school, so Dad told Sarah she was staying home. For the next two weeks we three girls took turns being home for Monica. But by the third week, we were again fighting about it. Monica started to cry. I ran and picked her up. "Don't cry," I said. "I'll stay home for you. I'll be right here waiting when you get off the bus." Monica gave me a big hug. "Donna Jean, will you help me find someten ta wear today?"

"Let's go look," I said, as I carried her off to the bedroom.

"Don't put da big yellow pin on my pants," she pleaded. But again that day I used the diaper pin, which had the head of a duck, to hold up her pants. "You're so skinny. If I don't pin your pants they'll fall off of you. You don't want that to happen, do you?"

"I'd be mumbarressed if dat happened at kool. But I don't like ta hafta ask teacher ta get da ducky pin off my pants when I hafta go pee."

"Well, start eating more, and then your pants will fit better."

Every morning after that, I helped my little sister get ready for school. By the time she came home each day I had the dishes done, the floors swept and the beds made. It was exciting being home and waiting for her at noon. One day when it was windy and cold, I hung out clothes on the line. A bunch of towels, washcloths, and my long nightgown that I'd received as a Christmas present from my godmother instantly stiffened up. It looked huge all spread out, like it would fit my dad. Monica and I laughed as we watched my stiffened nightgown blowing in the wind. That afternoon as I peeled potatoes and corn for supper, I made up a song about it. Later that evening I sang the song to my sisters and Dad.

> Whistling wind is coming to town.
> My daddy thinks he got on his nightgown.
> But it's not true; it's not true,
> Because his is white and my daddy's is blue
> Whoo, whoo, whoo,
> Whoo, whoo, whoo.
>
> Whistling wind came knocking at my door.
> I wouldn't let him in so he knocked some more.
> He just might get you in spite,
> So lock your doors and lock them up tight.
> For whistling wind,
> He comes right in, Whistling Wind.

"You didn't make that up!" Bernadette said sarcastically. "You must have heard it on the radio."

"Did not!"

"Did so!"

"I did not!" I cried.

"Well you certainly couldn't have made it up in just one day!"

"I did too!"

"Come on, now," Dad said. "Do you think she'd know all the words to a song after hearing it only once on the radio?" Bernadette cocked her head. I was just about to say, "Ha, Ha! So there!" When

Dad added, "Use your head! Do you really think they'd play such nonsense on the radio?"

Eleven

ᘓ

The smell of cocoa and toast topped with peanut butter greeted Monica at noon each day. As we ate our lunch, she'd tell me all that happened at school. One day before I had a chance to prepare our lunch she arrived home, so we ventured to the garden to pick the last of the potatoes. Dad had said that snow was in the forecast and I should dig them up before the ground froze. The garden was next to the pigpen, but we weren't afraid because the pigs were fenced in. But when the pigs saw the potatoes we'd picked, it was a different story. They snorted loudly and kept trying to dig their way under the fence. Suddenly the middle-sized pig jumped right over the fence and ran toward us. I didn't know what to do. Then I remembered the mother Killdeer we'd seen earlier in the year.

We'd been out walking in the field with Dad when we noticed a bird in the ditch with what we thought was a broken wing. My sisters and I started following it. We called for Dad to come and see the wounded bird. He looked at it. "Move away from that bird. That's a Killdeer. She's faking being hurt so you'll follow her instead of going after her young ones. She's afraid you'll hurt them."

The pig oinked louder as it sniffed the ground. "Run to the house, Monica," I screamed. Then I pretended to be hurt and made chirping noises as I dragged my leg. Sure enough, the pig came running toward me snorting and squealing, nostrils spreading. I threw a potato toward it, then another and another. As it stopped, sniffed and snorted, I ran as fast as I could to the house. Monica was holding the door open for me. "Hurry," she hollered.

For the next couple days we refused to go outside. But a few days later it snowed and we couldn't resist the thought of playing in it. We made a fort, two tiny snowmen and lots of snow angels. Doing so made me realize how much I missed being with my friends, and Mrs. Knuth, too. I longed to once again recite poems before the class and beat everyone in a spelling bee. I wanted to make Thanksgiving turkeys, Christmas bells and paper chains and paper lanterns, and to bob for apples at the Christmas party. But the more I stayed home, the more afraid I was to go back to school. At the end of the first marking period Mrs. Knuth had sent my report card home for Dad and me to look at, and for Dad to sign. It had all I's on it for incomplete. She had also sent a note with the card saying she missed my presence at school and was hoping and praying I'd soon return to school.

After the second marking period, we had a visit from a social worker. A few days earlier, Dad received a letter saying that she'd be visiting our home to see why I wasn't in school. The letter stated that Dad had to be there when she arrived. She'd already been to our house a week earlier when I was home alone. "You need to get back into school," she said. I was too scared to say anything. Dad had told me if people came nosing around, I wasn't to say a word. So I didn't. She eventually left, but before she did, she wrote a note and asked me to give it to Dad. She said that she'd be expecting a reply. He read it and threw it into the fire. When he received the second letter by mail, he was mad. "That's all I need is to miss another day of work! But she's coming, so get this place cleaned up before the Old Duck gets here."

Just the thought of her arrival made me sick to my stomach. My heart was pounding loudly when she knocked on the door. To my surprise, when Dad invited her in he was extremely polite and was acting as if he was glad to see her. He pulled a chair out from the table and motioned with his hand for her to take it. She inspected it, wiped her hand over the seat, and then sat down. Her action ticked Dad off — his face told me that much. Behind her he raised the back of his hand as if to strike her head. I knew he'd never do such a thing. It was rare for Dad to ever give spankings. But I quickly turned my head. I was afraid the lady would see him. She'd definitely send me back to school then.

"Coffee?" Dad asked, with yet another smile on his face. She looked to the stove and to the old blackened metal pot. "Oh, no, no coffee for me. We need to get down to business." Dad took a chair next to her and across from me.

"Mr. Jacques, why isn't your daughter in school? Did she give you my note and letter telling you that by both state and federal law your daughter *must* attend school?"

"I got them, and I told her she had to go back."

"Well, Mr. Jacques," she said sternly. "It's up to you to make sure she's in school by tomorrow or the police will bring her there." I began shaking all over. I was more afraid than I'd ever been.

"I don't have any shoes to wear," I butted in, which was by no means a lie. I had long ago outgrown my shoes. My toes had pushed holes through the top ends and the heels had nails poking through the bottoms, despite my efforts of hammering them down each day. She pulled her chair next to mine and lifted my foot to her lap. She slipped off my worn-out shoe and looked inside and outside of it trying to find the size, seeming not to notice the holes in both ends of my socks. "It looks like about a size four or five. Does that sound right?" I shrugged my shoulders. "That's about average for your age, I believe." At that very moment, for some weird reason, I found myself wondering if my own mother's shoe size was "about average" when she was eleven. Another half hour or so went by before the lady left. I was relieved that I'd bought myself a few more days before having to face my classmates. But the following day she returned with a pair of black shoes that had colored stripes of red, yellow, blue and green on the top above the toes; the prettiest shoes I'd ever seen. "Do they fit?" she asked.

"Yes," I said along with a smile and nod. I was afraid that if I told her the shoes were too tight, she'd take them back.

"Well, I wish you would've told me about this problem earlier, but, oh well, now you're ready to return to school." Just when she thought it was all said and done, I still wouldn't agree to go back. A zillion bugs seemed to be flying around in the pit of my stomach. No way was I going back to school. I found myself bargaining again. "The only way I'll ever go back is if Monica can come into my room after she's done with kindergarten each day; then she won't have to be home alone."

"Your Dad will have to make other arrangements for her."

"No! Monica only wants me. I'm her mother now!" In truth, I was saying whatever I could to keep from going back to school. I was afraid my classmates would make fun of me if I returned. The lady looked at Dad and nodded slightly. "I think I might have a solution to this problem. What if Monica spends the first half of the day in her grade and the second half in first grade?" I tilted my head and turned my eyes toward Dad and then back to her. "Can she really do that?" I asked.

"You can't ask for a better deal than that," Dad said, scratching the top of his head a bit. Still I wouldn't commit to return to the fifth grade.

"Remember," she said, "it's the law. You really don't want a policeman to come and get you and bring you to school, do you?"

"No," I said trembling, nearly crying at the thought of a policeman coming to pick me up. In fact, that scenario sounded even worse than the thought of having my classmates make fun of me, so I agreed to go back to school the following day. The lady was so happy that she kissed my cheek. Before leaving, she left round yellow gel vitamins to keep us from getting sick. She'd left them in the past. It was the only thing Dad ever thought she was good for. We hated the vitamins. They smelled and tasted terrible and the taste remained in our mouths long after swallowing them. But each time the lady brought them, Dad made sure we took them until they were gone. All but Monica managed to choke them down. Whenever she tried, she would vomit. We tried hiding them in different foods, even in ice cream one time, but she'd always find the vitamin. Dad told her that they'd make the pains she'd been getting in her legs go away, but even that didn't matter to her.

Monica cried a lot during the night because of pain in her legs, but she wasn't the only one who Dad got up for. Someone was always calling for him. He rubbed liniment on our aching legs and arms, blew smoke into our ears to soothe earaches, put droplets of whiskey on our toothaches, made hot lemonade for our coughs and colds and somehow managed to scrape up a quarter for the quart of ginger ale needed for the one who had a sore throat or the flu. Doctor Dad always helped to take away our aches and pains.

Twelve
ca

My legs felt like straw as I walked down the driveway to get on the school bus. Eyes stared as I climbed the steps and took my seat with Monica and Anna at the back of the bus. At that moment, I wished I were a bee to sting the on-lookers or to sit inconspicuously in a corner so no one could see me. Two stops up the road the bus got stuck. The ordeal took attention away from me, but it was short-lived since the snowplow came up from behind and pulled the bus back on the road. By the time we got to school, the morning bell had already rung and classes had started. Hesitantly, I walked to my room and, for a few minutes, stood back away from the door. I peered through the window. "Why, oh why couldn't Gary have been on our bus today?" Gary was the only other classmate to ride the same bus as me. We rode the mini bus. "Why, oh why did our bus have to be late?" I asked myself as I watched the kids dig through their desks for supplies as Mrs. Knuth handed out the daily lesson plan.

My heart beat like a drum as I ventured closer to the door. "Run home!" I told myself. But I knew Dad would make me go the following day, and since Christmas vacation was only two weeks away I tried to focus on the fact that I only had to go for a few days before I'd get time off. "It's now or never!" I told myself. I noticed my friend Anne. Seeing her gave me the courage to turn the doorknob. My body was shaking so bad that my schoolbooks and the new tablet Dad had bought for me nearly jumped from my arms.

"Hey, Mrs. Knuth!" Richard hollered when he saw me opening the door. "The big school skipper's back!"

"Faking being sick?" Edwin asked, as he stood sharpening a pencil.

"Edwin! Sit down this minute," Mrs. Knuth bellowed.

"She's just lazy," another added.

"Enough! All of you," the teacher said as she set down her book and came toward me. She took my hand and led me to where my desk had been moved. "Right here, honey." She lifted the top of the desk and inspected the inside, and then removed a bunch of waded-up papers from it. "I see you have your books with you."

"All but my spelling. I couldn't find it," I said nearly in a whisper.

"That's okay, honey. I have a couple extras." I sat down and placed my books inside my desk.

"Why are you shaking?" Anne asked. I shrugged my shoulders, like I did for other questions that came my way. I lifted the top of my desk and ducked under it. I peeked at Anne. She looked beautiful in her red plaid Kiltie, white Ben Casey blouse and the big red bow on the top of her hair. She was sitting as calm as a flower in the summer sun, while I trembled like a weed on a winter's day. She lifted her desktop and looked at me and smiled. She tried to tell me something but I couldn't hear her, so she wrote a note. "I'm glad you're back." I smiled. I took a deep breath. Afraid I'd get in trouble, I grabbed some paper from my desk and put the top back down. I started writing down the arithmetic problem that Mrs. Knuth was putting on the board.

"Anne!" Mrs. Knuth shouted. "Do you have a problem today? Do you have ants in your pants? Maybe you'd like to spend a little time out in the hall." Anne mumbled something as she grabbed a sheet of paper and started writing down the problem. I was glad she hadn't gotten in trouble because of me.

At the first recess everyone circled around me and wanted to know why I'd skipped so many days of school. I didn't know what to tell them. It was Eileen McDermott who finally broke the line of questions when she grabbed my hand and took me on a run into the hallway. "Hurry, get your boots on so you can come and see the snow fort that Candy and I made yesterday."

"I'm just going to wear my shoes," I said.

"Those are pretty. But hurry, get your coat on!"

Together we ran to the playground with the other girls from my class following behind. They all wanted to be my friend. The boys were much less accepting. Again they called me names like "Lazy," "School skipper," and to my shock, "Teacher's pet!" At one point in time, I'd fallen in love with each and every boy for at least a week, sometimes two, and they with me, but by the tone of their voices and the names they were calling me, I was sure none of them would ever want me for their girlfriend again.

Two days after I started back to school, Mrs Richards, the school secretary, came to the door. She talked to Mrs Knuth for a while and then my teacher motioned me into the hallway. "What is she in trouble for now?" Douglas hissed as I was leaving the room. My face grew hot. "Am I in trouble?" I questioned. "Follow me," Mrs. Richards said. I obeyed.

Monica had fallen off the slide and was crying for me. I sat in the Principal's office on the big burgundy chair and waited for Mrs. Boudreau to bring her to me. She sat her on my lap. "I told Mr. Johnson where your dad works. He has sent Bon (the custodian) to get him.

He'll have to take your little sister to the hospital. She might have a broken arm." Monica put her head on my chest and softly cried. Mrs. Richards handed me a tissue. I wiped Monica's runny nose and then swiveled us around in the chair while we waited for Dad. Quite a while later Shirley Peterson, a high-school girl, came into the office to use the ditto machine. She laughed because Monica kept giving me kisses. I smiled.

"She sure loves you, doesn't she?" she was saying when Dad came into the office. He lifted Monica from my lap. Mrs. Boudreau came back into the office and helped Dad put Monica's coat on her. She explained to Dad that Monica had fallen from the top of the slide and should be seen by a doctor. So Dad left for the hospital and I went back to my room, dreading every step I took down the long hallway. When I entered, everyone wanted to know if I'd gotten in trouble again. "Was it for missing so much school?" Richard asked.

"No," I said, my eyes welling with tears.

"Donna Jean, why don't you tell everyone why you had to go to the office?" Mrs. Knuth suggested. When I did, they all thought I was once again the lucky one for not having to do schoolwork.

After school Dad told us that Monica had broken her arm, so we'd have to be careful with her. When we were eating supper (leftover bean and rice soup) Dad asked Monica to tell us what the doctor had told her. To his amazement, she exclaimed that the doctor said she could no longer eat bean or rice soup, and she pushed her bowl away. We all laughed.

"Sarah," Dad chuckled, "put her soup on the counter and give her some cheese and crackers. We wouldn't want to disobey the doctor, now would we?"

"See," I said, "having a broken arm isn't so bad, is it Monica?"

"But it willy hurts!" she said, looking up toward the ceiling.

The next day, Mr. Annelin, the sixth grade teacher, came into our classroom and asked if a boy from our class would be willing to play the lead role in the sixth grade play. "None of the boys in my sixth grade classroom will do it," he informed us. Neither would any of the boys from our class, so I raised my hand and asked if I could do it. He cocked an eyebrow, and looked toward Mrs. Knuth. She nodded and smiled.

"Sure. Why not?" he said. So I did. I was Willy! I had five long verses and other lines memorized in just two days. With britches and a flannel shirt on, along with a big straw hat, I played the lead part in *Jest 'Fore Christmas.*

> Father calls me William, sister calls me Will,
> Mother calls me Willie, but the fellers call me Bill!
> Mighty glad I ain't a girl, ruther be a boy,
> Without them sashes, curls, an' things that's worn by Fauntleroy!
> Love to chawnk green apples an' go swimmin' in the lake,
> Hate to take the castor-ile they give for bellyache!
> 'Most all the time, the whole year round, there ain't no flies on me,
> But jest 'fore Christmas I'm as good as I kin be!

By the end of the second week, I once again started spending nights at my friends' houses, especially Krystal and Anne's. Each day continued to get better and better. As the days went by, even I forgot I'd missed so much school. I anxiously waited going each day and looked forward to times table races, spelling bees and penmanship class. One day Mrs. Knuth held up my paper for all the class to see. "Doesn't Donna Jean make her alphabet letters well?" she asked. My stomach tickled from the praise.

Each and every day of the second half of fifth grade I was thankful to be back in school. The days flew by and before I knew it springtime had arrived and along with it marble games and jump roping contests at recess times. I was very sad when the school year came closer to an end. I told Dad that I wished it could last forever. "Me, too!" he said.

On the day before Monica graduated from kindergarten, my friend Krystal helped me wash and iron Monica's dress. Dad had bought her a pretty new one but she had worn it to church and gotten it dirty. It was red suede on top and the bottom was of white eyelet ruffles. We made sure she had clean white socks to wear, too. Krystal spent the night and in the morning we helped Monica dress. She looked beautiful. When Dad arrived at school, he came into my room to get me so I could see her graduation ceremony. I sat with him looking at all the little kids when suddenly I noticed that Krystal and I had forgotten to polish Monica's saddle shoes. Instead of being black and white, they were black and black!

"It's too late now," Dad complained, when I pointed it out to him. "I told you long ago to make sure everything was ready for her." I lowered my chin. *How could I be so dumb?* I asked myself. But the following day I was again proud of being me. I'd thought for sure that Mrs. Knuth was going to flunk me because I'd missed so much school. She called me to the front of the room and had me sit in the little chair, which was by the side of her desk. She told me I was doing very well and that she was pleased with all that I'd accomplished during the second half of the year. "I'm going to pass you into the sixth grade because I know you'll do just fine." My eyes grew big. I jumped from the chair. "Thank you so much, Teacher," I said as I threw my arms around her.

Thirteen

CR

All eyes were on the new student as he walked to the front of our sixth grade room. He looked much too mature to be the same age as my classmates and me. All but a forehead wave of his blonde hair was slicked back from his face. His gray eyes were framed by long, straight eyelashes and his mouth was shaped into a natural "disgusted with everything" look. His casual pants were pressed with pleats; the light blue slipover shirt he wore followed the contours of his stomach. He looked smart, presidential, authoritative, more like a teacher. Marvin was joining our sixth grade class. My eyes were glued to him as he shook the teacher's hand and introduced himself. His presence seemed to mesmerize the whole class until his sister walked into the room.

Maybe it was my impressionable age, but that day burned into the memory bank of my mind. As Rosanna made her way to the front of the room, I couldn't help but notice she was everything I wanted to be. Each of her graceful steps in those black patent-leather shoes made me envious, from her delicate white socks edged with ruffles to her locks of brunette curls that cascaded down her back. I wanted to scream. I wanted yesterday back. I wanted my mother back. I wanted my mother's hands to curl my hair again, which lately looked and felt like straw upon my head.

Rosanna seemed untouchable. Yet not more than a week passed before I spent my first night, of what would be many nights, at the Rochefort home. Their house was beautifully decorated. Rosanna and her sister Pamela's bedroom looked like a room in a dollhouse. Their canopy twin beds were covered with pink satin spreads, with pillow shams and curtains to match. Each had a child-sized chair that had a heart-shaped back, upholstered with pink fur. I felt like a princess in that room, a jealous princess! Just when I thought Rosanna to be the luckiest girl in the world, Marvin and her Dad entered the house. A barnyard aroma followed. The parents seemed as unlikely to be farmers as *Green Acres*'s Lisa and Oliver Douglas. Her mother was a blonde beauty and her father looked much more like a banker than any farmer I'd ever seen. The farm odor soon faded. The only thorn left in this house of roses now was Marvin.

Rosanna often had pajama parties and invited nearly all the girls from our small class. Her parents would go visiting, trusting us to behave while they were gone. We'd get on the phone, which at the time was to be used solely for important things, but we'd dial numbers and ask for a name, like Rudolph, thinking we'd never find anyone with the reindeer's name. One day a man answered and said, "This is he!" I quickly hung up the phone.

Marvin would follow us wherever we went, and we hated it. One by one he'd try to get us to be his girlfriend. When that didn't work, he threatened to use his special eyeglasses on us when they arrived in the mail. He'd ordered them from the back pages of a *True Story* magazine. The glasses were guaranteed to see right through women's clothing. One day when I was there, his glasses arrived. I was afraid to be around him, so Rosanna and I ran to her bedroom. Quickly I turned the skeleton key. Weeks later I regretted not being his girlfriend, or at least letting him see through my clothes. Maybe then he would've overlooked a fault of mine instead of bringing it to the attention of the whole class.

Marvin was voted treasurer of our sixth grade. Our first fund raiser was selling boxes of chocolates. The money raised was for our eighth-grade class trip to Mackinac Island, which was still two years away. Each student received — and was expected to sell — twelve boxes of chocolate-covered candies. Soon after arriving home with them, the aroma invaded our house. All my siblings wanted some, but of course I couldn't give them any. I explained that I had to sell them. As the weeks went by Dad's car was either not running, low on gas, or Dad was too tired to take me around to sell them to the neighbors, none of whom were within close walking distance. In the back of our closet, the chocolates lay waiting to be sold, while the smell of them lingered in the air.

When the last day of the sale came, all the money raised was to be turned in. I felt stupid going to school because I knew I'd be put on a list of students who wouldn't be allowed to go on the class trip. The teacher had stated quite clearly that if we didn't work on the fund raisers, we shouldn't expect to take part in the fun. Since I hadn't sold a single box, I decided to stay home that Wednesday. I didn't want to show up as the only student who hadn't sold any. However, I couldn't get up the courage to go on Thursday or Friday either. On Sunday night before bedtime, Dad told me I was to be on the bus in the morning or he'd take me to school himself.

"Can't you at least buy one box of the chocolates?" I begged.

"I don't have five bucks for *candy*," he snapped. I had thought he'd be able to buy at least one of the boxes so I'd secretly opened a box and had been snitching from it since the first day. I'd eaten over half! Reluctantly I went to the bedroom to retrieve the chocolates as I thought of excuses I could use when my teacher learned I hadn't sold any and that one of the boxes had been opened.

I tried to think of things I could tell him, like, "The box came open and they spilled to the ground," or "One of my little sisters dug into them." Or I could say, "They were like this when I first received them." I was hoping one of the excuses would suffice, but I knew I'd still be expected to pay for the open box.

Reaching deep within the closet, I grabbed the big box that held the twelve boxes of candy. I counted the boxes to make sure they were all there. Then I reached for the one I had been taking the candy from. I didn't think I'd eaten almost the whole box, I thought to myself, feeling regretful. As I was placing the opened box back into the larger container with the others, my eyes did a double take. Lifting box after box, I was shocked to see all but five of the boxes had been eaten from, all over half gone! I screamed. It was as if I was already there, standing in front of the class and the teacher. At that moment I wished I were a fifth-grade dropout again, tending the fire, washing, hanging and ironing clothes, scrubbing floors, cooking and baking; each task seemed easy in comparison to what I'd soon face. Anything would be better than returning to school with the half-eaten boxes of chocolates without the money to pay for them.

Dad and my siblings came running. "This better be a matter of life or death," he said as he entered the room.

"It is!" I shouted. "Everyone has eaten the chocolates!" My sisters and John suddenly disappeared. "Now what am I going to do?"

"Well, the dirty little stinkers!" Dad said.

"I can't bring these back tomorrow!"

Again I begged him to pay for them. He pulled his empty pockets out of his pants and as burnt matches and wood chips fell to the floor, he said, "Do you see any money in these pockets? If I had some, I'd give it to you." When he left the room I opened the full boxes and poured some of the chocolates from each full box into the others that had been eaten from. When done, all the boxes were filled, but just barely over the top of the little cellophane window. "There," I said, hating what I'd just done. "Maybe no one will be able to tell they've been opened."

My cheeks were already hot as I climbed the steps of the bus the next morning. By the time I got to school and made my way to my homeroom I felt like a blob of Jell-O. I could already imagine the ridicule and laughter. It had happened for nearly every extra event that took place, like exchanging gifts by drawing names at Christmastime. Whispers would quickly pass through the room. None of the kids wanted me to get their name. They knew from past experience the gift they'd receive would be a dud — something stupid — like yellow work gloves or a pair of dusty potholders that had sat on a shelf at the local store for years.

Marvin, being treasurer, had to collect the money from the sales, so I made my way to the front of the room where he sat. I gave him the box that the candy was in. Taking it, his eyes gleaned the top. "You couldn't even sell *one* box, now could you? I don't think you'll be going on our class trip."

"My dad's car was broken!" I said turning my back on him and walking away as quickly as possible. I took my seat at the back of the room. Marvin sat down. He seemed to be tallying up the sales. "Oh, dear," I said to myself, taking a deep breath. Marvin hadn't noticed the missing chocolate. I tried to converse with my friends, as if I didn't have a care in the world. I wanted to shout for joy, run to the moon or even do a belly flop on water. Then the morning bell rang.

"First things first," Mr. Annelin said. "Marvin, can you give us an account now of the sales and how much money the class made on the fund raiser? In fact, why don't you come to the board and put the numbers up." My heart started beating faster and louder than ever. I was certain everyone could hear it. I'd found out that every person from my class had sold at least some of their candy; most had sold all. They'd been bringing in money from the sale since the day after it began.

Marvin did as he was told. Then he looked straight at me and announced, "We would have made more money if Donna Jacques would have sold at least *one* of her boxes." I lowered my head and thought, If this is all I have to endure, it'll be okay. Marvin put the numbers on the board and then took his seat. I tried to relax and ignore my friends asking me why I hadn't sold any. We took out our spelling workbooks. I could barely think of how to spell even the simplest of words; words that normally I would have been the last one standing for during a spelling bee. I tried to write the words in the workbook, but could hardly hold my pencil. "Please God, *help me*," I pleaded. Suddenly Marvin raised his voice and went running back to the front of the room with as many of the boxes of chocolates as he could carry.

"Oh my God, Mr. Annelin! You're not going to believe this! Donna Jacques's boxes of chocolates are *all* half empty!" At that moment I wished to be a spider, a poisonous spider, a tarantula! Not to bite Marvin, but me! I put my head down.

"Marvin," Mr. Annelin scolded. "It's not the end of the world. Calm down. Just put them away for the time being. I'll take care of it later." But Marvin pressed on.

"Didn't you hear me? Donna Jacques's boxes are half empty." All eyes turned to me.

"MARVIN!" Mr. Annelin said, this time raising his voice, his face getting nearly as red as my own. "I'll take care of it later! Now take your seat!"

"Okay, okay," he said, dragging his feet back to his desk, "but it's our loss."

Later, at recess time, Mr. Annelin excused everyone except me. When all had left the room, he asked me to come to his desk. He took some of the boxes of chocolates out and looked at them. "What happened to the chocolates?" he asked nicely. Breaking down into tears, I told him the truth.

"Because you were honest with me, I'm going to take care of this for you, so don't worry about it. Now go and play."

"Thank you," I gasped as tears continued to stream down my face. I didn't run to the playground, but to the bathroom to let out the big cry that I'd been holding back, and then hurried to join my friends. When they saw my red eyes, they assumed I'd been sent to the office for a paddling. I tried to tell them what actually took place, but they didn't believe me.

Fourteen
CR

Field trips, tug-of-war and baseball games during school hours was a sure sign that another summer in Chicago was just around the corner. I couldn't wait to be free of the duties of home. Although leaving was still days away, I packed my bags to be ready when Luke came to pick me up on Memorial Day weekend. It was 1964, the summer before my seventh grade year. This summer I'd be staying with my cousins Betty Jane and John and their four kids, so I was extra excited about getting there. Betty Jane was fun to be around. I learned "lady things" from her, like shopping for clothes and styling my hair. Her family had moved to Berwyn, a suburb of Chicago, so Luke moved there, too. His apartment was only a couple blocks away.

A few hours before we left for Chicago, Catherine decided not to come. I was sad, but glad that Tina, a friend of Luke's who lived in Chicago, would be riding with us. She drove Luke's brand new red convertible GTO. We had the top down and our bathing suits on so we could get a tan during the seven-hour trip. Guys honked their car horns, whistled at us, blew kisses at Tina and me, and one guy even mooned us.

"Oh, my gosh!" Tina yelled, waking Luke who was in the backseat sleeping off a buzz from the night before. She laughed. "You missed it, Luke. Some guy just mooned us!"

"What the heck do you mean, he mooned you?" he asked while trying to get his wits about him.

"A guy just pulled down his pants and stuck his big butt out the window," I said, laughing.

"You saw it, too?" I nodded, laughed and placed my hand over my mouth. "What's this world coming to?" he asked.

"You sound like Dad now," I said. Tina chuckled and told Luke that if he couldn't handle the quirks of the road he should go back to sleep.

I liked the excitement of the city. Things there were never predictable like in the small town of Garden. I saw and experienced new events that I never would have at home. I had more opportunities to earn money, like with the job I'd gotten babysitting for two little kids whose parents paid me two dollars an hour. (Back home the rate was fifty to seventy-five cents an hour.) In the city I was able to shop at supermarkets that had every kind of food imaginable. Taking taxicabs to malls and going up and down in elevators and escalators while shopping for clothes, shoes, and things I didn't even need, like make-up, was also a part of the city experience. I could go to Burger King (one of the first in the nation) to eat my fill of anything on the menu. I especially liked the fish sandwiches and chocolate milkshakes.

"Luke, Luke," I yelled one day, running up the stairs to his apartment, "I just saw a sewing machine at a garage sale in the alley. It's only twenty-five dollars! Will you *please* buy it for me? *Pretty please, with sugar on top*? It even has a cabinet!"

"Slow down," he said, laughing at my breathlessness. "I can tell I'm not going to get out of this one. Give me a minute and we'll go look at it."

After we got the machine to Luke's apartment, I made him take me to a store to buy material so I could start sewing. That night I stayed at his place, cutting quilt blocks and sewing them together. It took the entire next day before my baby-size quilt was completed. Luke and my relatives said it was nice, but I knew they had to have noticed that it was much wider on one end than the other. My next project was doll clothes for my sisters' dolls. The dress was my own creation and turned out nice, but I'd forgot to allow a space in the back for a zipper or buttons. The head hole was only the size of a quarter, so I took the dress and put into the side compartment of the sewing cabinet. So ended my summer sewing.

Being away from home meant staying up late, very late, stargazing the night away on lawn chairs with Betty Jane and some of her neighbors, from ten at night until two or three in the morning. It was learning from Tina how to put make-up on my face. She darkened my eyebrows, painted my lashes, covered my cheeks with pretty pink rouge and put traces of light blue shadow on my eyelids. Feeling all grown-up, I would try to catch glimpses of Elmer, the good-looking guy next door, who was much too old for me. Being in the city gave me the opportunity to see a talent show, a spectacular performance of a song and dance by a teenage girl. It brought such joy to my heart that I memorized every word and movement she made to the song by Millie Small called *My Boy Lollipop*!

> My boy Lollipop, you made my heart go giddy up.
> You are as sweet as candy; you're my sugar dandy...

That night as I lay in bed the lyrics ran through my mind. Butterflies did cartwheels inside of my stomach as I thought about the good-looking neighbor with the dazzling smile, twinkling eyes and silky looking hair. I was in love! Was he *My Boy Lollipop*?

The rush of the city took away the sting of my mother's death. Life there was sugarcoated, with places like Riverview Amusement Park with its fast, high roller coasters, realistic parachutes, house of mirrors and haunted mansion. Each of these experiences added pages to my book of life. A very special time, a carefree time was going to my first family reunion, held at a beautiful park. At the reunion of my mother's relatives I played with Betty Jane's kids and with Dean and Danny, Donald and Delores's boys. I pushed them when they were on the swings, caught them when they came down the slide and ran with them to get treats throughout the day.

At the reunion, I met my mother's first cousin, Emery Greenwood. He was the first adult male to talk to me about my mother since her death. He didn't shy away from talking about her the way so many others had whenever I asked questions. Instantly, I felt bonded with him. I was amazed that he didn't cry about her, like her sisters and some of her brothers did whenever I brought up her name. Most unusual, he didn't only talk about her death, but about her life, too! I learned that he and my mother had grown up in the same community of Upper Michigan, and had lived across the road from each other. He shared how he thought I looked like my mother and preceded to tell me that she was the flower girl and he the ring bearer at cousin Lizzy's wedding.

At that point in our conversation I exclaimed, "I was a flower girl at my brother's Mark's wedding!"

"See, you already have something in common with her. Did you say you were seven when your mother died?"

"Uh-huh," I answered as we walked toward the swings.

"That's the age your mother was when her mother died." I stopped. I looked up at him with a surprised look on my face. At that moment I was as happy as I'd ever been. It was thrilling to be reassured that I *indeed* once had a mother and that we shared something in common.

After the reunion Luke had no choice but to take me to visit Emery every now and then.

Emery was a rarity, a handsome, pleasant and soft-spoken man. If he ever thought some people were bad, I never knew it. He spoke only about the good of people. One day he told me that he, too, had been just a child of four when his own mother died, and that his aunt had raised him. "That aunt was Lizzy's mother," he said. He talked to me as if I were his equal and able to comprehend things. When I asked where his children's mother was, he explained that he was divorced and told me what divorced meant. The conversations we had gave me more faith and courage to survive my mother's death.

Martin Luther King, Jr. was also a big part of my city experience. I learned about other cultures, religions and races. I learned about human rights. My city relatives shared in Rev. King's dreams. They agreed with his values. I came to realize they were right in doing so. His values were the same values I knew both God and my mother would want me to have. Despite my dad ranting every now and then, I came to know that the black race was every bit as good as the white race. I wasn't going to let Dad's prejudicial ways influence me any longer. He didn't talk much about equal rights, but when he did, it was in a derogatory manner against blacks.

Still, the best thing about the city was getting away from home, not just from housework, washing and cooking, but also from Dad's friend Ernie. Sometimes Ernie would bring Dad home from the bar, and he'd come in with him, even if it were one, two or three in the morning. He and Dad would expect one of us girls to jump right out of bed, wear a friendly smile to the kitchen, and cook them something to eat, despite the fact that it was a school night. Ernie made me nauseated. He'd rub his back on the door casing while leering at me. One time as I made them eggs and toast, he stood by my side and continuously tried to grab my boobs and to kiss me. "Keep away from me!" I hissed. My anger gave him another thrill, and Dad was too out of it" to notice.

Ernie had fondled me when I was younger. At first I thought it was neat when he would offer to take us younger girls off of Dad's hands for a while. I felt privileged sitting on his lap while steering his car as we drove down the back roads of Garden. Though I despised the smell of whiskey on his breath and the prickliness of his billy-goat whiskers rubbing against the back of my neck, I wanted to drive his car. His front teeth were missing, and when he smiled or laughed he looked scary. "Don't, Ernie," I'd say when he'd put his hand under my blouse to try to *tickle* me. "You're going to make me run into the ditch." I'd keep pulling his hand out from under my blouse or away from my crotch as I tried to steer the car. I'd beg him to stop bothering me. At the end of our ride, he'd take us to the store and buy us each a Popsicle.

"DON'T," I shouted one day when he was tickling me once again. "I hate that!" He became angry at my yelling and dropped me off at home. "Your Popsicle days are over!"

"Come on," I said to my sisters. "Get out of his car!"

"No," they complained. "We want to get our Popsicles!" A few times later, Catherine realized that what Ernie was doing wasn't right.

"Don't you like Popsicles anymore?" Anna asked me one day when I tried to tell her that Ernie was doing bad things to her and Monica when they went riding with him. "Monica's afraid of Ernie. She won't sit on his lap anymore."

"Well, *you* should be afraid of him, too," I scolded, scaring her enough that neither she nor Monica ever went riding with him again.

Still, every day he was in our home. The minute Dad would leave the room he'd try grabbing at us and/or speaking sexual innuendos. "Let me rub your back. I'll give you a good backrub," or "I'll give you a dollar if you do this or that," he'd say as he moved his lower extremities in a sexual way. Sometimes he came over when Dad and

101

my brothers were gone. We'd run and hide but he always managed to find us in a closet or under a bed. He even flashed Catherine one day. Another time when Catherine and I were home alone doing the wash, he came over. We jumped out our bedroom window and ran and climbed the tall tree. Toward the top, we settled ourselves between its huge limbs. "Even if he finds us, there's no way he'll ever get up here. He's too fat!" Catherine said. We felt safe and secure in the arms of the big maple. We stayed there that day for nearly an hour after he'd left.

A few weeks later, I was home alone doing the wash when he showed up. I was in the utility room passing blankets through the wringer of the washing machine when I saw him standing in the doorway. My body felt like it was going to collapse as he gave the door a tap and walked in. I wanted to run, but my legs felt glued to the floor. I wished for Dad to come home early from work. I started to cry. "Tell your Dad I stopped by," he said, and left.

Shaking uncontrollably, I grabbed the wash machine plug and pulled it from the outlet. I ran to the kitchen and grabbed the last butter knife from the drawer. Trembling, I placed it between the trim of the door and the casing. I breathed a sigh of relief and headed for the bedroom. I crawled on the bed and pulled the covers over myself and cried uncontrollably. "Please, God, don't let him come back," I prayed. Suddenly I found myself wondering if my own mother had to fend for herself when she was little. A few days later Ernie was back, although this time other family members were home. He was back to his usual teasing and saying sexual innuendos. Ernie enjoyed bugging us girls, especially Sarah. He knew it bothered her the most. But he'd still chase her around the kitchen table until she couldn't take it anymore and would retreat to the bedroom. "Oh, my little Sarah," he'd screech.

"Dad, Ernie plays dirty," my little sisters said one night at bedtime.

"If he doesn't want to play fair, don't play the game," was all he said.

Although returning home at the end of the summer meant going back to deal with Ernie's hateful behavior and also him and Dad coming in at all hours of the night, I still was anxious to get home. I always missed my family and couldn't wait to return to see them and to share my experiences from another summer in the city and to get caught up on the things going on back home.

Fifteen
CR

The following year Dad's drinking continued, but now I didn't mind when he came home late. He had hired Jim, a sixteen-year-old high-school dropout, to work with him in the woods. On the weekends, he'd stay at our house. He'd pay for the booze that Dad bought and they drank it together. Jim was a person with a lot of restless energy. Hunting deer out of season was one of his passions, especially knowing we could use the food. He helped Dad cut and split stove wood and fixed Dad's car when it broke down.

Being twelve going on thirteen, I thought it was pretty cool having Jim around. He was older, attractive, and had taken a real liking to me, despite my age. Some nights when Dad had too much to drink and went to bed early, I'd sit up with Jim until midnight or later, innocently flirting and occasionally letting him kiss me. Fortunately, the only thing that ever took place was for me to really fall in love for the first time. He knew I was off limits as an actual dating partner, yet he teased me that someday he was going to marry me.

Those who knew him well called him Bones, but in actuality, he was a stocky, rough character with a mean streak, yet always nice to me. More than once he'd gotten into trouble with the law, by drinking and driving and getting into fist fights. No one ever wanted to tangle with him when he was sober, but drunk was another story. Smashed on peppermint schnapps, time and time again, he'd instigate fights. His drunken state cost him many times, like the night he picked a fight with a well-built schoolteacher. Jim ended up with a broken nose and a few gashes. That night, like many other nights of fighting, he came to our house to get his wounds taken care of. I put a makeshift ice pack on his broken nose and wiped blood from his cuts.

"Thanks, Florence," he said, still sitting half-drunk on the kitchen chair.

"Florence?"

"Haven't you ever heard of Florence Nightingale?"

"Oh, so I'm your nurse, now?"

"I love my nurse," he said wrapping his arms around my waist.

"Stop it, right now!" I complained, hating when he was drunk and slobbered over me. "I think you better get to bed!"

"Well, I can see when I'm not wanted," he said as he stumbled his way to the door and then took off in his car despite my pleas for him not to drive.

As time went on my mad love for Jim turned to hate. His presence sickened me. I blamed him each time he brought Dad home drunk. He was the bad guy, the one responsible for getting Dad messed up and bringing him home at all hours. He was the one causing Dad to blare the stereo at its highest volume in the wee hours of the morning.

I couldn't hide my dislike for Jim, not from him or from my Dad. Dad tried to deal with my anger by reminding me that it was Jim who gave him the money he needed to pay the property taxes and Jim who paid for the parts to get his car back on the road, but my dislike for him didn't change. One night they came home around two and tried to coax me out of bed to make them something to eat. I informed them that their all-hours waitress had quit and I wouldn't get out of bed, so Dad pulled me out.

"I have school tomorrow!" I screamed in his face at the top of my lungs. As I fried up leftover potatoes, they laughed. Jim told me that I didn't have to look so mean and ugly, and Dad referred to me as an old hen. All the time, I was wondering how I could get rid of Jim, once and for all. The fact that he was still coming around after the way I'd been treating him astonished me. I wondered if I'd have to come right out and say those three nasty words of "I hate you." Dad was acting like a teenage boy instead of a father because of Jim. Many times I contemplated leaving home, never to return.

Dad's getting drunk on occasion never bothered me. When he'd come home all snockered up and grab one of our hands to get us to dance with him, my sisters and I would giggle. We didn't mind. I figured it was the least I could do to take my mother's place, knowing that they had loved to dance, especially the polka. One by one, Dad would dance with us, both at home and at wedding receptions. It was a time of fun and making good memories. But lately, I didn't want to even touch my father's hands. In years gone by, springtime was a time when Dad put together a priority list of repairs around the house and decided which crops he'd grow in the garden. During the past two years, he hadn't as much as picked up the Gurney catalogue, let alone done his ordering.

The more I showed disdain for Jim, the nicer he was to me. Yet I still found him disgusting. His peppermint schnapps breath may not have been the worst smelling breath of a drunk, but I despised having to be around it. But despite my ugliness toward him, he still tried to approach me, as if I were still silly in love with him.

Looking forward to spending my summer in Chicago now was

more of a reason to escape home life than for a chance to see and experience city life. Chicago was now my haven. I couldn't wait for the end of the school year. I had to leave Garden. I counted the days until I could escape to the city. With just fourteen days to go, I received a letter from Luke. I thought I'd die when I learned he wouldn't be able to come and get me because he was working seven days a week again. Still, there was no way I was going to be stuck with Dad and Jim for the entire summer. "Maybe I can hitch a ride with relatives or take the bus if I can earn the money for the ticket," I contemplated. I'd get there somehow, even if that meant hitchhiking!

Bright and early on a Saturday morning, I walked to the corner store and asked Cal if he had any jobs I could do. He put me right to work cleaning and stocking shelves. The following week he told me that Leola, his wife, had things for me to do at their house. I crossed the road and took the path up the hill to their big white house. Leola was waiting for me and explained what she needed me to do while she was gone shopping.

The dust in the driveway hadn't settled before I turned the hamper upside down and started sorting the clothes into piles. "I should have asked her how these machines work," I said to myself, lifting the lid of the wash machine. "White clothes can go in with the towels... these must be Cal's," I said as I hurriedly tossed his giant underwear into the machine, embarrassed that I'd seen them. I was glad when I heard the water spraying inside the machine. "It must be working. Now, I can do the dishes while the first batch of laundry washes." It wasn't until the dryer signaled that the second batch of clothes were dry that I found Leola's note on the table, sitting atop the toaster.

Donna Jean,

Do not put any of my brassieres in the dryer or Cal's green wool pants. Wash the whites in hot water and the colored in cold. Hang them on the line out back. I'll take them in when I get home. Shake all the area rugs outside — not in the house.

Clean and scrub the bathroom completely, and do the dishes,
too. You'll find the Spic-n-Span in the same cupboard as the
washing detergent. Don't feel you have to rush through everything. Take your time, so that it's done right. There are candy
bars on the table and pop in the refrigerator for you. When
you're finished, Cal will pay you.

Thank you darling,
Leola

I threw down the letter and quickly grabbed Leola's three brassieres from the basket of folded clothes. Within seconds they were
hanging on the clothesline in the summer sun. Returning to the house,
I opened the dryer and retrieved Cal's two pair of green wool pants
from among the colored clothes. They were already dry but I ran them
to the line and hung them up also. While vacuuming, I happened to
glance out the window. Cal's pants looked only big enough for a midg-
et to wear. I panicked. I ran to the line and tried pulling on them to
make them longer and wider, but it was of no use. Returning to the
house, I finished my last task and left for home. I was glad I'd completed everything on the list. I returned to the store and Cal paid me for
all my days of work. I'd earned enough to buy my ticket to Chicago.

When Dad arrived home on Friday night, I didn't have the heart to
ask him if I could go to Chicago. Instead I told him that I was taking
the bus there. I'd already sent Luke a letter asking him to pick me up
on the day and time of my arrival at Union Station.

"Do you have money for a ticket? Because I don't have it," Dad
said.

"Yes, I have it!" I couldn't believe my dad was letting me go without a qualm, and even agreed to take me to catch the bus. Since he
was going to do something nice for me, I promised myself I'd clean
the house the day before leaving. Early the following Friday my three
younger sisters helped me with the cleaning, since my two older sisters had jobs. We washed clothes, scrubbed floors, changed around the

living room furniture, dusted, cleaned the refrigerator, picked lilacs for the table, and loved every minute of it. Dad was going to be so proud, we just knew it. But he didn't come home for supper as we expected. It was almost midnight when I finally heard the doorknob turn. I got up to let him know how disappointed we were that he hadn't come home as planned. Once again he was plastered and Jim had brought him home.

"How could you do this again?" I shouted at Dad. "We've been waiting all night for you to get home."

"Donna, Donna, Donna! You'd better wake up and die right!" he said, slurring his words together. "See, I only have one boss around here, and that's me!" He turned to Jim and laughed, put up his chin and said, "No woman's going to dictate my life!" Then he called me by one of my aunt's names; an aunt that he never liked and had talked derogatory about at times. Jim got a big chuckle out of my angry response to Dad's unkind words. His laughter infuriated me, so I shot back.

"Just what are you doing bringing him here?" Of course, Dad knew whom I was talking about since there was no one else around. My sisters were sleeping and John had gone out on the town. Dad, who rarely had a mean streak, suddenly picked me up, hauled me as far as the bedroom doorway and threw me across the floor. I screamed. Next thing I knew Jim had Dad by the throat against the wall in the hallway. "If you ever do that to her again, I'll smash your face in."

"Settle down," Dad told him. Shocked at what just happened, I lay there on the floor, practically under the bed. Jim came into the room and lifted me from the floor and onto the bed. "Are you okay?" he asked in his raspy voice. I nodded. He kissed my cheek, brushed the top of my head, and then left the room. I heard the outside door close. Then his car started up and he sped away.

Awakening, Catherine asked, "What was that all about?"

"Nothing much," I said. But throughout the night I thought about what Jim had said to my dad. I couldn't believe he had stood up for me. It made me question if he was the true culprit in Dad's drinking. That night I realized if I should be mad at anyone, it was Dad.

The following morning came. I was worried that Dad wouldn't take me to the bus station. I knew I had to leave, now more than ever. I was sure that Dad was as sick of my behavior toward him as I was of his toward me. I thought about how he hadn't cared one iota about my leaving, so it didn't really surprise me when he kept his promise to take me to catch my bus. He did admit on the way to the station that he wasn't happy about my taking the bus alone.

"I don't want to find out you ended up in Timbuktu."

"I'll be okay, Dad," I reassured him as the bus pulled into the restaurant parking lot. I hurried out of the car and grabbed my small suitcase from the back seat.

"Stay out of mischief," he said as he walked me toward the bus. As I stepped aboard, I looked back at Dad. He was rough looking, more unkempt than ever. He hadn't shaved in days and still reeked of booze from the night before. Though I was excited to leave my troublesome home life, I was crying by the time I took a seat. It seemed strange that I was missing Dad so soon, especially since it was him I wanted to get away from, him and his drinking, drinking with a capital D. As the bus began moving, I wanted to run to the door. I wanted to ask the driver to "Wait a minute!" I wanted to run to Dad, to hug and kiss him, to tell him how much I loved him, and to let him know that everything would be okay. But I wasn't sure if it would ever be okay. So I sat down, adjusted my seat, and silently cried until I transferred to the Chicago bus at Green Bay.

Sixteen
CR

Thinking the Windy City would help me forget all my troubles like it had in the past, I'd taken a bus to Chicago. But before I even got to my destination, I knew my decision in leaving home for the summer was a mistake. Dad had always been there for me, and now when he needed me most I had turned my back on him. My three youngest sisters would care for him, of that I had no doubt, but I knew it was selfish to expect them to do it alone. Nevertheless, it didn't take me long to forget about the guilt once I saw my cousins and started going places.

Compared to multitude of responsibilities back home, I only had one here, which was keeping Luke's apartment clean. Actually it was exciting doing the job for him because he let me keep whatever money I found as pay for the job. Once a week I'd vacuum, dust, do the dishes and change his bedding. By the time I'd leave I was usually twenty to thirty dollars richer. I found coins under the couch cushions, on his night stand, dresser, kitchen table, and even on the bathroom sink. Betty Jane laughed one day when I told her I'd collected nearly forty dollars.

"Are you sure your brother's not planting the money there for you?" I'd never thought that could be the case. If there was a chance of it, I wasn't going to let on that I knew. I didn't want my summers of Christmases to end.

Being with the Kuta family was somewhat bittersweet. Betty Jane was a reminder of what our family was missing. The love and affection she gave to her husband John and their children kept me longing for my own mother. I desperately wanted to see my mother again. I yearned for her hands to cradle my face and for her to swoop down and plant kisses on my forehead. I longed to hear her whisper "I love you," in my ear. Knowing that I'd never hear those words again was heartbreaking. The thought of never putting my hands into the big pockets of my mother's apron again or see both Dad and her together again was frightening. I'd searched the small picture box many times and even asked relatives if they had any pictures of the two of them together, but no one had any.

Betty Jane and John loved bringing smiles to their kids' faces. Something as simple as giving their kids money for an ice cream cone brought joy to their hearts. I was glad to be surrounded by such happiness. Yet it made me feel bad for Dad. He loved making us happy, too, but rarely could because of being both busy and broke all the time. Many mornings he faced outstretched hands as each of us hoped to get his last dollar for a week's worth of hot lunch or a dime for an event going on at school. I remember the day a magician came to perform at the local town hall. The whole school was going to be bused downtown to see the magician perform, so long as they had the admission fee.

"Don't you at least have ten cents?" I begged Dad that morning.

"If I had it, I'd give it to you. Certainly someone will loan you the money," is all he said. After we came home from school, Dad kicked over the little wooden stool and then kicked it again clear across the kitchen and into the hallway when he learned that my sisters, brother and I, along with a couple kids from other poor families, were left behind at the school because we didn't have the *measly dime* to get in to see the show. Later that evening, Dad played Johnny Cash's "Pickin' Time." It was the song he'd played over and over and over after my mother died. Whenever he played it, we girls left him alone. We figured he was having "Mama moments," and needed time to himself.

Pickin' Time

Well I got cotton in the bottom land
It's up and growin' and I got a good stand
My good wife and them kids of mine
Gonna get new shoes come pickin' time
Get new shoes come pickin' time

Ev'ry night when I go to bed
I thank the Lord that my kids are fed
They live on beans eight days of nine
But I get 'em fat come pickin' time
Get 'em fat come pickin' time

Corn is yeller and the beans are high
The sun is hot in the summer sky
The work is hard 'til layin' by
Layin' by 'til pickin' time
Layin' by 'til pickin' time

It's hard to see by the coal-oil light
And I turn it off pretty early every night
'Cause a jug of coal-oil costs a dime
But I stay up late come pickin' time
Stay up late come pickin' time

My ol' wagon barely gets me to town
I patched the wheels and I watered 'em down
Keep her in shape so she'll be fine
To haul my cotton come pickin' time
Haul my cotton come pickin' time

Last Sunday morning when they passed the hat
It was still nearly empty back where I sat
But the preacher smiled and he said that's fine
The Lord'll wait 'til pickin' time
Yes the Lord'll wait 'til pickin' time

From the time of my mother's death, Dad had been there for us. Sometimes he spent a good portion of his day going from one of us to the other, tending to scraped knees, removing slivers and pieces of glass from our feet. He put cold cloths on burns and fevers, pulled out our loose baby teeth, and played Fairy Godmother when called for, sometimes having to use his collectible Indian head nickels to do so. The bigger we became, the smaller the house seemed to get. Tensions sprouted like dandelions on a spring lawn. Dad often said that there were too many chiefs and not enough Indians at our house. With each of us trying to discipline the other, it not only frustrated Dad, but made him crabby, too. His usual nature was gentle and playful. If we didn't get out of bed in the morning he'd sing to us. His favorite was "Lazy Mary," which he'd direct to my youngest sister.

"Monica Mary will you get up, will you get up, will you get up, Monica Mary will you get up, so early in the morning?" Sometimes when she was in a good mood, she'd sing the response. "Oh, no dear father, I won't get up, I won't get up, I won't get up, oh, no dear father, I won't get up, so early in the morning!"

If we still weren't out of bed after his second call in the morning, he'd sneak his hand under the covers and tickle our feet. If that didn't do the trick, his final option was the cold-water treatment — drip-

114

ping drops of water from a glass onto our heads. We'd scream while he laughed. But times were changing. When we slacked off on our chores, he'd be so frustrated with our lack of obedience that he'd resort to verbal abuse. "Oh the little jackasses!" he'd holler. "They didn't wash any clothes yet. What the hell am I going to wear to work today, the same dirty, half-wet pair of pants as yesterday?" Or he'd find a half kettle of goulash sitting on the stove from the night before. "Well, son of a bitch! There goes a meal out the door!" We were expected to look around to see what had to be done, and never wait to be asked to do a task that needed attention. It might be too late by then was Dad's philosophy.

After I'd finished cleaning at Luke's apartment one day, I went over to my friend Gretchen's house, which was just two blocks away. Although we were friends, I was uncomfortable being at her house when her dad was home. He talked gruff and one time he struck Gretchen because she'd thrown out perfectly good food. I felt sorry for her, but I knew my own dad would've been mad at me had I done as she had. To Dad, wasting food was a cardinal sin, especially when it was carelessly left to spoil. Food was usually an issue at home. The first problem was to recall which two girls' turn it was to get supper on the table. Second was to decide what to have, which meant asking ourselves questions like, "Do we have time to cook a venison roast? Or will it be better to use the last can of Kennedy pork or beef from the surplus commodities?" Dad might have suggested using a chunk of salt pork from butchering the pig to make rice soup, but no one wanted to take on such a task. None of us could ever make it as tasty as Dad. It was almost a given that there would be plenty of complaints, especially if the cook used too much rice and didn't cook it long enough. Spaghetti usually sounded the best to most of us, but making it meant a trip to the store. Would there be any change left under the doily on Dad's dresser to buy the ingredients?

Another issue was whether there be enough food to go around.

It was common for my sisters and I to misjudge how much food was needed. And if Dad and the boys came home hungrier than usual, it didn't take long for it to disappear. Even when Dad was the chef, it didn't guarantee there would be enough to go around. So whenever he chanted, "The first man up is the best man fed," we knew we'd better get to the table fast if we wanted to eat. On school days, if we were too poky getting to the breakfast table, it usually meant it would be suppertime before we'd have another chance to eat.

Being hungry at school was both physically and mentally draining. I made it a point to sit by the door in the classroom whenever possible so the noise from my stomach wouldn't be heard. Some days the sounds were so loud and lingering that they got more than just my attention, especially when schoolwork was being done in silence or it was test-taking time. I'd fake a sneeze or several coughs to block the groaning. My face would flush with embarrassment whenever someone asked if I was hungry. I'd deny it. I had to. If I didn't they'd expect me to eat lunch, but I didn't have any money. I forced myself to concentrate on reading, writing or arithmetic but the ruckus within my stomach, along with the aroma of good-smelling food floating down the hallway from the cafeteria, distracted me. Just the smell of the food would increase the growling, which forced me to be even more disruptive. I'd lift the top of my desk, wrinkle papers or pretend to be looking for a pencil or tablet under the rubble of schoolbooks and papers.

"Miss Jacques," the teacher would bellow. "It's no wonder you're doing so poorly. You never pay attention! Day after day you're disruptive, always talking to your neighbors and fidgeting around as if you have nothing better to do!"

Sometimes I'd get moved to the front of the room, or worse, out into the hallway. Students with hall passes, on their way to and from the office or bathroom, would tease me for getting into trouble. "Shame, shame," their fingers would say as they passed by. Or they'd shake their heads while pressing their lips and rolling their eyes as if to say, "Not again!"

Occasionally my disruptive behavior got me sent to the office. Each time I was scared to death that I'd get the paddle! "This is the third time in a month that you've been sent to me," the principal said one day. So from behind the world map he reached for the large paddle while I begged for mercy. "P-p-p-please, I'll behave. I won't cause any more trouble!" The first two times my pleas for lenience had worked, but this time even reciting the Biblical passage, (that he should) "forgive seventy times, seven times," did nothing in my defense.

"Bend over," Mr. Lundell said, pointing to his desk.

"Ohhhhh," I screamed, as my eyes fell upon school board notes and I wrapped my hands around my bottom.

"Do you want your hands hit, too?" I pulled them away, right before the first strike. The paddle whistled through the air and landed onto my bottom five times, each strike worse than the first. I never cried, but the whole school must have heard my screams.

"Why do you shake?" Gretchen asked one day as we walked back from the Berwyn community pool.

"I'm not really sure but my dad said that I inherited it from my mother because she always shook too."

"Do you always shake that bad?"

"No," I laughed, "Sometimes I shake even worse, like when I'm hungry at school and don't get to eat." Gretchen listened intently as I told how a teacher of mine had called me up to the blackboard to do a math problem during one of the shaking episodes from not eating. "It was awful," I said. "My hands were trembling so bad that I could barely hold the chalk let alone write on the blackboard or concentrate on the problem. My trembling made my classmates laugh. To make matters worse, I'd started my monthly on the way to school and didn't have a nickel for the Kotex machine, so I'd used toilet paper."

"Toilet paper?"

"Yes," I said, "and I was so afraid that I'd flow through my clothes and onto the tile floor. I couldn't even move. My teacher got upset with me for just standing there, doing nothing. 'Miss Jacques, think! Use those brains God gave you! Work out the problem!' I thought I was going to faint because the room got dark and then starting spinning around me. I couldn't remember how to multiply. So I didn't answer the teacher when asked if I understood the problem. 'Oh, go sit down!' he said, totally disgusted with me. Then he called a less-than-brilliant student to the board. Within seconds the student had solved the simple problem. Once again all eyes turned to me. I was so embarrassed. Most of the kids laughed again. I could tell that even my best friends were wondering how I could be so dumb."

After a couple weeks of chumming with Gretchen, her family moved away. I was devastated. Finally, I'd found someone in the city my own age. She was a person I felt comfortable sharing things with. I told myself that God was punishing me for having so much fun while poor Dad was miserable at home. I went back and forth and back and forth between feeling guilty and justifying my leaving home for the summer. A part of me felt that I deserved to be riding in taxicabs to shopping centers, playing baseball in the park or riding a bicycle for miles. Going for midnight strolls to the Dairy Queen was something I never wanted to give up. Other kids were allowed to sit around all day watching television and reading books. "Why shouldn't I be able to?" I asked myself more than once.

Over time, I left the guilt behind. It was as far away as home itself. It probably wouldn't have returned if I hadn't seen the wino at Riverview Amusement Park. Seeing the man all dirty, staggering back and forth, and looking as if not a person in the world cared about him was heartbreaking. By the time the double Ferris wheel brought Luke and me to the top, my first tear for Dad had fallen. I looked out over the sights so my brother wouldn't notice. After all, he was trying to bring a little bit of heaven to my world. I didn't want to seem ungrateful, so

I asked what ride we'd be going on next. On our way home, I decided to spend the night at Luke's because I wanted to be alone. After he left for work, I climbed into bed. There between the percale sheets that I'd placed on my brother's couch, I let my sorrow out. It had been piercing my heart throughout the day. I was glad to finally be alone, to cry if I wanted to without anyone to hear me.

"It's no wonder Dad has been drinking," I said to myself. "He has nothing but worries in his life. He can forget that the house is no longer insured or if it burnt down we wouldn't have a place to stay, or that he might not get us all out in time. When he's drinking he doesn't have to think about how he's going to buy our school clothes... or... or..." Suddenly my thoughts wandered to our school picnic that was held a couple days before school got out for the summer. Dad had extended his workdays by a couple hours each day to earn extra money to buy us windbreaker jackets in time for our picnic. We'd all begged for them, since they were the rage. Dad beamed when he announced he'd met his goal. The extra money would be included in his weekly pay. But on Wednesday the refrigerator quit working and he had to replace it. About the same time, Sarah needed a tooth pulled, so we settled for special picnic lunches of bologna sandwiches, apples, chips, Twinkies and a bottle of pop.

My throat tightened. "Why did I come to Chicago this summer?" I asked myself. Now here I was feeling so sad for Dad, and not even able to call him. I needed to know that he was okay. I tried to tell myself that he was safe in bed sleeping the night away, but the fear of him walking home from the bar on the long dark road and getting hit by a car hounded me. I tried to sleep, but my mind was like a radio with many stations trying to tune in. The thought that won out was Christmas during my fourth grade year. Relentlessly, I'd begged Dad for a black corduroy skirt and blue cotton blouse. "If Santa doesn't bring them, then he's a fake!" I yelled, a few days before Christmas.

I hadn't believed in Santa for quite some time, but hoped by asking for the things I wanted, I'd get them. Dad watched that Christmas morning as my sisters and I tore through the (nameless) wrapped packages from the Salvation Army — bobby socks for each, a checkers game, hair rollers with picks, two Santa coloring books, a kitchen apron, two dump trucks, a grader and a big red fire engine. Our faces hung to the floor. Dad rubbed his wide hands back and forth over his face for a few minutes before he got up and went into the kitchen. Some of us followed. "Look here," he said, with a grin on his face as he opened the big, deep bread drawer. We ran and looked inside. It was filled with apples, oranges, grapefruit and 2 bags of hard candies. Our earlier sorrow turned a bit joyful as we grabbed the fruit and ran to the table with it. The smell of the Macintosh apples and oranges made it seem more like Christmas to all of us.

After Dad had prepared dinner that Christmas, he sat down on the kitchen floor. One by one he put us on top of the big toys and showed us how to use our little legs to scoot them around on the kitchen floor. Soon we were taking turns racing those trucks, grader and fire engine around the kitchen table, timing each other to see who could make the lap the fastest. By New Year's Day the linoleum had given way to the plywood below, adding visible lanes to our racetrack. After some major tumbles and a few hundred crashes into the lower cupboards, we rounded the corners of that track faster and more smoothly than any Indy driver ever could.

Recalling how concerned Dad was for our happiness that Christmas, I broke down into sobs. I was glad the man in the apartment next to us had his music blaring. I let the tears pour out until not a single one was left. It was the first time in years that I'd cried so hard. The last time I missed my dad so much was when my mother was still alive. It was in the dark of night when Mark went for help. Our neighbor came and took Dad to the hospital because he was in lots of pain. A few days later he returned after having passed some kidney stones.

My last big outing of the summer of '65 was a trip to the Cermak mall with Betty Jane, followed by a visit to see Emery. I learned that Emery was a good cook, but not for food like Dad made. The food he cooked was fancy. He served us lasagna and we each had our own individual bowl of salad. For dessert we had orange sherbet with dainty little sugar cookies he'd bought at a bakery. Seeing Emery one last time before leaving for home and finally meeting his girlfriend made me happy. But as I hugged him goodbye, I felt sad because I knew I wouldn't get to see him for a long time.

"So you're going home by bus tomorrow morning?" he asked, kissing my cheek.

"Early tomorrow morning," I replied.

"Yes," Betty Jane added. "Our cab's on the way, Uncle Emery, so we have to get going."

When the bus pulled into the Escanaba station, I looked out the window to see if Dad was there to pick me up. I could hardly believe my eyes when I saw him. Not only had he remembered to pick me up, but he was leaning against his car and looking like the most handsome dad in the world again. He was dressed in a pair of new, light-gray casual pants and a yellow short-sleeve slipover shirt. I'd never seen him in a short-sleeved shirt before. He was beautifully brown from the summer sun. His hair was cut and he was clean-shaven. When he saw me step down from the bus, he smiled and cocked his chin upward as he lit his pipe. I started running toward him.

"Get your suitcase," he hollered. Taking it from the driver, I ran to tell Dad how much I'd missed him and to ask how *his* summer had been.

Seventeen
CR

The months following my arrival home that year went much smoother. My sisters and I had a serious talk and agreed to do the majority of our weekly chores on Saturday. Two of us, always a younger and an older one, would take on the task of cleaning and changing around the living room furniture, dusting, sweeping and cleaning the bathroom. Two others would do the washing and hanging out, and the folding and ironing of clothes. Monica and I usually did the dishes and mopped the floors. We also assisted Dad in the kitchen. He usually took over the cooking and baking on Saturdays during the winter months. The summer months were left to my sisters and me.

Dad had become a great cook and baker during his years in the CCC (Civilian Conservation Corps) camps. I loved to bake with him. For my thirteenth birthday I made myself a banana cake with peanut butter frosting. I could tell Dad loved it but I wanted him to tell me that he did. He was never too generous with compliments. That day I finally received the affirmation I'd been waiting a long time for. "This is real good!" he said. Before I had the chance to rejoice, he added, "What did you do, make a mistake?" I hadn't planned to tell him, but with that comment, and him smirking, knowing his teasing was getting to me, I said, "No, I bought a cake mix!" It was a rare happening, but I had the last laugh. To him only homemade food was worth eating and praising.

Although things at home were going better, at school my grades were slipping. Things were always popping into my head, which sometimes got me into trouble. One day I decided we eighth grade girls should break the school dress code. If those responsible wanted us to wear skirts to school, then skirts we would wear, but mini skirts, the newest fad in the world of fashion. Word passed quickly through our homeroom. "Wear a mini skirt on Friday. Wear a mini skirt on Friday." Although I didn't own one, I'd already decided what I would do. As we waited for the bus on Friday morning, I began rolling the waistband of my skirt over and over itself until my skirt looked like an official mini skirt. Sarah saw what I'd done and objected. "Mind your own business," I screeched as I boarded the bus.

Shortly after the morning bell rang, the door of our classroom was banged open by the fist of Mr. Lundell. "Girls, to the blackboard!" he ordered. Candy was first as he made his way down the line, yard stick in hand, measuring each girl's skirt to see if it was one inch or less above the knee. Candy, Cindy, Krystal, Rosanna and Anne were already told they had to go home and change. Those who lived too far from school, like Janet, had to call home to have a change of clothes brought to the school. I trembled as I fought to bring my skirt length down.

"Hey, Donna's cheating," Edwin hollered. Mr. Lundell quickly stood and turned around. His face got blood red. "Who just spoke without being asked?" Edwin lowered his head and pretended to be reading. I lowered my shoulders and breathed a sigh of relief. As he reprimanded him, I hustled to complete my skirt makeover while the boys coughed and coughed trying to get our principal's attention directed toward me. My knees were knocking when Mr. Lundell knelt in front of me. "Well," he said as he finished the measuring of the final few. "It looks like a few girls have common sense." With the yardstick he tapped the toes of Cheryl, Gloria and my shoes. "You three may sit down."

"Cheater, cheater," was being whispered as I made my way to my desk at the back of the room. I had escaped the punishment of a week of after-school detention. However, escaping punishment the next time around for acting up in science class was not to be.

Krystal and I were caught talking while the teacher was presenting some information, so we were moved to the front of the room, smack in front of the teacher's desk. We felt picked on because half of the class had been talking. We resented having been moved, so at lunchtime she and I came up with a riddle to say to the teacher during his class the following day. After he'd taken his seat, we extended our arms out toward him and, pretending to cock a gun with our pointer fingers, we sang to a verse of a sixties song, changing the words.

> One, two, three
> Kill Mr. C
> Three, two, one
> Shoot him with a gun.

Then we laughed along with everyone else who had heard our song. Mr. C's nostrils flared. "To the office!" he demanded, jumping from his chair and grabbing the two of us by the back of our necks. He marched us down the hallway and practically pushed us into the office. After giving Mr. Lundell the lowdown, he left. I was ordered to take a seat on the big burgundy chair. There I sat as he lectured Krystal and then paddled her, a hit on the rear for each year of her life. She was crying but managed a smirk my way when she left the office, as if to say, "Ha, ha! Mine is over. You're next!"

Mr. Lundell didn't get as mad at me as he had at her. "I'm disappointed with you," he said. "I thought you were one of the students I could count on to be a role model."

"A what?"

"Role model — a student who sets a good example for the others." His words shocked me. I couldn't believe he thought so much of me. I felt ashamed. With each hit of the long wooden paddle, I vowed to be that role model that Mr. Lundell could count on. I would make him proud. He opened the office door and called Krystal back in and then informed us that our behavior was so hateful that he had no choice but to suspend us for three days. The thought of time off from school was already being calculated in my mind as a blessing in disguise. I could finally get some of the walls and windows washed at home that hadn't been done in the spring. Suspension smelled as wonderful as wild summer roses until he informed us that we'd be washing school windows during our suspension. "Oh, dear," I thought, already feeling the humiliation of it all.

Krystal and I were put at opposite ends of the school. One time when Bernadette passed me in the hallway, as I scrubbed away with the ammonia and water, she chuckled. She had gotten a hallway pass to the bathroom, I'm sure, just to poke fun at me. "You two are getting what you deserve," she said as she passed by, then gave her long blonde hair a flip.

Maybe we were getting what we deserved because it wasn't the first time she and I had been, at least somewhat, in trouble that year. One noon hour the two of us decided to skip school and ride around with a guy and girl who'd dropped out of school. They were drinking beer and asked if we wanted some. Krystal sipped from the girl's bottle. I did, too, but I was afraid to take more than the one sip because a friend of Bernadette's had drunk pickle juice with aspirins in it at the junior high dance and she ended up thinking she was Frankenstein. Two of the chaperones had to take her to the hospital.

Skipping school and riding around in a car made me nervous. We were pretty sure some kids had seen us leave. As I got on the bus after school, I hurried to the back. "Boy, are you in BIG trouble," Sarah said loudly. I put my finger over my mouth to shush her. "No, I'm not going to shush. When the bell rang, some kids said they saw you and Krystal getting into someone's car today, and they told the principal."

"Krystal took me home for lunch. She does that a lot, so I can eat."

"Oh, then tell me what you ate?"

"Toast with peanut butter and jelly, with some coffee! So there!" I said wishing Krystal and I would've made up an excuse together before returning to school.

"Wait until I tell Dad you beg people for food. And that you had coffee!"

Actually, I'd tried coffee a couple different times at Krystal's insistence, but I never liked it. Most often I drank orange juice, which was a real treat. As we'd eat, we'd do each others fortunes, which consisted of nothing more than writing seven columns of seven entries each on a piece of paper, such as seven choices of boys we'd marry, seven kinds of homes, cars, rings and how many kids we wanted to have. Then the person doing the fortune would add an item of his or her own choice to each category. We'd then pick our lucky number and the process of elimination would begin until there was only one item left in each of the categories.

The games usually ended with us laughing until we'd nearly pee our pants because of the results of our fortunes. I'd marry a monster, move to Siberia, have a horse and buggy for a car, live in an outdoor toilet and adopt thirty kids! One time we were laughing so hard that we didn't hear her father return early from work. "Get your little asses back to school where they belong," he shouted while giving us a boot out the door. Even I knew that Krystal's dad's bark was worse than his bite, so our laughter continued until we took our seats at the sound of the noon bell.

As Sarah had predicted, the following morning Mr. Lundell was waiting for me at the door when we arrived at school. He asked me to follow him to the office. Krystal was already there. "Please step out for a minute," he said to her. He closed the door. "I was told by a reliable source that you left school property yesterday. Is that true?" I nodded. "Where did you go?"

"To Krystal's house."

"And what did you go there for?"

"We had lunch."

"What did you have?"

"Peanut butter and jelly toast with coffee. Actually, I had orange juice and Krystal had the coffee."

I knew what I'd told him was a lie but I was afraid to tell him the truth because his face was so red when he first met me at the door. He opened the office door and called Krystal back in. I was certain that our stories had conflicted because she'd told the truth. I felt faint when she reentered the office. "Okay," he said, "I believe you, but next time get *permission* from your homeroom teacher before you decide to leave school property. Now get to class!"

Neither of us said a word as we walked to our homeroom. Everything that needed saying was being said through our eyes and the grins on our faces that day.

However, this time we didn't get off so easy. As we slaved away each of the three days of suspension washing the school windows, I was mad at myself for doing something so stupid. Added to that, I was getting further and further behind on my schoolwork. "I'm going to become the model student Mr. Lundell thinks I can be. From now on, I'm going to school to learn!" I told Dad that night before he started to lecture me again.

"You bet you are," he said, "and you're going to help me out more, too. You can start right now by washing these paint brushes."

"Paint brushes?"

"Yes," he said, "paint brushes. Now get moving, or you'll get my boot on your behind."

That fall Dad repainted what needed redoing on both the inside and outside of the house. He remained busy with chores that needed to get done before the cold months arrived. Sometimes he was still outside after dark, which made me uneasy. My nervousness got on my brother John's nerves a lot, but never as much as in November of '65. While Dad's friend Carl was hunting deer he came across a skeleton in the woods near the Fayette State Park, about nine miles from our house. Although the body was decayed, our community soon learned that it was a man that had been shot in the head, dead for months. Everybody was in shock. People wondered who would do such a horrible crime.

Night after night I'd hear Dad talking with John about the murder. I wondered if the murderers were nearby, and if a member of my family or I would be next to die. As darkness crept over the land each evening, I became terrified. I feared the killers were still in the area, maybe right outside our house, watching, waiting, ready to shoot one of us. It was as if Lucifer himself was on the prowl. Not having locks on the outside doors added to my fear. One night while doing the dishes, as I was washing the big butcher knife, I saw my reflection in the window and thought it was someone outside with a gun. I screamed as if my life depended on it. Everyone came running. John had little patience with my imagination. He thought I was just trying to get out of doing dishes and didn't believe me when I told him I'd seen someone outside the window with a gun.

"Finish the dishes, you big pansy," he said.

"Then it's your fault if I get shot!" I snapped.

A few nights later I was on my bed listening to Bernadette's transistor radio. The Beatles were in America and I was waiting to hear their latest release, "I Feel Fine," although I was anything but *fine* knowing the criminals were still at large. Suddenly I heard a ruckus in the living room where Dad, John and my sisters were watching Bonanza. Quietly I tip-toed out of the bedroom. Strangely enough, when I got to the kitchen, everything in the living room went silent. I couldn't even hear the television. I froze. "Dammit, be quiet so I know what's going on," I heard Dad whisper.

"I just heard the noise again," Sarah said softly.

"Dad," John whispered, "I think it's coming from over here." My heart was beating so loud that I thought for sure the murderers would hear it and come charging into the house and grab me before I could get to Dad. As much as I tried to control my fear, it took over and out came the most wrenching scream, worse I'm sure, than any scream ever heard on the face of the earth. Everyone came running into the kitchen. "What the hell's the matter now?" John asked.

"Are they outside?" I whispered, not understanding why they'd all run to the kitchen and left the murderers to do as they pleased.

"Who are you talking about?" Dad asked.

"Well, I heard you all whispering, like someone was outside."

"Oh, real swell," John said. "It's her dumb imagination again!" They all went back into the living room and left me standing without an answer. I followed, knowing the problem obviously had nothing to do with the killers.

"I just heard it again," Bernadette said.

"Me, too," Monica added. Dad started accusing my sisters of humming or making some other sound to bug him. Even though they all denied it, he said if he caught the one making the noise he was sending her straight to bed. Before long, I heard the noise, too. We began looking at each other trying to see which one was making it, but everyone was standing perfectly still.

"Just a minute," Anna said. "It's John who's making the noise. He's meowing like a cat."

"No, John's not meowing like a cat!" John said sarcastically.

"Listen, everyone," Dad pleaded.

"It's John, Dad," Anna insisted. "Because the sound is coming from behind him."

"Hold on," Dad said, walking over to where John was standing. We stood quiet. "Sounds like it's coming from inside this wall, doesn't it?" We scrambled to the wall and placed our ears against it. Sure enough, we could hear meowing coming from inside the wall.

"John, go to the pump house and get my crowbar, and make it snappy," Dad said. In no time John was back. Dad used the crowbar to pry the paneling from the wall, then the drywall. On the floor between the studs lay six newborn kittens. "Well, the mother cat must have made her bed up in the attic and her kittens have fallen through," Dad chuckled. My sisters and I each grabbed a kitten. "Follow me to the barn," Dad said. John put a pile of hay in the manger and we put the kittens on top of it. "Now let them be. The mother will reject them if you keep pestering them, and they're way too young to survive without her."

"Do we get to keep them?" I asked.

"Aren't the twenty-two we already have embarrassing enough?" John asked.

It was true; cats were everywhere, twenty-two of them fending for themselves. After the long U.P. winters, their bodies would look like they'd just found their way out of a cemetery. Many mornings when we went outside to get on the bus the cats would come running from every direction and follow as if we were Pied Pipers. I disliked when they did that. Being teased about being in a family of a lot of kids was bad enough. I hated being harassed about having cats all over the place, too. "Shoo, get away from here," we'd say, each trying to get rid of them before the bus made it to our stop.

From the night of the kitten rescue, Dad referred to us six girls as his six little kittens. Whenever John would pester us, Dad would say,

"Oh, let those little kittens alone." Boy, did that bug John. But lots of things bugged him, like when we jumped rope, practiced cartwheels in the house, or when we did the hand motions to "Did You Ever." (A chant written for hand motions.) But it never bugged him to boss us around or cheat our little sisters out of pop. "Drink for drink or sip for sip," he'd say whenever Dad treated us to our own bottle of pop. Anna and Monica were gullible when it came to John's schemes and they'd willingly give him a gulp of their drink. When they saw that the bottle he held behind his back was empty they'd go crying to Dad. John would take off outside. One time after his trickiness we made up a ditty about his meanness and sang it to him.

"Meany, meany tuska tinny oou walla, walla beany ump belly oh-a-doe, oh-a-doe and dotton, dotton." He hated when we'd sing that. But he especially disliked when we'd spy on him, like we did the day we looked through the keyhole of the pump house and saw him smoking Dad's old pipe while he rode Monica's big tricycle around and around the pump. Together we chanted. "We... see... you!" Within seconds he was chasing after us. "You girls must want a knuckle sandwich, don't you?" he hollered.

"Ahhh!" we screamed as we ran to the house for Dad to come to our rescue.

"Don't always come running to me for protection," Dad complained. "If you mess with the bull, you get the horn!"

Eighteen
 CR

Dad sold a load of pulpwood just before Christmas and gave us each some money, according to our ages, to go shopping with. He told us to spend half on ourselves and the rest on gifts for each other. We were thrilled. Dad smiled at our giddiness. I couldn't believe that I had *forty-five* dollars to spend.

"When can you take us shopping?" Monica asked.

"Next Friday night. That way you'll have more time to shop because the stores are open until nine."

"I'm not going," John said. "I'll go with some of my friends some other day." But John didn't wait. That very night he used some of his money to take his girlfriend Sally to a movie. Ever since she'd told him that his eyes were as beautiful as violets he was going bonkers over her. So much so that nowadays he was always jolly. He'd go around the house jumping up and trying to touch the ceiling, not with a hand anymore, but with an elbow! He was so happy that he was even *nice* to us girls.

Keeping his word, Dad took us to town on the following Friday night. When we got to Escanaba he dropped us off behind the Fair store and told us to be at Mark's house by nine fifteen. "You know how to get there from here, right?"

"Through the alley, past the National food store, and then two more blocks and we'll be at Mark's," Sarah said.

"That's right, and stick together! I'll be waiting for you, so be on time."

We were so excited about being able to Christmas shop that we didn't realize we were running on icy sidewalks until Monica landed on her behind. "Ouch," she cried. We helped her up, brushed the snow from her coat, skirt and tights and were off again but moving cautiously toward the music of "Silver Bells." On the corner of Ludington and Ninth there was a little shelter, about the size of an outhouse. Hooked on top of it was a loud speaker that the music was coming from. Standing next to the shelter was an old lady dressed in navy blue from her prairie-style hat to her boots. She was ringing a bell and asking for money for the poor. We stood momentarily, wondering which direction we should go, toward Montgomery Ward or J.C. Penney's. We marveled at the beauty of the street. The streetlights and businesses were all decorated with huge Christmas balls and colorful lights. Women and men with packages were rushing by. Many of them stopped to put money into the little red kettle.

"Come on," Sarah said. "We're wasting time just standing here looking around." We followed her as she headed in the direction of the town Christmas tree.

"Wait!" Anna hollered. I turned around. Anna was putting money into the little red kettle.

"Anna, no! Don't put your money in there," I hollered. But it was too late. "Oh, Anna," I said, grabbing her hand and giving her the "don't be so dumb" look. "Come on, we have to catch up with the others." I tucked my freezing hands into my coat pockets and suggested she do the same.

"That money's for poor people, so I gave them one of my dollars and three of my quarters. That was a nice thing to do, right, Donna Jean?" she asked as we entered Kresge's, the store I'd seen my sisters go in to.

"Yes Anna," I said. "It was a *really* nice thing to do. But don't do it again or you won't have much money to spend." Part of me wished I had been as generous, but another part was glad I hadn't parted with a single penny. I was planning on buying a couple of bras even if it meant using every bit of my money. I was tired of being teased for wearing an oversized bra to school. It was the only bra I had, one I'd got out of a box of hand-me-downs. It was wear it or no bra at all! My puberty buds, which had seemed to appear overnight, seemed to draw everyone's eyes toward me. Using the oversized bra didn't bring much comfort. A couple boys nicknamed me Falsies. That word stung worse than the elastic back they pulled every chance they got. I was tired of the ridicule. New bras were the first item I'd thought of buying when Dad gave us the money.

"I want to buy a pair of boots," Catherine said, as we looked around the store. "My feet are always cold when we play outside at school."

"Let's look," Sarah said, guiding her to the shoe department. Bernadette and I took Monica and Anna to the little girls' clothes and helped them pick out under shirts and panties that had either blue, yellow or pink flowers on them. Bernadette picked out some blonde highlights for her hair and I found some bras. Catherine found the boots she wanted and Sarah found shoes she needed. We paid for our things, but before leaving the store Sarah said she was treating us to root beer floats at the soda fountain. "Really, Sarah?" we asked, hoping she wasn't joking.

"Yes," she said, "I planned to do this with some of my money before we even left home."

As we feasted, we thought of different gifts to buy each other and decided to pair off into three different stores so we wouldn't be able to see what we were buying for each other. Every half-hour we'd regroup and switch partners so that our Christmas would be full of surprises. Our final few minutes were spent picking dad out a flannel shirt and a bottle of cologne. We bought John a belt and socks.

After getting home, we hid Dad's gifts out in the woodshed. Unfortunately, two days before Christmas, right after putting up the tree, Sarah went to the pump house to get Dad and John's gifts so that we could wrap them. But Dad's cologne had frozen and the bottle had broken open. His new shirt was all stained. Despite the cold weather, Sarah bundled up and walked to Cal's and bought Dad a package of Plowboy tobacco, a new corncob pipe, and a box of matches, so that he, too, would have gifts to open on Christmas morning.

After John finished his chores Christmas morning, he put on his new shirt that he'd bought when he went shopping with his friends. It was a beautiful slipover shirt, made of many different colors. "That's a nice looking shirt you have there, so take care of it. Don't be letting it drag on the floor," Dad said.

"You don't have to worry about that," he replied. "This is the best shirt I've ever had. I plan to take special care of it."

John guarded his shirt even more diligently than he did the refrigerator when it had pop or ice cream in it. The second his shirt got a spot on it, he hurried to the sink to wash it off. When it needed a full bath he washed it by hand, in cool water to keep it from fading. I was in the kitchen the morning his shirt got another bath. "Why are you washing it today?" I asked.

"What concern is it of yours?" he asked as he lifted the shirt in and out of the sudsy water.

"Just wondering, that's all."

"Well, if you really want to know, I have a *hot date* tonight!"

"With Sally, right?".

"Sally? That's over!" he said as he carefully wrung out his shirt and then hung it over the back of a chair. He turned on the oven and opened the door. He grabbed the chair and pulled it closer to the oven. As his shirt began to dry, John ran to get his pile of wood split. Returning once to check on the shirt's progress, he brushed his hands against his pants to make sure they were clean, then flipped his shirt to the other side. Before leaving he asked me if I could keep flipping it over so it would be dry by the time he finished his job.

Every few minutes I turned his shirt from top to bottom and over, too. Still it felt damp and John's woodpile was shrinking. I wondered how I could get it dried faster, to make sure he could wear it on his date. Like in other situations, a brilliant idea came to mind. I moved the chair away from the oven and grabbed the potholders. Gripping the top rack, I pulled it out. Carefully I lay John's shirt upon it. After a few minutes I reached in and felt it. It was dry! I carefully took it out and set it on the table. "John will be so happy." I thought. "I'll fold it just like it was folded when he first spotted it on the shelf of the F & G store." I laid it on the table and buttoned the three little buttons on the front and fixed the collar. Terror struck when I turned it to the other side. The back of John's beautiful shirt was scorched with oven rack lines. "Ahhh!" I screamed, causing my sisters to come running.

"Boy, are you in big trouble!" Catherine said when she saw it.

"I'm glad I'm not you!" Sarah added, as her eyes shifted toward the door.

"I'm getting out of here before he comes in," Bernadette said.

She had barely moved a foot when in he came, whistling away. He whipped his coat off and threw it on top the freezer chest and then pulled off his old shirt. "Is it dry?" he hollered on his way into the bathroom. "I'm going to wash up and then I'll be right there." No one said a word. Again he asked if it was dry. Again no one answered. He swung himself around the wood casing of the utility room and into the kitchen.

"Can't you idiots hear? I asked if my shirt was... Oh no! No!" he shouted, grabbing it from the table. I slid into the narrow spot between the refrigerator and wall. "What the hell did you do?" He hurried his shirt to the kitchen sink and tried with all his might to scrub the scorch marks out, but they wouldn't budge. In some places it was so badly burnt that it had left holes in the material. He looked like a giant gorilla with bulging red eyes and flaring nostrils as his footsteps followed my backward steps out of the kitchen. Quickly I turned and ran, my long hair flying every which way. He caught me under the crabapple tree and knuckled the top of my head. "Did you hear... me... tell you... to put... my shirt...*into the oven*, you dumb little shithead? Well, did you?" He asked jerking my hair.

"No!" I screamed as I followed my hair to the ground.

"Well," he said, knuckling my head a couple more times. "Next time listen to me, you misfit!" Then giving my hair a final tug he let go and walked away. I ran back toward the house crying for Dad, but I was afraid to go back in the house because I wasn't sure where John was. A few minutes later I opened the door a crack and saw him standing in the kitchen pulling up the sleeves of his red sweater with the gray trim, the same red sweater he always wore.

"Tell Dad I'm not coming home tonight," he said to Sarah. When he turned his back I snuck in and hid in Dad's bedroom. A couple minutes later I heard the door slam so hard that it sounded like the glass of the window had broken. Then I heard him trying to start the car. I felt bad for him. I lifted the window shade and peered behind it and prayed that the car would run. Without realizing it, my eyes had found his. He waved at me, but with just one finger. "Whew," I said to myself, "he must not be that mad or he never would've waved." I smiled and waved back, but for some reason it made him mad again. His face turned gorilla-like again. "Do you want your face smashed in?" he shouted, his words coming at me as if through a megaphone. Quickly I dropped the shade and crawled under Dad's bed and didn't come out until the sound of the car faded into the distance. At that moment I was glad John was a senior and would soon be leaving home for good.

When John's Junior/Senior prom came around, it gave him something else to think about other than me ruining his shirt. One day he came home from school and told Dad that no one from the junior class could think of a band to play for the prom so they asked the seniors for ideas. "As I sat there thinking, it dawned on me that Aunt Geraldine and her brothers have The Gorsche Orchestra. So I told the junior class about them and they agreed to hire them."

"I don't think that's a good idea," Dad said. "I've heard they're not very dependable."

"Oh, that's just swell!" John replied. "I already called Aunt Geraldine from school and booked their band."

For the next few weeks John waited with anticipation the coming of the prom. Despite Dad's misgivings of The Gorsche Orchestra, John had faith in them and was proud that he'd been the one who'd suggested them for the evening. John was optimistic that the evening would be a memorable one. And memorable it was, but not in the way John had hoped. During the band's first break, Aunt Geraldine's brothers left the hall and went to the bar next door. When they didn't arrive back for the next set, Aunt Geraldine left to go get them but they still wouldn't leave, so she asked John to help her coax them back, but the men wouldn't budge.

"They were so drunk, Dad, they could barely stand, let alone play instruments and sing," John said the next morning, still mad at what had happened. Sitting on a kitchen chair, puffing on his pipe, Dad seemed not to be paying attention to the whole scenario. Finally he stood from the chair, pressed his lips together, cocked his head and chuckled, "Did I, or did I not predict that that would happen? Didn't you ever see the show *Father Knows Best?*"

"Don't go laughing." John scolded. "I'm never going to live this down. Half of the kids are blaming me for what happened."

"Well, John, you should've listened to what I told you and stayed away from that prom. Remember, 'Father knows best!'"

"Miss my last prom? Very funny."

"But now who's laughing?" Dad smirked, once again rubbing John the wrong way.

"I'm certainly not sticking around here all day just to listen to this crap." He took off and didn't come back until later that night, just in time to watch the Ed Sullivan Show. A couple Sundays later it shocked me when he asked Bernadette, Sarah and me if we were planning on going to his graduation.

"I'm going for sure," Bernadette said. "I'm in the choir." John then looked at me for an answer.

"Me?" I asked, pointing to myself. I wanted to be sure it was me he was referring to, because since the scorched shirt incident, I'd made him mad again by telling him that Dad was buying him a car for graduation. Needless to say, when he found out the truth he came after me, took me by the feet and held me upside down, then cracked me a good one on my behind. "It wasn't me who thought of telling you that. I'm just the one who said it!" I screamed. But he didn't care who had thought it up. I was the one he was angry with. I was the one dumb enough to tell him the lie. I didn't think he'd believe it.

"Me! Really? Go to your graduation?"

"I wasn't speaking Greek, was I?"

"Sure, I'll go," I said, delighted because I'd never been to a graduation before.

A few weeks later I was sitting in the bleachers with other friends and relatives. The parents were sitting on chairs. Dad looked proud as we all waited for the graduates to march into the gymnasium. John would be the first from the family to graduate. When the ceremony finally began, I took in each and every thing that took place. I nearly cried when Bernadette and the other choir members sang "When You Walk Through a Storm" and "I Believe." But when they sang, "When You Leave the Halls of Garden," I couldn't hold back the tears.

> As you leave the halls of Garden,
> · That surrounds you here today,
> We will not forget, though you be far, far away.
> To teachers bid adieu, your high-school days are through.
> The future lies ahead with something new.
> And as you sadly start your journeys far apart,
> Every heart will linger near.

Hearing the song made me sad that John really would be leaving home for good. He and his friend Lonnie had joined the Army under the buddy system and planned on leaving shortly after graduation. As the speaker began talking, I found myself already worried that John would be sent to Vietnam and never come back alive. Then for some weird reason, as they were passing out the diplomas, I thought about something that had happened to John during his elementary years of school. Over the years, he'd tell us about it every now and then. He had felt humiliated at school each morning the three years he'd had Mrs. Rost for a teacher. She'd make all the farmers go out the backdoor of the school to shake themselves off. "She thought we stunk!" John would say each time he retold the story. My sisters and I would laugh as he reenacted how he'd shake himself off. "Hey, think how I felt," he declared one time. "We must have looked like idiots out there!"

My thoughts then drifted to earlier in the week. As John began packing some of his things that he planned to take with him to the Army, we girls were rejoicing, not because we wanted him out of our lives, but out of his bedroom. His leaving meant we'd finally have just three girls to a bedroom, instead of three girls to each double bed in one room. We'd be able to claim not only his room, but the airplane as well — the bed that sat high off the floor. The airplane was equipped with two mattresses on top the box springs, neither of them good for anything; at least that's what the boys thought. I had tried the bed out. I felt like the princess from "Princess and the Pea" on it.

Fights between my sisters and me for the "new" bedroom had already begun, as if his room was some kind of magical place. We all wanted to take up stake in *that* bedroom. Every time we asked Dad to decide for us, he'd chuckle and say, "Let me sleep on it." Finally he had us draw straws that he'd pulled from the broom. Bernadette, Catherine and Anna had gotten the longest ones. John tried to make Sarah, Monica and me feel better about losing the draw by telling us how many nights he was attacked by the bedsprings. "They make their way up through the mattress and poke me between my ribs or into a thigh or some other place on my body."

Still I was disappointed. I wanted to be one of the three that would share the boy's bedroom. I wanted that bedroom as much as I'd wanted my black skirt and blue blouse, which I received the following Christmas, one year after asking for it. Like my skirt and blouse, I knew getting the boy's bedroom might take a whole year, but unlike my skirt and blouse, I knew I'd eventually get the bedroom. Switching beds with my sisters every so often was a given. Fights between us were always taking place. It was just a matter of time before one bad enough broke out between Bernadette, Catherine and Anna. And I couldn't wait until it did. It didn't matter to me if sleeping on the airplane meant being attacked by bedsprings. It wouldn't be the first miserable night's sleep I'd ever gotten. John had once put burrs from the sumac under the blankets of each of our double beds. He placed them way down at the foot of the bed. They didn't attack us until during the night. We kept blaming each other for having sharp toenails. In the morning we found the burrs and instantly knew who'd put them there.

For now I'd have to make do with the canoe. We'd given it that name because the bed was very low to the floor and the mattress was so worn out that we tended to roll toward the center of it. The other double bed in our room was Miss Jane, named after Mr. Drysdale's secretary from the Beverly Hillbillies show. Miss Jane's mattress was thin and hard. Sleeping on it was like sleeping on a board. Sometimes during the night Miss Jane would suddenly collapse to the floor, box springs and all, leaving us startled. Dad would come running. After about the tenth time of this happening, he cut some boards and used them to secure the frame. Though Miss Jane was, as of lately, treating us with the utmost respect, by unanimous decision it was the bed we decided to throw away once John was gone.

Strange as it may sound, as the graduation speaker talked on and on, I was already missing Miss Jane. I found myself thinking about all the secrets we'd told while gathered upon her. They were secrets about boyfriends, best friends, old friends and friends we hoped to someday have. Miss Jane knew all about our menstrual cramps, high-school champs, of headaches, colds, fevers and chills, the flu and throwing-up, too. She could tell of chicken pox, holes in socks, of pillow fights, jumping jacks, Duck Duck Goose and feelings of being smothered. People's ears would ring if she told of everything, like tickling backs, our little spats, tattooing with pen each others' arms and legs and some-times faces, too! Over the years, Miss Jane had heard us giggling late into the night. She had witnessed our REM dreams, midnight screams, yawns and dawns, but most of all the tears we'd cried for Mama.

"John Joseph Jacques," Mr. Harju, the Superintendent, said, call-ing John to the front and me back into the present moment. As my brother took his diploma, I found myself no longer caring if I got to move into his room. It now seemed insignificant. For the first time in my life, I knew I was going to miss having my brother around.

Nineteen
CR

Following eighth grade, I decided to spend the summer of '66 at home rather than in Chicago. I was at the boy crazy age, as were Krystal and my other friend Janet, so I spent a lot of time with them. Janet didn't have sisters, but Krystal had older ones. It was fun listening to them talk about their boyfriends and watch when their dates came to pick them up to take them to a show or to the teenage hangout, Roy's, where the older kids sat around a big wooden table playing cards and talking about sports, cars, boyfriends, girlfriends and whatnot. Whenever Krystal and I were at my house, we couldn't go to Roy's. Dad didn't think it was a proper place for a thirteen-year-old, but at Krystal's we were allowed to go there, although I didn't share that with my dad.

Neither of us usually had money to spend, but on one particular night we did. I loved grape soda and whenever I had extra money

I'd buy peanuts to put in it, as I did this evening. Krystal bought her favorites also and we sat at the soda fountain, eating our treats while unintentionally eavesdropping on the conversations of the older kids. We were barely finished with our goodies when their eyes stared us down, telling us in no uncertain terms that it was time to shove off.

When we left to go back to Krystal's, we were hoping to see some boys along the way. The wide-open sky was magnificently sprinkled with stars. Although the view was heavenly, I started singing "The End of the World."

> Why does my heart go on beating?
> Why do these eyes of mine cry?
> Don't they know it's the end of the world?
> It ended when you said good-bye.

"Ooh, that song! Why do you always sing it?" Krystal asked.

"Sister Theresa hated my singing, too!" I said, as I began to tell her how Sister said my singing off key usually messed up the whole choir.

"No!" Krystal interrupted, giving me a slug in the arm. "You moron! I didn't ask, 'Why do you sing?' I asked, 'Why you sing *that* song?' I just wondered, why that one?"

"Promise not to tell?"

"Crisscross my heart," she said, making the gesture.

"Because I feel my life *ended* when my mother died."

"That's what I thought," she exclaimed, without further comment.

Despite the fact that Krystal had a mother, she somehow seemed to understand my loss. She was always sympathetic to my situation. She would join me in song, even though she couldn't hold a tune much better than me. We'd sing our hearts out to Mama. I came to trust Krystal with most of my secrets. She knew even before my sisters that I'd fallen in love with Jim. I even trusted her enough to cut my waist-

144

length hair. Her sister Sonya had cut Krystal's hair, so I figured Krystal could cut mine.

"Do you really want *me* to cut it short?" she asked, with scissors in hand, as I sat in front of her bedroom mirror.

"Yes, cut it off," I said. But as she lifted the scissors, I cried out in a pitiful voice, "Oh poor me, poor me!"

"Forget it! I'm not cutting it."

"I'm just joking," I laughed. I had to re-talk her into cutting it. But again I went back and forth with the "poor me" until she got mad, grabbed a chunk of my hair and lopped it off. "There, now it has to be cut."

Krystal proved to be a much better friend than beautician. Sonya had to straighten up her jagged mess. Still, it wasn't enough to quit trusting her with my life issues. Before the night was over, I confessed to her how I liked a certain guy and she confessed she liked his best friend, which got the two of us thinking, and like usual, that meant trouble!

The next day, Saturday morning, around eight o'clock, we left her house for mine. At least that's what we told her mother. We were really walking to Fairport, a neighboring community about twelve miles away where our so-called boyfriends lived. We'd been walking for about two hours when a neighbor of mine pulled up in her car and asked if we'd like a ride. At first I hesitated, fearing Dad might get wind of our adventure, but because of our blistered feet and tired legs, and realizing that it was Eileen Lovell, we got in.

Eileen lived about a mile down the road from our house with her son and daughter. Another son was in the service. Her husband worked on the ore boats, so was rarely home. Her daughter Charlene was as nice as her mother. Often, one or the other would invite Catherine and me over to play Bingo. Each time we played, Catherine and I were amazed because either she or I would win the games, even when we weren't paying attention. Over a two-year span we carried quarters, dimes, nickels and pennies home with us each time, leaving the two of them all smiles.

Eileen and Charlene not only played Bingo with us, but also listened to our many stories. They loved hearing about the things we were doing at school, like Catherine slugging the baseball over the fence or punching a boy in the gut. They felt bad when I told them about my first dance, how I didn't have any high-heels to wear like all my girlfriends. "So what shoes did you wear?" Charlene asked.

"These," I said, taking my foot out from under the table and lifting it high. "My cheering shoes."

"So you had to wear your tennis shoes to the dance?" Eileen questioned. I nodded.

"But she had fun," Catherine exclaimed.

"At first I didn't. When I entered the hall, I had to stand on my tiptoes to make myself look taller. My girlfriends were standing in a corner and were looking all grown-up and important, like women. I started to turn around and run back down the flight of steps, but then Janet caught my eye, so I joined them. The boys were in their own corner talking loud and laughing. I thought it was because of my sneakers. Then, without notice, a sharp-looking guy tapped me on the shoulder. 'May I have this dance?' he asked."

"That's when her sneakers felt like Cinderella's slippers," Catherine butted in, and then continued on. "Tell them about your eighth grade class trip, too, Donna Jean. Tell them how your class got to go by ferry to Mackinac Island. Tell them how you and Rosanna rode a bicycle built for two. Tell them how you had to take Candy to a doctor to get that boil-thing on her arm popped! Tell them, Donna Jean! Tell them!"

"Why should I, Catherine? You just did. Why don't you tell them something about yourself, like the time you decided to sleep on the ironing board and it collapsed to the floor?"

"Why should I?" she said. "You just did!"

"Where on earth are you girls headed?" Eileen asked when we got into her car on that bright sunny morning.

"To my friend Janet Bouchard's house," I told her.

"Babe's daughter?" she asked as she lit a cigarette.

"Yes," I said, breathing a sigh of relief that I'd come up with something to say other than that we were going to see our boyfriends. But now there was a glitch. In my haste to answer, I'd forgot that my friend Janet also loved the guy Krystal did. Needless to say, after being dropped off at Janet's and finding out that she wasn't home, I was relieved. We continued on by foot to our destination, hoping Eileen wouldn't see us since she'd continued in the same direction as we were headed.

Finally, after making it to Fairport, I knocked on my boyfriend's door. Soon Krystal and I were riding around with the guys in a car named Put-n-gin. We rode for hours on all the back roads before Krystal and I began the long walk home. "Did he hold your hand or kiss you?" Krystal asked. "My guy held mine and kissed me a lot."

"He didn't hold my hand, but I almost touched his twice," I said as I looked at her watch to see what time it was. "Oh, no! It's already four o'clock. My dad told me to be home by three. Plus, I haven't even asked him if you could come over."

"Just great! At our speed, we're not going to get to your house until seven or so." But luck was on our side. Eileen was on her way back to Garden and once again picked us up.

As I had surmised, when we got dropped off, Dad was at the door to meet us. I quickly ran through the doorway, but Krystal was too slow and Dad swatted her with the broom. "Gosh almighty," she said running to the bedroom. "How'd your old man find out we walked to Fairport?"

"I'll ask him," I said, not even thinking he knew nothing about our adventure.

"You did what? You went where?" Dad hooped and hollered until

I finally shot back.

"You always get mad at your own kids when they do something wrong, but the day we saw that girl jump out of her mother's car, you felt sorry for the girl! You got mad at her mother instead! So why are you getting mad at me for misbehaving? Walking to Fairport isn't as bad as jumping out of a car!"

"That girl's mother just kept on going. She didn't so much as slow down. That's why I got mad at her instead of her daughter. So you hush your sassy mouth." Dad's teeth were clenched. "Get out of here, both of you. And don't think you're tramping around any more."

A few weeks later, on a Saturday night, we left Krystal's and went to Roy's, skipping, singing and talking about boys. Shortly after we left the hangout, a red Mustang with Indiana plates pulled up. My heart sank. Inside were a couple of great-looking guys. The passenger rolled down the window. He looked Italian with his shiny black hair, eyebrows that stretched from one to the other, and beautiful tanned skin. His dark brown eyes seemed to pierce right through me as Krystal and I peered into the car. The driver had curly red hair, was fair-skinned and stocky.

"You guys lost?" Krystal probed.

"Hell, no," the passenger replied. "We're wondering if you cuties would like to go for a ride."

"No, thanks," I blurted before Krystal had a chance to answer. I didn't want to take a chance of getting in trouble with Dad because I'd asked him to take me to see Lizzy, Delores, her two girls and little Danny who were staying at Lizzy's summer cottage just outside of Escanaba.

"Well, I don't know about her, but I sure the hell do," Krystal said.

"Great," the guy answered, as he opened the door. I got into the back, thinking Krystal would follow, but instead the passenger did. Krystal took the front seat. As we rode the back roads, I felt nervous being in their car. It didn't take long before my trembling hands caught the attention of the guy sitting next to me.

"What the hell's the matter with you?"

"I'm cold."

"How the hell can you be cold? It's ninety degrees yet!"

"Oh, she always shakes," Krystal said as she popped the glove compartment open and began fiddling with things.

"Close that," the driver demanded, but not before Krystal had grabbed something from it.

"Is this a rubber?" she asked. I couldn't see what she was holding. I figured the rubber she was referring to had come out of a can of Monkey Grip, a tire patch kit. Dad always kept both big and little pieces of rubber in the can inside of the glove compartment for when we had a flat tire. I wanted to act intelligent and grown-up, so I said, "My dad always keeps rubber in his glove compartment, too."

"You're quite the comedian, aren't you?" the passenger chuckled. I didn't think anything was funny, but since the three of them laughed, I did too. As the driver and the passenger talked, I caught their names. Bobby was the driver and Kevin was next to me. He had a high-school ring on his finger. The year on it was 1965. "You're nineteen?" I asked as we headed out of town.

"Bingo," he said.

"Where we going?" I asked, feeling more and more afraid that Dad would find out that I was riding around in a car with boys. More than ever, I was thankful he was letting me spend the night at Krystal's.

"There's an outdoor theater up the road. How would you two like to see a movie tonight?" Bobby asked. This time I said nothing. I'd never been to a movie, not even in Chicago, so I waited for Krystal to speak. If she said, "Yes," I'd agree, and if "No," I'd agree with that, too.

"Sure," she said, "I'm all for it."

"How are we going to get away with this," I thought as the guy grabbed my hand.

On our way to Manistique, Kevin and Bobby chatted back and forth. They talked about girls back in Indiana, one that Kevin got "knocked up." I had no idea what they were talking about, but Krystal did. She joined in and told us about a girl she knew who was shacking up with a guy because she'd gotten knocked up. They laughed, so, once again, I did too. When we arrived at the drive-in, I was surprised. I'd seen a side-view of the movie theater several times from the highway, but I had no idea the screen would look so spectacular stretched out across the wide-open sky. I scrunched down on the backseat so I could see the entire screen.

Kevin grabbed my feet and put them on his lap. It surprised me. I thought he'd just continue to hold my hand. When he untied my sneakers and took them off and then took off his own, I felt uncomfortable and was ready to ask him why he'd done such a thing. But before I could say anything my pedal pushers and underwear were off and he was jamming something inside of me, and that something didn't feel very good. It hurt! I felt paralyzed. I couldn't move. But worst of all, for the first time in my life, I couldn't scream. My ears began ringing and the inside of my head felt picky, like it was filled with insulation. I wasn't sure what was happening to me, but I surmised it had something to do with how girls got pregnant. When we were in third grade, Richard Lester had told me that his cousin told him that the way babies were made was when a man laid on top of a woman and rubbed elbows together, so I kept mine as far away from his as possible.

From the front seat I could hear Krystal giggling. I could see men and women, both young and old, passing by the car. I hoped they couldn't see him on top of me, forcing his hands up my shirt, while he slobbered his mouth against my neck. I closed my eyes. As his body moved up and down and up and down and up and down on me, I let out the loudest silent plea ever heard. "Mama," I cried. "Help me, Mama!" Instantly, I could see her hovering above me like an angel, dressed all in white, with white billowy wings. She swooped down and kissed my forehead, then my cheeks, and pressed her lips hard against my lips. As she lowered her hand, I desperately tried to reach for it. But the hand that grabbed mine was HIS — Satan's. "C'mon," he said, "Help yourself. Get up!"

"What the hell do you think you're doing?" I heard Krystal shout as she slapped Bobby across the face. Then, as she shouted a litany of obscenities, she punched at him as he swatted at her hair. "If I tell my old man what you were trying to do, he'll KILL you, you bastard!"

Quickly I pulled my pants on and pushed as far to my side of the car as possible. Giving my arm a light punch he asked, "Popcorn?" I said nothing. He opened the door.

"Get back in here!" Bobby shouted. "Let's get these babies home where they belong." He started the car.

"Hold on," Kevin shot back. "I gotta get my popcorn."

Bugs Bunny was leaving the screen as we drove out of the drive-in. I felt like puking. I wanted out of that car. I wanted to never smell Vitalis hair cream again. For the first time in my life, I understood the word *hate*. The nuns from religion class had talked about hate since my first CCD class, but I'd never given it any thought. I had always liked everyone. Sister Janet Marie had said we should never hate anyone. I never thought I ever would, until now. Hate was the only thing I could think of. On the ride back to Garden I argued with Sister in my mind.

"I hate him! I hate him! I hate him!"

"No, you shouldn't hate anyone!"

"Will if I want!"

"You must forgive those who hurt you."

"No, I won't! I never will!"

"You need to."

"Never, never, never!" I continued until we got dropped off at Cal's store.

151

My feet had barely touched the gravel when they sped off. "You little witch!" Krystal shouted. "You knew I was in trouble. Why didn't you help me? Why didn't you say something?"

"I'm sorry," I said. "I couldn't help. I have to go home."

"You can't! Your dad thinks you're staying with me."

"I'll tell him I got sick and wanted to come home."

"And what should I tell my mother?"

"Tell her I got sick," I said, then immediately started walking home. On the way I didn't smell the lilacs, or clover, or wild pink roses. I didn't hear birds chattering, trees swishing, or see grasshoppers hip-hopping in the grass. All I could see was his face. All I could smell was Vitalis. All I could hear was my own voice. "What a CREEP, what a CREEP, what a CREEP!" I said until I turned the doorknob of our house.

"You're in big trouble!" Anna spurted when I walked in. "Dad's out looking for you right now. When he went for groceries, somebody told him they saw you and Krystal get into a car with some boys. He already went to Krystal's to see if you were there. Her parents are mad, too, and are also out looking for you two… Donna Jean… what's wrong with you?"

"Nothing!"

"Something's the matter," Monica said.

"Where did you go?" Sarah asked, walking into the kitchen.

"To a stupid movie with some weirdos, that's all."

"That's not all it's going to be when Dad gets home."

"I know," I told her as I made my way to the bathroom and locked the door behind me, saying not another word until Dad pounded on the door an hour later and demanded that I get out to the kitchen immediately.

"I'm taking a bath," I hollered. I heard my sisters telling Dad how I hadn't even warmed any water for the bath, like we usually did. In the tub of icy cold water I washed, not once, or twice, but three times draining the water and refilling the tub each time. My skin was red from the cold and the scrubbing when I finally made my way to the kitchen. Dad looked me in the eyes.

"I made a promise to your mother that if anything ever happened to her, I'd make sure none of you became tramps, and, by golly, I plan on keeping that promise. Now get to your bed before I take the black-snake to you," he scolded.

As I lay there on my bed, the thoughts of what had happened wouldn't leave no matter how much I begged God to take them away. Around 4 a.m. that next morning, in dawned on me that the date was June 26 and that exactly one year earlier as I lay on the bed listening to Bernadette's transistor, waiting for the Big Beat, the nightly news had come on. "Oh, great! News!" I'd said to myself. I'd always hated when the news came on. Dad loved listening to it so much that we had to sit still and not say a word until it was over, whether it was the local news with Al Holtine on WDBC or Walter Cronkite on CBS television. However, that night, the first story got my attention. "Oh, no! Oh my God! Dad! Dad!" I hollered as I ran outside to see if he was still working on the hole in the muffler of his car.

"What's the matter?" he'd asked, pulling his body out from under his car.

"It's Lizzy's son, Donald!"

"What about Donald?"

"The news just said that he's presumed drowned and someone found Dean and Danny floating on top of the water. Dean is dead, too, and little Danny is in serious condition because of exposure to the sun!"

"I'll tell you what happened," Dad said. "Their fishing lines got tangled. Donald tried to untangle them and the boat capsized." According to the news the next morning, Dad had been right about the cause of the accident. Six-year-old Danny had told the police the same story. Donald's body was recovered a few days later. Mark was called to identify it.

For three days after the deaths of my cousins I had laid in bed not caring whether I lived or died. "Get up and move around," Dad would say each day. "There's nothing we can do about it but get on with our own lives."

Now here I was, a year later, once again refusing to get out of bed, not caring whether I lived or died. On the third day after my ordeal, Janet's dad drove her to our house to see if I could spend a few days with them. I didn't think Dad would let me go after the trouble I'd been in but he told her that it would be okay. I got out of bed and packed a bag. "Behave yourself this time," Dad said as he gave the top of my head a rub with his matchbook. I nearly cried, not because it hurt, but because it was one of the little quirks Dad sometimes did to show he cared.

Twenty
CR

Janet and I had become closer friends and confidants during our eighth grade year and we looked forward to spending time together during the summer before starting high school. During our eighth grade year, I'd stay at her house as often as her mother and my dad would allow. I loved being with her family. She had a cute, cozy bedroom, all to herself. We'd lie on her bed eating candy lipstick, telling each other how many kids we planned to have and what their names would be. Willow would be her girl's name, Robbie for a boy. Mine would be Onna and Douglas. She agreed with me that I should adopt my kids rather than take a chance of dying while giving birth to them. Sometimes we'd still be talking and giggling at two or three in the morning. Her mother would come into the bedroom and threaten to never let me stay again if we didn't get to sleep. Reluctantly we'd give in to the night.

Janet's olive green eyes were framed by a set of double eyelashes that were thick, black and long. She had a joyful personality — nothing ever made her mad, except for her dark thick eyebrows that she thought made her look boyish. I was envious of them. I thought she was lucky to have such a defined brow, since my own were so blonde that I practically needed a magnifying glass to spot them. Her lips were thick and rounded, mine thinner and peaked in the center. One thing we had in common was thick, kinky, curly dark hair that did exactly what it felt like doing no matter what we did to control it. The only part of our 'dos that went the way we wanted were our sideburns, which we shaped into spit curls.

Spending time at Janet's house meant being there for meals that I didn't have to help cook. Her mother, originally from Tennessee, made different foods than what I was used to. Since I'd tasted her grits, I didn't want to taste any of the other strange concoctions she made, but she'd put a small piece of the barbecued chicken or a couple fried green tomatoes on my plate anyway. "Try them, you'll like them," she'd say in her southern drawl. There were two foods she made that I absolutely loved. One was her salad, because she put chopped apples into it, and the other favorite was her blackberry cobbler, which she topped with ice cream. One time she laughed at me because I ate three pieces.

During those three days I spent at Janet's house, I learned that she was much more than a confidant; she was my kindred spirit friend. "Okay," she said, after we arrived at her house and made it into her bedroom, "tell me what's wrong."

"Nothing," I said.

"You're not going to tell me that. I know when you're not yourself. You can probably fool even your sisters, but you can't fool me anymore." At that moment I wanted to tell Janet everything. I wanted to tell her about the monster that had attacked me without warning. I wanted to tell her how I never wanted to smell Vitalis again. I wanted to tell her that, though Sister Theresa and Sister Janet Marie had taught us about forgiveness, I was never going to forgive the Creep. I wanted to tell her that, though my mother and dad had read from the Bible that we were to love as Jesus loved, I was going to hate the Creep forever. But I knew if I started to tell her what had happened, I'd start to cry, so I said I'd talk to her later.

After supper I desperately tried to concentrate as Janet's mother tried to teach me how to knit. "Knit one, purl two, knit one, purl two," she said as she put the yarn over and between the two needles. "Here, you try it, Donna," she said handing the yarn and needles to me. "Knit one... whoops... knit one... sorry... knit one, *here*, Mrs. Bouchard, I can't do it!" I said, and took off running to the bedroom, with Janet right behind.

"It's okay, honey. It takes time," I heard her mother say as I threw myself on the bed.

"Gosh, oh gee," Janet said, as she stroked the back of my hair. "I knew something was wrong, but I didn't think it was this bad."

About ten minutes later her mother came into the bedroom to tell us that she and Janet's dad and brother were going visiting for an hour or so. The outside door had barely closed when both tears and words began to flow, though none of the words were making sense.

"Out... door... movie... seeing... Bugs... Bunny... popcorn... some boys... girls were sitting... on... on the hoods... of their cars."

"Oh, my gosh. What happened to you?" Janet probed, as she patted my back. "Come on, let's take a walk outside."

"I can't. My body is buzzing all over."

"Then tell me what happened!" I sat up and moved to the edge of the bed. Covering my face with the palms of my hands, I shamefully told my friend how Krystal and I had snuck out with some boys we'd never met before and had gone with them to an outdoor movie theater. I told Janet every detail that I could recall of the dreadful experience; even how the Creep had insisted on going to the concession stand afterwards to get some popcorn though the other guy said we were leaving. I told how he had handed me the surprise from the inside of the crackerjack box, as if he was doing me a big favor, and how I'd taken it because I was afraid not to. I told how I'd thrown the wrapped trinket into the ditch as soon as I'd gotten out of the car. I explained how Krystal had no idea what had happened to me.

"Sit down," Janet said, pointing to her vanity bench. In front of her mirror she forced me to look at myself. "Okay, when I count to three, we'll both say, "He's a creep. He's a creep. He's a creep."

We repeated this mantra often as she brushed my hair one hundred strokes, then two hundred, then polished my fingernails pink and my toenails red. When I saw her eyes trying to close at around 3 a.m., I repeated the phrase until she was wide-eyed again.

"You brat," she laughed. "Well, now that I'm awake, what do you want me to do?"

"Tell me the story of *Black Beauty*." Janet knew it was one of my favorites. She knew the story by heart. I loved when she'd tell me it at night when we were in bed. The ending of the story was so comforting that I'd usually drift off to sleep. But it didn't happen for me this night. As Janet kept vigil with me, she snuck out to the kitchen to get pop and candy or whatever else I wanted. It was the first time in both of our lives that we were still awake when the sun came up. The pain I'd felt the night before as the sun sunk deep into the earth had somewhat dimmed.

As the weeks went by and our ninth grade began, we rarely talked about the incident. Instead our free time was spent discussing clothes, hairdos, make-up and boys from our class. I was heart-broken in the spring of the year when she and her family went for a whole week on vacation to Tennessee. I was lost, both at school and at home. I counted the days until her return. When she came back, she brought me back a charm bracelet of the fifty states. I was thrilled. I couldn't believe it! A bracelet all my own! Only mine! The only other thing I owned that belonged to me alone was a fountain pen that I'd won in school a couple years earlier.

At school Janet hooked the bracelet with its dangling fifty little charms onto my wrist. "Do you get to spend the night?" she anxiously asked.

"Tomorrow night," I said. "My dad said I could stay the day after your family got back."

Dad liked the Bouchard family, so I knew when I'd asked him that he'd let me go. Plus, I was doing a lot better at not sassing him. He'd also been really happy with me after talking with Mrs. Tatrow, our class advisor. He'd come to pick me up at school after a fund raiser and she'd told him that I had been an excellent worker for the turkey dinner that our class put on to start earning money toward our senior class trip. I felt butterflies of pride as she talked to Dad, with me standing next to him. Unfortunately though, she also told him how I'd thrown away the heart of the celery, which she thought was the best part of the stalks.

"I can't believe you wasted the *heart* of the celery," Dad said as we rode home.

"I didn't even know celery had a heart," I told him.

"Yi, yi, yi, yi, yi," he blasted, looking at me like I was stupid.

"I suppose *you* knew celery had hearts when you were fourteen?"

"Let's just forget this conversation ever took place," he said, shaking his head. "The main thing is that you showed your schoolteacher what you're made of — that you know how to work." I smiled.

The next day at school I felt nauseated. Time seemed to tick by. "I think I have the flu and should go home," I told Janet. Janet was disappointed, but understood. Dad wasn't home when we got off the bus. It was the first time in a very long time that he'd gone to the bar. He got home real late, so I didn't get to tell him that I was sick. During the night, I vomited twice. Stomach cramps woke me in the morning, but when I went to tell Dad, Matthew said he'd already left with Ernie. By early afternoon the pains were so bad that Matthew asked Jim (Bones) to take me to the hospital. Sarah came with and sat in the back with me. The louder I moaned, the faster Jim drove. He was a good driver, but going so fast scared me. One time when we girls were coming back from Escanaba with him and Matthew, the hood of Jim's car flew up over the front windshield and blocked his view. Before he got the car stopped, it broke off and flew into the ditch. I was afraid something like that might happen again.

"Oh, my Lord," Sarah exclaimed. "We're going nearly a hundred miles an hour."

"I'm trying to get her there as soon as possible. Listen to her. She's in a lot of pain!"

Sarah pulled me down and placed my head on her lap. There I stayed until we arrived at the hospital. Jim carried me in and set me on my feet at the registration desk. That's when everything went black. "Catch her," I heard someone say. I awoke in a wheelchair, with a nurse next to me. As she began to ask me questions, I fainted again. The next thing I knew I was in a hospital bed, in my own room.

"You're a sick little girl," a nurse who lived in a neighboring town said. I was shivering so Mrs. Labadie tucked the covers up, around and under my feet. After taking my vitals and getting me all situated, she allowed Sarah, Jim and Matthew to come into the room. A few minutes later they all left to go home. The next day, Sunday, seemed three days long as I waited for Dad to come and visit me. I wanted to tell him that my doctor needed to talk to him. But it was after seven that evening when he finally showed up, and he smelled of booze.

"What the hell are you in *this* place for," he mumbled.

"The doctor said I have a kidney infection."

"They'll never be able to fix you up. Look what they did to your mother!" He walked up to my IV that was hanging near the bed. "What's all this contraption that they have in you?" he asked, fumbling back and forth between the IV container and the syringe they had placed in my arm.

"Dad! Don't touch that! It hurts my arm when you do. Stop it Dad! You're going to knock it over! I'm going to get in trouble if you break it."

"What are they putting into you, poison?"

"Something that will help me feel better. Dad, why don't you go home now and get some rest?"

The heaviness I felt for Dad when he left the room made my heart feel the size of Texas. First I cried and then prayed that he'd get home safely, and that God would send someone to pick me up the following day. I didn't dare ask my dad to come back for me. The doctor had informed me that he expected me to be well enough to go home on Monday. I was released just after ten in the morning. I felt stupid not having someone there to pick me up, but we didn't have a phone, so I couldn't call anyone. I told the nurse that my dad told me to sit in the lobby to wait for him. As people came and went, I wanted to hide. Everyone seemed to stare at me as they came and went from the hospital. My hope was to see someone from Garden. Finally, just before two o'clock, acquaintances of Dad's, Henry and Julia Doyle came to visit a relative of theirs, so I asked them for a ride home. Although they said they'd be glad to take me home, I figured I'd have to wait a couple more hours until afternoon visiting hours were over. But within minutes they were back in the lobby taking my bag from the floor and practically carrying me to their car.

Donna Jean Pomeroy

Twenty-One
ᏃᏒ

My favorite class during my freshmen year was home economics, especially since I was interested in sewing. We also had lessons in cooking and needlework. The class was exciting, which made the entire school year fly by. Before I knew it, May had arrived. One day after arriving in the cafeteria where the class was held, our instructor, Mrs. Winter, informed us that she had a different project for us to do. "Since someday you'll be mothers yourselves, I'm taking you over to my daughter Lynn's today to get hands-on experience bathing an infant. But before we leave I need to measure you from the top of your neck to your waist and your arm length, too, so you can make yourselves a simple nightgown next week, which will be the final project of the year."

Hoorays were shouted, especially when she said that the home ec-fund would provide the material for those who couldn't afford to buy their own. Then she asked everyone wearing a sweater over a dress or blouse to remove it so she could get a more accurate measurement. Suddenly the idea of making nightgowns didn't sound so wonderful. One by one she began measuring the students. Some kids kept hollering to me, telling me that Mrs. Winter had asked us to take off our sweaters."

"I can't," I said, "I'm too cold."

"How can you be cold?" Anne asked. "It's hotter than heck in here!"

"I don't know," I said, turning away from her. "Everyone else is sweating to death. You must be sick," she said.

My body felt like it was spinning. Then it dawned on me that Anne had provided me with a way out. "Yes," I told to myself. "I can be sick!" I hoped being sick would be enough to keep the teacher from asking me to take off my sweater. I looked out the corner of my eye to see if Anne was still standing there. She was running toward the teacher.

"Donna Jean is sick!"

Mrs. Winter finished measuring Rosanna then came walking toward me. "Anne tells me you're sick. Is that right?" I nodded. I knew I was telling another lie but the last thing I wanted was for her to make me take off my sweater. Underneath it was a blouse with only one sleeve. Sarah and I had gotten into a fight and her finger had gotten stuck in a rip on the shoulder seam. When she tried to break away from me, the sleeve went with her.

Mrs. Winter went over to the light switch and turned it on and off. The room got quiet. "Listen everyone," she said, "please take a seat. Donna Jean is sick, so I'm going to measure her next so she can lie down for a while to see if that helps." She took a quilt from the cupboard and placed it on the floor in a corner of the room. Now even my legs were trembling. I stood by the cafeteria table barely able to breathe. I bent over to sneak some air while holding onto the table.

"I think she's getting ready to throw up," Kathy shouted. At that very second I wished to be anyone but me — my dead mother or even the Wicked Witch of the West with water being poured on me, so I could disappear. Whispers circulated throughout the room as they watched me walk to the wooden platform where Mrs. Winter had been measuring the others. No longer did I need to pretend being sick. Now I was!

Mrs. Winters tried to gently pull the sleeve of my sweater down over my wrist. I yanked it back up. I saw Sarah and Bernadette. They were both looking at me. Sarah motioned no with her head and Bernadette rolled her eyes, as if to say, "You better not take it off. I told you not to wear that blouse."

"No," I said to the teacher as I pulled my sleeve back up, "I'm too cold to take it off."

"Oh, it'll only take a minute, then you can lie down on the quilt." This time she tugged my sweater from the top of my neck. Quickly I pulled it back over my shoulders. To my surprise she helped me, then refastened the top little button on the front.

"My gosh!" she said. I wanted to run out of the room, to flee like a panther, to get as far away from the school as possible. I wanted to run to heaven, where my mother supposedly was. There was no doubt in my mind that Teacher's "My gosh" meant one thing: she'd seen my one-armed blouse and was about to ask me in front of the whole class why I was wearing a *rag* to school. I froze.

"My Lord, you do have the goose bumps and you're shaking uncontrollably. I better measure you right over the top of your sweater so you can stay warm." I looked at her and forced a smile. She winked at me. My pounding heart began to subside as she walked me over to the quilt. "Rest now," she said as she gave my leg a couple pats before calling Janet to the platform. After everyone had been measured, she told us to gather our belongings to get ready to go to Lynn's.

"Donna Jean can't come with us today, can she? 'Cause if she's too sick to take off her sweater, she's too sick to go with us to your daughter's, right?" Patsy questioned.

"Yes, I can!" I hollered. "I'm feeling better now."

"That's not fair," I heard some of the other kids saying.

Mrs. Winter again came over to me. "Let's see," she said as she put her hand on my forehead. "Why, of course she can come. She doesn't seem to have a fever and her color is returning. All she needed was a little rest." I smiled and again she winked, before telling me to fold the quilt and return it to the cupboard. I obeyed and then hurried to get my shoes on. Fifteen minutes later we were following her down the sidewalk to her daughter's house.

Lynn was ready and waiting for our arrival. We gathered into the house and then around the kitchen table. She carried a little bathtub of warm water into the room and placed it in front of us. "Donna Jean and Rosanna," Mrs. Winter said as Lynn approached with the baby, "I'm going to let you two help wash my little granddaughter, Delia." She carefully took the baby from her daughter and gently lowered her into the water.

"We're lucky," I whispered to Rosanna, "we get to bathe her." Rosanna didn't share my enthusiasm. "I don't especially like babies," she said.

"Listen carefully," the teacher advised as we watched her demonstrate how to properly care for the baby so she'd be safe at all times.

"I like babies," I said as I soaped up the mini-size washcloth. "But I'm *never* going to have any of my own because my mother died having a baby and my grandmother died shortly after having my Uncle Elmer."

"Quit blabbering," Bernadette said as Rosanna poured warm water from a plastic cup over Delia to rinse her little body. "Nobody wants to hear about all that."

Everyone marveled as the teacher wrapped the baby in a towel and then gently placed her on a blanket at the other end of the table.

Lynn promptly emptied the bath water. "I'm not having kids because my mother said it hurts when you have to push the baby out of your stomach," Tricia said.

"My sister said it feels like your head is going to explode," Cindy offered.

"Okay, let's get Patsy and Kathy over here to put the powder and lotion on the baby and then Eileen and Candy can dress her."

After those tasks were accomplished, we were shown how to wrap an infant in a blanket, and then we gathered into Lynn's living room. While Mrs. Winters rocked her granddaughter, Lynn passed out Dixie cups of ice cream that her dad had sent over from his store, Roy's.

"Does anyone have a baby story they'd like to share?" Mrs. Winter asked. No one responded, so I spoke up.

"When we were little, my sisters and I thought that dolls could become babies," I said.

"Speak for yourself," Bernadette blasted.

"Yeah," Sarah said, putting her hand over my mouth.

"Don't!" I said, ripping it away. I didn't say another word though I really wanted to because I thought it was funny that when we were little we'd actually believed Luke when he told us that dolls could become babies if we took good care of them.

Every night we cuddled our dolls in bed with us, and every morning before leaving for school we gently covered them so they'd be warm when we were gone. After school we hurried into the house to see if any of them were alive. The care of our dolls came before housework or schoolwork. They were cradled, breast fed, burped, diapered and rocked to sleep. We gave them vaccination shots, haircuts, baths, spankings, yelled at them, talked to them and whatever else was necessary to make them human. No longer did we have to run to grab a doll out of the way of a brother's foot that was about to catapult it to a new location. In fact, for that entire summer and into the fall my sisters and I patiently waited, each hoping it would be their doll to

166

join the ranks of the living first. I begged God, and my dolly, too, to be first. I could hardly wait to hear her cry. Finally it happened! As I was lying at the foot of Dad's bed one day watching Laura through the bars of my little sister's crib, I was surprised to see one of her eyes flutter. "She's alive!" I hollered as I jumped off the bed to pick her up. "Now I'll never have to go to a hospital to have a baby like Mama and Grandma did. Now I'll never have to die!"

"Oh my darling little Laura," I said as I gently cradled her to my neck. "You're alive!" But days went by and still no cry, and her skin remained hard. "You're dead! You're dead like Mama!" I said as I threw her to the floor and jumped up and down several times on her hard little body. Anna happened to come into the room. She screamed at me and picked Laura up and held her softly to her face. "Poor baby," she said, giving my doll kiss after kiss. "Why are you being mean to Laura, Donna Jean?"

"Do you want that dumb doll?" I asked sarcastically.

The adoption occurred that day. Anna became Laura's new mother and much more loving to Laura than she'd ever been to her own little Nellie, who lay helpless on the threshold, her naked body scribbled with ink, her hair cut to the scalp. That day, my *living* doll became my baby sister Monica. I carried her everywhere I went. I spoon-fed her at meal times (even though Dad opposed it) and wrapped her in a blanket. The big, deep kitchen cupboard drawer became her day bed, which she loved, so long as I left the drawer open. But her favorite thing was when I rocked her to sleep at night.

"Well," Mrs. Winters said as we placed our empty Dixie cup containers into the trash, "if we're going to make it back to school in time to catch your buses home, we better get going."

On the bus trip home, Bernadette was mad at me. "If you had told that *doll* story to the class, I'd never have forgiven you. Can't you ever think before you speak?"

"I do," I said.

"No, you don't," Sarah agreed.

"Okay, from now on I will. I promise." But unfortunately it didn't take me long to goof up again. It was the day of my cousin Dickey's wedding. Since our mother's death Dad rarely went to such events. He hated going places alone, especially to wakes and funerals. When people he knew died, he never wanted to go to the funeral home alone, so I would go with him. I went to Ejard Bernard's, Pepper Martin's, Harry Green's and others. I didn't mind seeing dead people, they helped me know my mother would have company in heaven, people she knew.

Not since Mark and Sandy's wedding, where I had been their flower girl, had we gone to a wedding. At the reception there had been lots of people eating, drinking and dancing, but not Luke. Although he was best man for the wedding, during the reception he'd sat in a corner crying most of the night. It had only been a year since Mama had died and he'd felt bad that she couldn't be there with us. Many other people including Mark had tried to cheer him up, but he'd just kept crying. Pretty soon a bunch of our relatives had been crying, too. Since then, Dad stayed away from weddings. That's why we were so surprised when he told us that he was taking us to Dickey's wedding.

Bernadette and I decided to wear nylons. We'd gotten some garter belts and nylons in a box of hand-me-downs. Sara didn't want to have anything to do with them, but she helped us hook ours. Then she put the lipstick and powder on us that Aunt Geraldine had given her. I wore my tan pleated dress with its big, white, to-the-hip belt. Bernadette wore her black skirt with her plaid blouse that had patches on the sleeves. That evening when the band began to play, a very cute boy asked Bernadette to dance. I was jealous, then bored, so I walked around the tables where aunts and uncles and cousins were drinking beer and talking a lot. When my relatives weren't looking, I sipped from their glasses. Soon I was feeling tipsy.

"Hey, Bernadette," I yelled, to the top of my voice. "Come over here quick!" She came on a run.

"What on earth are you screaming so loud for?"

"I… I… don't… know?" I slurred. She was so intrigued with the boy that she hadn't noticed I wasn't my normal self. No sooner had she taken her place beside him on the other side of the room that I called out to her again. As before, she came running, but this time she was irritated with me.

"What on earth are you acting like a fool for? You're embarrassing me!"

"Why… do… you… say… I'mmmm… embarrassiiiing… you?" I laughed.

"Oh, my gosh! You've been drinking beer!" She guided me over to a corner. "What are you thinking? You're going to get into BIG trouble! Sit down here and keep your mouth shut. And don't you dare get up!" Again, for the third time she joined the boy in the corner. I planned to obey her, but a few minutes later my cousin Peggy grabbed my hand and brought me out onto the dance floor where a bunch of other kids were dancing. Within minutes I was face-to-face with one of the cutest boys I'd ever seen. For the next hour or so the two of us did the twist, tried to polka and did the waltz a few times. When his parents came to tell him it was time to go home, I graciously volunteered my dad to take him home later, which didn't sit well with Dad when he found out, since the boy lived twenty minutes away in the opposite direction. Between Dad's scolding me on the way home, along with the long ride, my stomach got queasier and queasier. Yet, I somehow managed to make it home before throwing up.

Twenty-Two
∞

Before my freshman year was over, I got a job working at a local restaurant as a dishwasher. Though the owners, Bob and Bernice, expected a lot from their employees, it was good to be earning money for things like clothes, shoes and new curtains and rugs for our room. Bob and Bernice were very cheap, always trying to figure out a way to save a dime, going so far as making me wash the plastic straws that their customers had used. It panicked me because I was afraid that I wouldn't be able to clean them good enough, so I asked if I could at least throw away the ones used for drinking malts, but they objected. "It'll keep you busy," she said. The only time we didn't have to do a ton of work was when Bernice lent a hand, which was only when she wanted to take credit for something.

In late July a group of golfers made reservations for supper. They'd be arriving shortly after their golf tournament. Though it was always the cook's job to make biscuits for strawberry shortcake, Bernice insisted on making them herself so she could get the credit. She also took it upon herself to set the table for twelve; making sure the best linen, silverware and dishes were used. We all knew she was putting on the ritz in hopes of getting the golfers back after each of their outings. Janie, the head waitress, was picked to wait on the table. Yet it was Bernice who had the honor of serving the luscious-looking dessert. The golfers oohed and aahed as she carried the tray of shortcakes to the table. As they began devouring the dessert, stories from their day were boldly and loudly heard throughout the restaurant, along with their laughter and even singing until abruptly one of the men jumped up from his chair and began cursing and screaming. Bob and Bernice ran to their table. Others in the restaurant froze in place.

"What the hell is this, a son of a bitchin' Band-Aid? In my shortcake!" he shouted with his hand extended so Bernice could see clearly what he was holding. She threw her hand over her mouth. Bob looked into the man's hand. His mouth fell open. He looked toward his wife. He seemed to be waiting for her to deny that she knew anything about it, but instead she explained that she had put a Band-Aid on her cut finger that morning before making the biscuits. She'd thought it came off while she washed her hands after mixing the dough. As the group prepared to leave, the owners ended up giving the whole group their meals free as an apology for what had happened. We workers hurried back to our task, chuckling amongst ourselves at what had taken place. I buried my hands into the dishwater and was taking out a handful of silverware when Bernice walked up. "Why didn't you tell me you didn't find my Band-Aid in the dishwater?" I was so dumbfounded at what she was saying that I couldn't even respond. "Don't look at me like that! The fact is, a good worker is one who doesn't have to be told things," she said as she grabbed the dishrag from my hand and stormed off into the dining room.

It had been a hectic day, so when Janie suggested to her mother

Donna Jean Pomeroy

Phoebe, one of the cooks, that we cross the highway and go for a midnight swim, we took her up on it. We were hot, sticky and miserable. The water looked inviting as we walked toward it. Under the moonlit sky, with the summer breeze gently blowing, we waded into the water and then climbed the slide and slid down into the waters of Lake Michigan, still in our work uniforms. After a few times, we got into Phoebe's old car and headed home, dripping wet.

On the way back to Garden, I noticed red in the sky. "Look!" I shouted, "I hope my house isn't on fire!" Phoebe floored the old car, giving it everything it had. When we turned down the Little Harbor Road my heart was beating rapidly, but within minutes I realized that it wasn't our house on fire, but that of our neighbors, Steve and Josephine. I ran from the car and into the house and woke my dad. Phoebe and Janie went to notify the volunteer fire department. Catherine got out of bed and she and Dad took off. I stayed home to be with my younger sisters. We were relieved when Dad and Catherine got home and told us that Steve and Josephine were okay, although the fire had destroyed their house.

There were other events that kept the summer interesting, also, like the Sunday after church when Bernadette and I went to the store for pencils, at least that's what we told Dad. We would never have told him the truth that it was for Kotex. That was way too embarrassing. Dad had never once talked to us about our monthly cycles; no one had until the day Aunt Melina did. She and Uncle Archie came to visit and Bernadette was in bed with terrible stomach cramps because of her monthly. Aunt Melina sat on the edge of the bed and talked to Bernadette about how girls have menstrual cycles. Bernadette was too embarrassed to tell her that both she and I had been having our monthlies for more than two years! We'd found out about them after starting just hours apart. It was the day she and I had a green apple-eating contest. She ate one hundred and I ate one more than her, just so I could beat her. Bernadette started her monthly that night and I started mine the

172

next morning. At first we thought it was from eating so many green apples until Sarah told us the difference. She had started at school one day and her teacher had told her all about it.

Whatever would, could or already did happen with our female bodies was discussed amongst us sisters only, because of the embarrassment we knew it would cause Dad, and us, too, if we talked about it with him. Even viewing the female body during television commercials made us squirm. Whenever the Playtex's Cross Your Heart bra commercial came on, and Dad was watching TV with us, one by one we'd make excuses to leave the room until the commercial was over. The last one, though, remained, feeling a bit foolish to also leave the room. I hated being the one left, to watch and listen to a *man* talk about brassieres. I'd try to make conversation with Dad about school, church, the weather, or sometimes unable to think of something better, I'd bring up the garden. The garden was something we all tried to avoid talking about. It usually got us a lecture about how it hadn't been weeded, hoed, watered, or the produce hadn't been picked often enough. Talking about the garden a little usually created a lot of work.

Under the pencil pretext, Bernadette and I left for the store, arguing all the way there about whose turn it was to ask Cal for the Kotex, which were stocked high on a shelf behind the counter above the booze and cigarettes. When we got there the store was filled with after-church shoppers. We walked around pretending to be looking for a certain item because neither one of us would ask for the Kotex. We kept pointing fingers at each other. "You ask Cal to get them down," I said to Bernadette.

"No way, I did last time!" she said, putting her hands on her hips. "It's your turn, and you know it! So get up there and ask," she insisted, giving me a dirty look along with a little push. I was glad to see that Leola was in the store helping Cal behind the counter. I figured it would be a lot easier asking a woman for the pads. I stood in line waiting for the opportunity, waiting for the courage to ask, but Anna

Leckson checked out, then Molly Guertin, and Pete Lambert paid for his can of tobacco and cigarette papers. Still I was too embarrassed to ask for the feminine product.

"What can I do for you, darling?" Leola asked. I looked behind me. I was just about to ask for the Kotex when Mrs. Lucas stepped up.

"Go ahead," I said, "you can check out."

"No, no, honey, you were here first. You go ahead. I have other things to get," she said, placing another item onto the counter then repositioning the baby she was carrying. I turned around to see where Bernadette was so I could tell Leola that it was really she who was waiting to ask for something. I looked off to the side to take a deep breath. I was startled to see Bernadette glaring at me from between the boxes of Rice Krispies and Corn Flakes.

"Come on now, darling. I haven't all day. What do you need?"

"Uh... uh... one... jaw... breaker... two... Black... Jacks... um... um... a... red... hot... burning... gum... and... um... a... Tootsie Roll... and — Ouch!" I turned around. "Quit stalling, you big pansy! Ask her!" Bernadette snarled. "Leola," she said, "Donna Jean needs to ask you to get her something." I panicked.

"Yes, child. What else is it you need?" My eyes fell on the Charmin. "Oh, here it is right here! I've been looking all over for this, and why, it was behind me all this time!"

Mrs. Lucas laughed. "Isn't that just the way it goes sometimes?" she said as I set the toilet paper on the counter top. Leola began tallying the pieces of penny candies and then fumbled to find the price on the Charmin. As she did, she squeezed the toilet paper a couple times. Once again, without thinking before speaking, in a very loud, serious and dramatic voice, I shouted, "Mrs. Richards!" She dropped the Charmin and slapped a hand to her heart.

"Darling, what in God's name is it?"

"Please don't squeeze the Charmin!" I said. The store had been getting busier and the checkout line longer. Everyone started laugh-

174

ing.

"Is Mr. Whipple here?" a man from the back of the store chuckled as he made his way to the front to see who was the jokester.

"Oh, my goodness. Why, you little darling. You about gave me a heart attack!" Again the customers laughed. She forced a smile. I signed for the items and grabbed the bag and went out the door, still laughing at my own joke. Bernadette was waiting for me in the car, not too happy with me.

"I can't believe you did that to Leola! That was so stupid," she said as she rolled her eyes. "Dad is going to hear about this! You should've told me what you were up to so I could've made a beeline for the door."

"Well, I didn't plan on saying that. It just came out."

"Gosh, Randy was in there. He heard you! It was so embarrassing! And you didn't even get what we came for!"

"Big deal. Who cares about Randy?"

"I do, that's who," she said.

"If I were you, I'd be more worried about Randy seeing you driving this noisy hunk of junk without a license," I said, still in a laughing mode. Bernadette snarled then gave my arm a slug.

"You are such a Dodo bird," she exclaimed as we pulled into the driveway. Together we went running to the house.

"Hold it," Dad said when we came in quarreling. "What the heck is going on?"

"She's always *embarrassing* me!" He listened as she told him the entire story, of course leaving out what we really had gone to the store for. With each word, I grew more and more hysterical. Finally I fell to the floor rolling in laughter, so much so that my stomach hurt.

"You have to learn to take a little joke," Dad told her as he laughed at my laughter. Then butting his foot up against my leg, he said, "Okay, enough of that! Get up off that floor. You two get out of my way. And, oh, by the way, leave me one of those pencils you bought. I never can find one when I need it."

I stood up and finally got my composure. Bernadette and I looked wide-eyed at each other as we slowly disappeared into the other room. "Oh, Bernadette," I said. "Did you see Mrs. Lucas's baby? I was going to ask her if I could hold it while she shopped."

"You were going to do WHAT?!"

"Ask her —"

"Oh, I know what you said! That would've been so dumb! You're not supposed to ask everyone you see carrying a baby if you can hold it!"

"Well, it just so happens that I like babies!"

"You're just going to have to wait until you have your own," she blurted.

"No way! I'm never having a baby. I'm adopting my kids."

"Adopt them! Have your own! Whatever," she said as she walked away.

Twenty-Three
CR

A cold fall followed the hot summer, and winter brought with it several days of sub-zero temperatures. It was on one of those below zero February nights that we got the news that John had been in an accident and was badly hurt. While at Fort Knox, Kentucky for his advanced training, the Army truck he was riding in the back of had overturned. Lonnie had called his dad, Gordon, to bring us the message that John had been thrown from the military transport truck and was seriously injured, and that Dad should go to Kentucky as soon as possible. Dad contacted Luke, and as soon as he got us kids farmed out, he left with Gordon for Chicago, and they continued on from there with Luke. I stayed with Lonnie's mother, Mrs. McPhee. She was a hot lunch cook at the school and had to be there early each morning, so I rode with her. After school each day I'd ride the #2 bus back to her house. I loved it at her house. It reminded me of our house, the way it was before my mother died, warm and cozy, and with the smell of homemade bread and cookies filling the air.

After supper she and I would do the dishes. There were just a couple glasses, plates and silverware to wash and dry each day. Compared to my house where tons of dishes were dirtied at each meal, it almost seemed like we were playing house. Several times I found myself thinking about my mother when I was there because Mrs. McPhee was a lot like her. Everything she did reminded me of my mother, from the way she washed, cut and curled my hair, kept her house so spic and span and treated me to cookies and milk before bedtime. But it was the kisses that she planted on my forehead each night that affected me the most. Each time she kissed me I'd nearly cry. Not just because of the kiss, but because I could smell Ponds on her, the same cold cream my mother had used. A part of me wanted to run away from her, yet another part of me wanted to stay there forever. That is, until Catherine asked me at school why I hadn't come home yet. I hadn't even known that Dad was back from Kentucky. I was confused. "Why didn't he come to pick me up, like he'd picked up all my sisters?" I wondered to myself. By the end of the day I was almost in tears. I was certain Dad didn't want me anymore. So I decided I was moving in with the McPhees for good. So that Friday, without asking, I *told* Mrs. McPhee I was going home after school to pack my clothes because I was moving in with her. "I'll have my dad bring me back on Sunday after church," I said. Mrs. McPhee didn't say a word.

Everything was a mess when I got home; the counter was loaded with dirty dishes and the house was cold and stunk of fuel oil. I was glad I wasn't going to be living there anymore until I saw that John was home. He was lying on the couch. My sisters told me that he had a brain injury. His face was black and blue and his eyes were so swollen that they were almost completely closed. His wrists were both broken and in casts to the elbows. Every time he moved, even a tad, he'd moan. "You girls help your brother out. I don't have the time," Dad said. I hurried over to John.

"Can I get you anything?" I asked.

"Scratch the top of my head," he managed to say. Then he asked if Dad had gotten the oil burner going. I looked to see. Dad was black with soot and cursed when the match he'd lit didn't ignite the flame of the burner within the oil stove. "It's not working yet," I said, going back by John.

"Well, I'm freezing. Find me another blanket." I ran to Dad's bedroom and pulled a blanket from his bed and hurried back to cover John with it, tucking it under his cold feet and around his neck.

"That's better," he said, still shivering. Then he told me how Dad had been working on the stove for two days and that the water pipes were all frozen and wouldn't thaw until there was more heat in the house.

Bernadette called for me, so I hurried to the kitchen to see what she wanted. It was much warmer in there. The utility stove was going, plus Dad had turned the oven and two back burners of the range on. "Here," Bernadette said, handing me a grilled cheese sandwich she had cut into small pieces. "Feed this to John."

"Sure," I said. It was nice seeing John again. Seeing him all bruised up and in pain made me realize that I should spend as much time with him as possible before I moved in with the McPhees. When I was feeding John, he kept biting my fingers. At first I thought it was because his eyes were so swollen that he couldn't see them as I gave him pieces of the grilled cheese. However, when it happened over and over, and he began to laugh, I realized that he was doing it on purpose. So I conned Monica into feeding him the rest of the sandwich. I knew he'd be nicer to her. "I'll finish feeding him but I'm not brushing his teeth again tonight. Last night he kept holding onto his toothbrush with his teeth and wouldn't let it go," she said. When she took the food from me, I quickly made my escape from the room and went to gather both my clean and dirty clothes.

Early the next morning, I hauled water from the pump house to fill the kitchen sink so I could wash my dirty clothes. After wringing them out, I put them on hangers and hung them to dry on the hooks above the wood stove. Later that evening, as Dad continued trying to get the oil stove lit, I asked him if he'd take me back to McPhee's after church the following day. "Mrs. McPhee will be expecting me. I'm moving to her house." Dad didn't seem to hear me. Yet, after church the next morning, without any questions or comments, he drove me there. I was happy to be back. I liked being warm and not having to do anything but my homework. I liked being served breakfast in the mornings and having Mrs. McPhee help me with my homework. I was tickled each morning when she gave me the twenty cents I needed for hot lunch. But, on Monday morning, unlike the other school mornings when I was there, she had me ride the bus, rather than with her. Later that day as I stood in the hot lunch line waiting for her to put some macaroni and cheese on my plate, she told me I was to go home after school. "I've already taken all your belongings back to your house," she said. My face dropped. I instantly felt embarrassed.

"Okay," I replied in a faint voice, already wondering what it was about me that neither she nor my dad didn't like. Throughout the remainder of the school day, I felt stupid. And I felt stupid riding the bus home that afternoon, since I'd already told the bus driver that I wouldn't be living at home any more.

"Can someone start the utility fire?" John asked as we came hurrying out of the cold after school. "The oil burner is still going, but it's cold in here again. And I'm starved!"

Catherine and Bernadette hauled in the kindling and other wood needed to get the fire going nice and hot, while Sarah and I got supper started. Kathy Guertin, Anna's best friend, and a neighbor, had gotten off the bus with us to stay a couple hours until her mother got back from town. She and Anna said they needed to go out and into the woodshed to work on a school project. Bernadette discouraged them from doing the project out there because the temperature had already dropped into the single digits, but they said they had to have it done by the next day. "Do you have all the wood hauled in for the fire?" Anna asked Bernadette.

"Why do you want to know?" she replied.

"Because we don't want anyone to see what we're making."

"Just get going, so you can get back in here," Bernadette told them. So the two of them went out while Monica sat on the wooden stool that John had made in shop class, diligently practicing her spelling words.

"I'm glad we're all back together, aren't you Donna Jean?" Sarah asked as we browned venison burger to make chili. I forced a smile. It was nice knowing that at least Sarah cared about me.

"I'll help you guys with supper in a minute," Bernadette told us. "First I'm going out to the woodshed to see what those two are up to." Shortly afterward she was back with the two of them by the back of their jackets. "Just what I thought! I caught these two smoking!" No sooner had she said that than Dad walked into the house. She turned the two of them around. Their faces dropped. "Boy, Dad, am I glad you're home. I just caught these two smoking a cigarette in the woodshed."

"Well, did you call the cops?" he asked. (Asking if we'd called the cops was Dad's way of joking things off, things that he didn't want to deal with at that particular time.)

"Very funny," Bernadette said. "You don't care what they do, do you? But you sure care if I do something wrong, like not doing my housework! In fact, you wouldn't care about me at all if it wasn't for work!" she said sarcastically, then ran to the bedroom. I followed. I could hardly believe what I'd just heard. She was feeling the same way I was, even though Dad had picked her up the very day he'd got back from Kentucky. So I shared with her how I was feeling.

"At least Dad cared enough to pick you up right away."

"That's only because he needed me to help him around the house. You're the lucky one. Mrs. McPhee told Dad that she was enjoying your company and that he didn't have to rush to get you. For what it's worth, I'm glad you're back," she said. "We sisters belong together."

"You're right," I told her, not realizing until that very moment that despite the inconveniences and the turmoil that often went on at home, I was happy to be back where I belonged.

Twenty-Four
ରେ

After one month of convalescence, John left for Kentucky to re-join the army. That same Saturday I went out on my first official date with a friend of Bernadette's boyfriend. We double dated. Thanks to the "dating game" our housework was done without procrastinating or fighting for certain jobs. We started our tasks early that morning and worked harder and faster so we could have the latter part of the afternoon to pamper ourselves with hot baths and to fix each other's hair and polish our fingernails. Anna and Monica couldn't understand our excitement over boys. As we were waiting for the guys to arrive, I could hear the two of them in the bedroom talking, so I quietly crept up on them. Both of them were standing in front of our old dresser. They had the mirror tipped down so they could see themselves better. Monica was putting rollers in her hair and Anna was busy ratting her hair. On the dresser sat two old China cups with saucers beneath. As I peeked in and listened closely, I realized they were mimicking Bernadette and me. I couldn't help but chuckle to myself when I saw them pick up their cups and saucers and pretend to sip their drinks as they sang, "I like coffee, I like tea, I like the boys, and the boys like me!" I started to laugh, which startled them.

"Get out of here!" Anna shouted.

"Just go on your date! We don't want you guys around here anyway!" Monica exclaimed. "Besides, once we get into our new school, we'll never get to see you!"

Our school had consolidated with two nearby schools during '67, but it would be the fall of '68 before the schools planned to come together as the school of Big Bay de Noc. Before that took place, school officials planned a couple of opportunities for the students to get acquainted with one another. One of these occasions was when the school of Cooks invited Garden and Nahma to join them for their championship basketball game. Buses filled with kids from each school met at a central location and then divided up so that each bus had a mixture of students from each area. I stayed on the Garden bus figuring Dennis, the guy I'd been dating from Nahma, would more than likely get on my bus, which he did. A couple minutes later Bryan, also a student from Nahma, walked on and asked Cindy, who was sitting directly across from me, if he could sit with her. That's the first time I remember seeing Bryan. My heart fluttered. Every time I stole a look his way, he was staring at me and would wink. His long eyelashes and pleasant smile were breathtaking. Like a magnet I found myself drawn to him. "Hey, Dennis, want to switch?" he suddenly asked, surprising me as much as an unexpected gift on Christmas morning.

"No!" Dennis declared. I jumped up, "I do!" I said. Dennis looked shocked as I crawled between him and the seat ahead of us. Cindy had no choice but to get in with Dennis. Bryan latched onto my hand and snuggled me next to him. Although we rarely talked, both on the bus and at the game, for some peculiar reason on the way home I told him my mother had died when I was little. I'd never before talked with any guy about my mother being dead. I thought maybe he wouldn't like hearing about my mother's death, but he said he was sorry for me, and to my surprise, he planted a kiss on my cheek.

We had made a connection, yet two more years passed before destiny brought us together again. Our attraction for each other was rekindled the beginning of our junior year. I'd spend nights at his cousin Sandy's who lived across the road from him. Sandy was dating a buddy of his and the two of them would stop by or we'd go to visit them. Bryan had a pool table in his basement so the guys would play while we watched. He'd flirt with me and I with him even though we were both going with other people. When the basketball season came around in late November, the coach suspected we admired each other and tried to keep us apart. When going to away games the coach made the cheerleaders sit to the back of the bus and the players to the front. His tactics didn't work. One night Bryan exchanged seats with the boy sitting in the last boys seat and I did the same with a girlfriend of mine. Bryan turned around and grabbed my hand and asked if he could take me to the movies on New Year's Eve. My eyes lit up. "Good," he said, though I hadn't said a word. I smiled. From that second on, I couldn't wait for New Year's Eve to arrive.

The house was quiet when Bryan came to the door that Tuesday evening. He winked. I blushed and took him by the hand to the living room. "Dad," I said, "this is Bryan."

"How are the ruts?" Dad asked just to give him a hard time.

"He's talking about the roads," I said, with a bit of a smirk as I tried to make the best of my dad's foolishness.

"Not bad at all," Bryan said. "But I never let a little blizzard stop me from going places." I knew my dad got a kick out of his answer. I could tell by his demeanor that he instantly liked Bryan. Yet, as Bryan and I headed for the door, Dad continued to try to intimidate him. He went to the front door and looked out the window of it. "I see you're driving a green '65 Ford Fairlane. Is that right?"

"Yes, Mr. Jacques."

"Well, if that '65 Ford isn't in this driveway by 10 p.m., it'll turn into a pumpkin." Dad's ways didn't faze Bryan. He smiled. "Okay," he said, and away we went, holding hands on the way to his car. Bryan opened the passenger door and I got in. He took the driver's seat, grabbed my hand and slid me over beside him. My eyes followed his every move, the way he chewed his gum, his hand as he shifted gears and his arm as he put it around me. My heart melted within me when he pulled me ever so close to him and then kissed my forehead. Although I was extremely proud to be with him, I found myself hoping that none of Dad's friends would see me sitting so close to Bryan. Dad had a rule when we were with a guy. He'd warned us several times that he didn't want to see any "double-headed driver" coming down the road.

Although we went to see a movie, it was Bryan whom I kept my eyes on all night. When he asked me if I'd like something from the concession stand, I said I wasn't hungry although I was starved. I knew I'd be too nervous to eat. Instead I watched as he devoured Junior Mints, an Almond Joy, a Hershey Bar and some Coca-Cola. On the way home he asked if I remembered our first date. I was shocked. "You remember that, too?" I asked.

"Some things you just don't forget," he said. "Especially since my dad died of a heart attack a couple weeks later. I kept thinking if Donna Jacques has lived without a mother since she was seven, then I can live without my father at fifteen."

"Oh, Bryan," I said. "I had heard about your dad dying. I felt so bad."

"I'm okay now, that was two years ago." But I saw tears in his eyes when the dome light came on as he opened the car door. He walked me through the blackness of the night to the dimly lit house. Looking at his watch, he checked the time.

"You'll never see anything in this darkness," I told him, feeling stupid that we didn't have some kind of yard or porch light.

"Yes, I will. My ma bought me this watch for my sixteenth birthday. The face of it lights up when I push the side attachment." He started to chuckle when he saw that it was 10 p.m. sharp. "At least I don't have to ride a pumpkin home!" I laughed. Several hugs and kisses later we gradually began to let go of each other. "I'll be waiting to see you at school on Monday," I said.

"Me, too," he whispered as he kissed me and gave me a final hug. We slowly parted until only our fingertips were touching. Again my heart felt like wax melting within me as I turned the doorknob and entered the house. A few minutes later I climbed into bed. "Sweet dreams," I said to him.

Being with Bryan gave me a whole new attitude. For the first time in many years life was good, it was worth living. Good things were happening, and I knew it. But by no means were all things peaceful. The more we dated the more nervous I got about Bryan wanting to be at our house for any length of time, especially at night when we got back to my house around midnight. When the temperature was freezing I had no choice but to invite him in for the final good-bye, which often took ten to fifteen minutes. I preferred one minute. The sooner I could get him out the door the better. But with the aroma of Dad's Saturday baking in the air, and Bryan always being hungry, he usually had to have one of Dad's homemade cinnamon rolls that were topped with luscious vanilla frosting. Most often one roll would lead to two or three, delaying his departure. The sound of teeter-tottering snoring from Dad's bedroom and from the living room where Matthew now slept (the couch had become his new bed after returning home) embarrassed me. But the snores alone didn't keep me from looking Bryan in the eyes. Sometimes the two of them would alternate at passing gas. Like fireworks on the Fourth of July the booming and popping was heard, or an occasional sound effect like that of a dud, squeaking and squawking its way to the ground.

But even the pride-punching fireworks didn't take away all my peace. What kept me uptight was my concern that Bryan would ask to use the bathroom. And heaven forbid if he had to go #2. "Would there be any toilet paper left?" This question and many others ran through my mind before we'd make it to my back door. One or two rolls of toilet paper under the sink before I left with him meant nothing, especially if six or more of my siblings, plus Dad were at home for the evening. "What if one, or two, or perhaps three of them had diarrhea or a cold and blew their nose half the night, or worse, the box of Kotex had gone dry?" I doubted very much that Bryan would understand that the catalog on the floor wasn't for placing an order. I certainly didn't want to explain to him that if he had to resort to the Sears Roebuck it meant taking the wipes with you to the utility room (which, thankfully, was next to the bathroom) and throwing them into the wood stove. The fear of having to teach Bryan our family bathroom etiquette tortured me. I finally came to the conclusion that it would be easier for him to go without the toilet paper and save us both the humiliation.

Bryan and I were on the bus, returning home from an away basketball game when he asked me to go steady. We had only been dating a couple weeks but I accepted his ring. I felt on top of the world until Bernadette tapped me on the shoulder. "Scoot over," she said.

"Bernadette, sit down!" the bus driver scolded. Bryan and I quickly moved closer to the window to make room for her.

"Will you go out with this guy tonight so I can go out with Herky? He's the guy from the other school I was sitting with at the game," she whispered.

"No way! Bryan just asked me to go steady!"

"Pleeeease?" she begged. "Herky doesn't have a car. The only way we can go out is if I get a date for his friend, the one with the car. You and Bryan barely know each other; you've only been dating two weeks!"

"That's not true! We know a lot about each other."

"Well, if you don't do this for me, don't ask me for any more favors!"

"Oh... oh dear... well, just this once! And don't ever ask me to do it again for you. And I'm *not* staying out late!"

"Thank you!" she said, as she squeezed my hand and took off to her seat in the back of the bus.

"What was that all about?" Bryan asked.

"Just *stupid* sister stuff," I answered as I lay my head on his shoulder. Sometime later, the bus stopped to drop him and the others from his area off. I dreaded what I had committed myself to doing. To make matters even worse, the guys had followed the bus. I was scared to death to go with strangers. I planned to tell Bernadette that she better help me out if this guy tried anything but she'd beat me to the bus door and was on her way to their car before I was even off the bus. I caught up with her just as she was about to open the car door. "What is this guy's name, anyway?"

"I'm not sure what his real name is, but they call him 'Fat Boy.'" My faced dropped.

"Oh, great," I said. Bernadette exploded with laughter. "It's not funny," I snarled, as I nervously opened the front door and got into the stranger's car. I knew I'd make my sister mad but I immediately said, "We only have an hour and we have to be home or we'll get a belting."

"Your parents hit you?" Fat Boy asked.

"Viciously," I answered.

"Don't worry," he said, "I'll have you home on time."

Everything went fine. I stayed as close to the passenger door as possible, while Bernadette's first and last date with Herky went by. I was thankful when we got dropped off. Before getting into bed I wrapped yarn around Bryan's class ring, then kissed his picture good night.

Although I became more comfortable with Bryan being at our house, I was sure after he found out what little of life's pleasures our family had he'd no longer want to go out with me. But a week later he asked if he could take me to the prom, which wasn't until April. My friends thought us to be the perfect match. Anna and Monica loved my new boyfriend. One night after school Anna asked me to thank Bryan for giving her and Monica money to buy pop and chips at lunchtime.

"I thank him every time he gives you some," I told her.

Catherine, on the other hand, wasn't so keen about him. She found my new love a nuisance because I'd stay up late doing homework more conscientiously, and for the first time in my life, I spent time on my appearance. I didn't wear make-up or highlight my hair like Bernadette, but I cared what I looked like. It irritated Catherine to no end when I'd get home late from a basketball game or date and put the bedroom light on so I could Dippity-Do my bangs, then Scotch tape them down. It was the only way I could get my natural curly hair to lie flat.

The second holiday Bryan and I would share was Valentine's Day. When I heard Dad saying that he was going to Manistique, I asked if I could go with, but he wouldn't let me. "Please," I begged. "Pretty please, Dad."

"I'm not coming right back," he explained. I knew what that meant. He was going to visit a few bars while there and probably wouldn't be back until much later, maybe well into the night. "Just tell me what you need and I'll get it." Reluctantly, with zero faith in him to do such a personal task, I told him that I needed a Valentine card for Bryan. He laughed. "Well, I think I can handle that."

"Don't come back with something dumb or I won't be able to give it to him." I'd already been feeling like the girl from the song "Rag Doll." Nearly every bit of clothes that my family and I owned were hand-me-downs from people we'd never met. For once in my life I wanted to feel "normal." I wanted to get Bryan a small box of Russell

Stover's like other girls were buying for their boyfriends, but I knew that would be out of the question. After Dad left I summoned every angel of heaven to remind him to buy a card, something decent. Again at bedtime I prayed myself to sleep. The next morning on the kitchen table lay a card, not one that I'd have picked out, but useable.

> From the girl whose always yelling out,
> To the guy she's cooped up with.

On the front of the card there was a chicken coop. Inside of the coop was a chicken and a rooster smooching with the words "True Love." I laughed. "It's okay," I thought, knowing that it could've been so much worse.

On Valentine's Day my bus arrived at school early, so I was waiting for Bryan's bus. When he came through the doorway, he winked at me. "Happy Valentine's Day," he said as he planted a kiss on my lips. Reaching into his inner coat pocket, he took out a small heart shaped box of chocolates and handed it to me. I was thrilled that it was small. Proudly I handed him my card. He laughed when he read it. "So you think we're cooped up?" he joked as he walked me to my first class.

As the next two months went by, Bryan and I joined other couples at Fishing Point — the teenage parking site that overlooked Garden Bay. Parking was fun so long as we weren't getting too serious. Anything beyond necking petrified me because I felt my mother was spying on me. One night I got so scared, I frantically hollered for Bryan to take off. "What's wrong?" he asked as he sped away.

"I think I just saw a UFO in the sky over the bay."

"Again tonight?" he questioned.

People had been going crazy because of UFO sightings all over the United States. One had been seen near Gladstone, a small city forty minutes from my house. To me, using the UFO frenzy as an excuse for my paranoia was perfect. It was much easier than trying to explain that my dead mother was watching my every move. Besides, she wasn't the only one on my case these days. One day Bryan and I had taken a walk in the back woods past Matthew's junkyard. We were lying together on the grass by the edge of the woods when we heard something. We looked up to see Dad. "You two, get back to the house," he said, pointing his finger at us. "And stay out of mischief from now on." But we didn't. Dad caught me in the kitchen sitting on Bryan lap face to face and he demanded I turn around that second and sit properly on Bryan or get my own chair. Then, just a few days later Mr. B, our school principal, called Bryan and I into the office because someone reported that we were necking on the bus. Bryan and I admitted we had been kissing a lot, but not necking. "I'm giving you two a warning this time. Next time you'll be punished. Do you understand me?"

"Yes," we said in unison.

"Now, get back to your classes and behave yourselves!"

Mr. B was a single man in his middle forties. His black-colored eyes penetrated through me whenever he looked my way. His voice was more frightening than the stern look embedded on his face. Whenever he hollered, most times it sacred me so much that I thought I'd have a heart attack. So after he reprimanded us, I didn't so much as look Bryan's way as we headed back to our classrooms. "I love you," Bryan said as we parted. I didn't respond. I turned the doorknob of my government classroom and went in.

It wasn't the first time Bryan had told me those three words of "I love you." The first time was when we double dated with my sister Bernadette and Gerald, a guy she was dating for the first time; a guy from the same town as Bryan. I heard Gerald share something with Bernadette that got my curiosity. He was telling her about his mother's death. That she had died while giving birth to her eleventh child. "It was January of 1961; both she and the baby died," I heard him say. I thought for sure Bernadette would tell him that a similar thing had happened to our mother in January of 1960, but that the baby had lived. She didn't say a thing. When we got ready for bed that night, I said, "Wasn't that awful about Gerald?"

"Yes," she exclaimed. "I was so embarrassed! When he opened the refrigerator to get something to drink, there wasn't anything!"

"I wasn't talking about that! I meant how his mother died while giving birth to her eleventh child, like our mother did."

"Oh, I don't want to talk about that sad stuff," she said, as we went to our bedrooms. "In fact, I didn't enjoy tonight at all. I'm not planning on going out with him again."

I continued to think about Gerald's mother that night, and for many nights afterwards. I was glad when the prom got closer. It gave me something better to occupy my mind. It was my junior prom so Dad said I could order a dress from the Sears catalogue. After looking through the book a hundred times or so, I decided on a sleeveless, empire style of chiffon that fell a-line to the floor. I knew the soft turquoise color would look good with my dark brown eyes and dark hair. The cost was twenty nine dollars, just under the thirty Dad had allowed me to spend. I could hardly maintain my composure when I went to the post office to pick up my C.O.D. order. After getting home, I quickly tried it on. It fit perfectly. I was so excited that that afternoon Bernadette and I went to Escanaba. With money I'd saved from babysitting, I bought a pair of white heels and then took them to be dyed the color of my dress.

At a rummage sale that my sister-in-law told us about, Bernadette bought the most beautiful white dress with gold sequins affixed to the bodice. Like mine, hers also fit to a tee. I knew that her new steady boyfriend, Terry, would love it. Unfortunately though, she put it in the trunk of Dad's car and when we got home we noticed that chainsaw oil had spilled over the lower front of it. We both screamed when we saw what had happened. I was thankful I'd kept my dress in the back seat. I'd taken it along to get the exact color for the dying of my shoes.

Monday afternoon Dad took Bernadette's dress to the cleaners in

Manistique, but they were unsuccessful at getting out the stain so, reluctantly, she had to borrow a dress from her friend Dawn. At the last minute a classmate of mine asked Catherine to the prom, so she burrowed a dress from my friend Krystal. Catherine didn't really like the guy, but she wanted to go, and he needed a date, so she accepted his invitation.

Two days before the prom the class gathered after school to decorate the gym. Bryan and some other guys from the class had a track meet so they couldn't be there to help. The theme was *This Magic Moment*. The plan was to transform the gym into a tropical paradise. We covered the walls completely with crepe paper. A scene of a palm tree with a guy and girl dancing in the moonlight had been purchased and placed as a backdrop. A trellis was covered with Kleenex carnations and set at the entrance of the room. Except for the table decorations the decorating was nearly complete, so I left the gym with Cheryl O., Bob and Louie.

We went to a cousin of Cheryl's and asked her to buy some beer for us. She refused but did allow us to have some of her own, as long as we stayed there to drink it. That's where I drank my first full bottle of beer. Needless to say, I felt tipsy after consuming it, yet when offered another I accepted. I didn't want to be called a "Miss Goodie Two-Shoes" like I'd been called in the past, not just by some classmates but also by some of my sisters. In actuality, I was too nervous to go to beer parties with them. Besides, the one time Bryan and I did go to a party, we both got so drunk that we had a hard time driving home. I had to have Bryan stop the car several times because I was so sick. After that night I promised myself to never drink again, which I hadn't done until this day after decorating for the prom.

When Bryan returned from the track meet he caught up with me and was thoroughly disgusted that I was drunk. I tried to act sober, but by then I could barely walk straight. He helped me into his car and then took me to his house so I could sober up before he took me home.

194

His mother seemed to know that I wasn't myself. She asked what was wrong, so I told her I had an upset stomach. "Well, I have the perfect cure for that. It has never failed me yet," she said as she grabbed a small pan from the cupboard, then poured milk into it. She lit the burner on the stove and placed the pan over it. She grabbed a medium size pan and ran water into it and put it on another burner.

"Oh, I know what you're making, Ma. The same thing you made me for my upset stomach the night I came in sick from camp." Then looking at me and smirking, he said, "You'll love it. It's dry toast with poached eggs on them, with warm milk over the top!" I nearly threw up just hearing what she was cooking.

"It'll knock any poison right out of your system," she said as she placed the large Melmac plate of food in front of me. I started to gag, but held back. I wanted to move from the table. I wanted someone to run the plate of food out the door and throw it into the field, like I had done the day Dad had bought home spoiled chicken from town. Instead, so not to lose his mother's respect, I sat there on that red gingham-covered kitchen chair and ate nearly every bit of the concoction, while Bryan grinned and chuckled whenever his mother wasn't looking. I didn't think I'd ever feel good again.

However, two days later, bright and early on the morning of the prom my sisters Bernadette, Catherine and I got ready to go to Escanaba to get our hair fixed. My sisters went with their friends and I went with mine, Debbie, Linda and Sandi. On our way to the Beauty Academy, Debbie shared with us that she had found out from a reliable source that she had received the most votes, so she would be crowned queen that night. I felt bad because I figured Bryan would be king and I had wanted to be his queen.

Later that afternoon, as my sisters and I were putting on make-up and then getting into our dresses, we were singing a line from *Cinderella*. "The prince is having a ball, the prince is having a ball, the prince, the prince, the prince, the prince, the prince is having a ball."

Even my sisters not going to the prom were being giddy with us as we sang, but inwardly I was sad. I'd always dreamed of being someone's Cinderella, and my chance of being Bryan's had come to pass, knowing Debbie was going to be crowned queen of the prom.

When Bryan came to pick me up it was the first time I'd ever seen him in a suit. He looked stunning. It was hard for me to quit hugging him. I thought for sure Dad was going to tell me to give the guy room to breathe, like he'd told me at other times when he thought we were getting too mushy. I couldn't wait to be alone with him in his car, to cuddle next to him and the fragrance of English Leather on his body. I'd given him the cologne for his birthday; it was the only kind he ever wore.

"You look so beautiful," he said as he placed a beautiful corsage of miniature red roses, with dipped blue carnations onto my wrist.

"You look handsome," I whispered.

After pinning a boutonniere to his lapel, we left. Following a wonderful dinner, we arrived at the gym. Everyone looked spectacular, though I felt bad for Catherine. Her hairdo was already falling out and the guy she was with was throwing a tantrum because he was the only guy without a boutonniere. "Get over it. It's not the end of the world," I heard Anne say to him.

At ten o'clock, those of us who had been chosen by the student body to be on court gathered in the center of the floor. Without the anticipation of wondering whether I would or would not be crowned queen, I felt extremely calm. Although I was still disappointed about not being queen, being totally relaxed was making everything very enjoyable. It continued to be that way as we lined up into our practiced positions of the queen and king's court. As the band began to play the music to the prom song, Christine, the queen from the previous year, walked behind the girls of the queen's court, trying to add suspense to the night. Inwardly, I was chuckling at it all, until, to my surprise, Christine placed the queen's crown upon my head.

I was flabbergasted! From the back of the room, I heard my sisters' screams. I thought my legs were going to collapse to the floor, and my mouth fell open. Christine then presented me with a dozen yellow roses, the smell of which I would always remember. As the band continued to play "This Magic Moment," Bryan and I led the grand march. I looked at him and said, "I get to be Cinderella for the rest of the night." He smiled and squeezed my hand tightly. "I'm glad," he said.

Donna Jean Pomeroy

Twenty-Five
CR

"It's hard to believe four years have already passed since John graduated," Dad said. "After tonight, I'll have two less around the table."

"I heard that, Dad," Sarah yelled from the bedroom, as she and Bernadette readied themselves for their graduation ceremony. "Sounds like you're counting the minutes until we're out of your hair!"

Dad laughed. "And the seconds, too!"

I knew he was just playing around, but was also glad to soon be relieved of more responsibility. For Dad's sake as well as my own, I was getting excited about leaving the nest, too. I was glad my junior year had come to an end. The sooner I could claim my wings and fly, the happier I'd be. But with only one summer left before the final bell would ring, I decided to enjoy it as much as possible.

Once again I went to Chicago, but returned three weeks later be-

198

cause I was so lonesome for Bryan. Besides, both Bernadette and Sarah were getting married in the fall so I wanted to be with them as much as possible. I was sentimental thinking about the times we'd shared, like the times when Bernadette and her friend Colleen and I would ride the town drag, over and over again, as if our car tires were glued to the trail. Colleen sometimes used her dad's car and sometimes we used our dad's. Bernadette always drove our car despite my having a license. She still didn't trust me behind the wheel. I thought her driving left a lot to be desired, too. In a two-week span she'd gone in the ditch three times!

The first time we hit the ditch was by the old Garden school. It was during the springtime and the unpaved road was muddy. Bernadette drove the car too close to the shoulder and we ended up in the ditch. We sat lopsided as we waited for someone to come by and push us out. A few days later we were sitting lopsided again, this time on the driver's side. While Bernadette was driving, she was messing around with the radio and before she knew it she'd lopped off a sign on the other side of the road, banging up the driver's door. That night she backed into the driveway so Dad couldn't see the damage. The third time she hit the ditch was while turning around in the funeral home parking lot. She backed too far across the road and the rear of the car ended up deep in the ditch while the front of it stuck up in the air.

It had always been a pact of ours that whoever laughed first after a driving flub-up had to go for help. That night it was Colleen who first giggled, so she went across the street and asked Nick Thennes to pull us out, which he did. We didn't dare tell Dad about the ordeal because we knew he'd be mad at us for bothering Nick. But as usual, word floated back to him as quickly as a hot air balloon blown up by gossipers. Dad threatened to keep the car from us, but it only lasted two days before we were riding the roads again.

Not having my older sisters around was going to seem strange. We'd shared so many things, included cigarettes in the bathroom.

One time Dad walked in shortly after four of us had shared one. We'd thrown talcum powder around to disguise the smell, but he still detected it. Sharing one cigarette and holding out long enough in the bathroom usually eliminated all traces of evidence. On the other hand, when each of us had our own cigarette it was as if a dense fog had rolled into the room. Early one afternoon as we were each taking delight in having our own smoke, Dad knocked on the bathroom door. "What are you girls up to in there?" he asked.

"Just fixing each other's hair," Catherine answered.

"You better not be smoking, because I smell smoke out here!"

As he spoke we were flicking the hot end of our cigarettes off into the sink trying to get them out in a hurry without damaging the whole cigarette. "No, we're not smoking" we replied. Sarah bit onto her thumbnail and Bernadette held a finger over her mouth to shush Catherine and me because we were getting the giggles. We were relieved when we heard him walk away. We quickly relit our cigarettes. We had no idea that Dad was quietly walking around to the back of the house, next to the bathroom window, which we had wide open to let out the smoke. He stood there silently for quite awhile listening to the different excuses we were planning to use for having been in the bathroom all at once, and for so long. Without us knowing, he stepped up to the window, reached in and pulled back the curtain, and watched as we each took our last drags of the cigarettes.

"So you're not smoking, are you?"

"Ahhh!" we screamed at the top of our lungs, looking in his direction. My sisters quickly threw their cigarettes into the toilet but mine went flying through the air and came to rest on the windowsill, smack in front of Dad's eyes. He picked the butt of the Pall Mall up as smoke continued to float his way. "Give me that pack of cigarettes," he demanded. Bernadette handed them to him. He looked her in the eyes. "Were you the one who wanted me to punish Anna for smoking?" She didn't say a thing.

When he got back into the house he broke them up in front of our faces. Bernadette, Sarah and I all thought it, but only Catherine was gutsy (or stupid) enough to say it. "Well, there goes our pop bottle money down the drain." Needless to say, that summer night none of us were allowed to go out on the town like we'd planned. Instead, Sarah and Bernadette got stuck weeding the entire garden, while Catherine and I scrubbed each and every floor throughout the house. It was the last time we chanced smoking at home, at least when Dad was there.

Although I wasn't in the fast pace of the big city, and was back home after just three weeks in Chicago, time went by fast during the summer. Before I knew it Bernadette was married and Bryan and I were in our senior year of high school. With him in cross country, and later basketball, and me as one of the cheerleaders, the fall and winter months also passed quickly. The spring months brought the extracurricular events of track meets for Bryan and yearbook staff for me. Needless to say, with all our activities the end of our school year was fast approaching.

It was a Saturday morning when I awoke to Bernadette moaning as she lay in bed. Terry had joined the National Guards, so she was staying at home again. My sisters and I got up and tried to take care of her so she wouldn't lose the baby that was growing within her — the baby Dad still knew nothing about. We were afraid to tell him about her condition because he might put two and two together — that she was expecting before she'd gotten married. No one wanted to tell him because he'd always said that if any guy ever got us "in a certain condition," he'd meet him at the door with his forty-four.

As the morning turned into the later part of the afternoon, Bernadette's pain worsened. When I suggested we leave for the hospital, she started to cry. That's when Dad came into the bedroom carrying a candy dish that Bernadette and Terry had received as a wedding gift. Dad moved the dish back and forth as if it were a cradle. When he left the room we agreed that he was trying to tell us that he knew she was pregnant and that he was okay with it.

Bernadette's teeth clenched as she grabbed the blankets and began twisting them around and around. Carefully, I lay beside her. "Oh, I wish Mama were here!" I said to myself. Pain after pain left Bernadette howling every few minutes. Again I asked if we should leave for the hospital. This time with tears streaming down her face, she nodded, so a few minutes later I helped her out to the car.

"You've never driven on the highway before. Do you think you can get me there?" she asked. She had little or zero trust in my driving abilities, and I felt somewhat the same but found myself saying, "I know I can! I drove on the highway during Driver's Ed."

"Oh, owww," she cried, hesitating a moment before telling me that she should probably be more afraid of my driving than having her baby early.

"I'm not that bad. Watch and see." In truth, I was panicked about taking her the fifty miles to the hospital. But she needed my help. It was no time to think I couldn't do what needing doing. I grabbed the key and started the car.

"Wait!" she said. "One final question: You're not going to leave me somewhere down the road are you?"

"Very funny," I said, knowing full well that what she was referring to was Dad's big, yellow '53 Cadillac, the day I'd abandoned it in the middle of the road. The car was so embarrassingly long that we hated going anywhere in it. Yet, Dad never could understand why we despised being in that car. He laughed whenever he had to go to downtown Garden. We'd duck because we were afraid to be spotted by friends, especially boys. Sometimes he'd tell us we already passed through town so we'd pop up only to find a group of young boys crossing the street in front of us.

One day while Dad was at work, Bernadette had coaxed me into driving the big yellow Cadillac to the store. "I can't! No! I can't! No! I'm too afraid!"

"Yes you can! Come on now!" she'd coaxed.

I had gotten about a quarter mile down the road and totally panicked. "Keep going," she'd encouraged.

"No, you take over." She wouldn't so I'd attempted to turn the big lug around. It stalled crossways in the road. It was so long that it completely blocked the road. I was petrified. I didn't know what to do. All Bernadette had done was laugh hysterically, that is, until I'd taken off running home and left her there. Up the road a ways, I'd turned around and seen her getting into the driver's seat. She'd seen me looking and started spewing words that were hotter than sparks from a campfire. "You witch! You turd! You fartface! Just wait until I get a hold of you."

Nearly an hour had passed before Bernadette came storming into the house. "Thanks a lot," she'd said, slamming the door and then running toward me. I'd tried to get away but she grabbed my ponytail and gave it a jerk. "You are the biggest pansy, ever! Three cars came by before someone had jumper cables to get that dumb car started. It was so embarrassing, all those people asking ME what I was doing with Dad's car! Don't ever expect me to ride with you again!"

"Well, you're the one who wanted me to take that big yellow mare down the road." To ignore her ranting, I'd run and turned on the radio. Realizing what I'd done, she'd come charging toward me. As she'd reached to turn the radio back off the song "Yellow Submarine" by the Beatles came on. "Hey!" I'd said, "We all ride in a yellow submarine!" Of course, I had laughed, as did my other sisters.

"You brat!" she'd said, pinching my arm. "Just wait until Dad gets home. We'll see then who rides in a yellow submarine!"

"Ouch!" I'd squealed as I'd run into Dad's bedroom and quickly pushed his dresser in front of the door. For the next two hours I had stayed in there, on guard, waiting for the sound of Dad's car and hoping that Bernadette would be too afraid to tell him what I'd done. I hoped she'd realize that getting me in trouble would get her in trouble, too, if he found out *we'd* taken his car out of the driveway.

My prayers were answered. She didn't tell. That night, despite her hesitation to sing along with our sisters and me, she'd joined in to sing "Yellow Submarine." From that day until the yellow Cadillac died and was put in Matthew's junkyard, Dad's car was known as the Yellow Submarine.

I knew the fact that I'd flunked Driver's Ed had something to do with Bernadette's reluctance to have me drive her to the hospital. Since I had been driving cars for years on the back roads of our property, I'd thought the course would be a cinch. Sally Nedeau, a friend of mine, had sat behind me in class and at my request would pull out split ends from my hair. It had relaxed me so much that I had usually been in a dreamy state during class. Only when Mr. Haindl had raised his voice or called on me was I startled into a coherent state of mind. I realized much too late, after taking the test on the book work part of the course, that I should've paid closer attention during the first six weeks.

The second time around I had passed with flying colors so I got to start driving. I had shared the hour slot of time with Cindy and Janet. Once when Janet was driving, she had taken a ninety-degree corner going so fast that our instructor had to throw his newspaper to the side. "What the heck are you trying to do, put us in the ditch?" he'd asked as he hit his brake and grabbed the wheel. Dust went flying. "What were you thinking?" he'd continued after he got the car under control.

"I tried caressing the corner," Janet had said, nearly crying. Cindy and I had almost exploded with laughter when we heard her choice of words.

"That was far from *caressing* a corner," he'd said. "You sure you weren't daydreaming?"

Janet had never been behind the wheel of a car before. She'd been looking in the rearview mirror at Cindy and me in the backseat. We had been making faces at her, faces as if our lives were about to come to an end. "Ahhh," we'd mouthed. She could see us in the rearview mirror.

Although I had been still trying to hold back my laughter, I'd felt bad we'd gotten her into trouble. After school on the bus that day, I had shared with Bernadette and some of the others sitting near me about Janet's reckless driving. I had been relieved to finally be able to let go of my laughter. "Well, you're the *last* person that should talk. Have you forgotten about the time *you* were driving Jim's car and jumped over the front seat and into the back just because you met the state police on the Churchill?" Bernadette had said loudly to her friends and then continued on. "She was so afraid of getting a ticket for not having her driver's license, that I had to hurry into the driver's seat and take over the car for her,"

"Oh, yeah, I forgot about that. But that was a long time ago," I'd said.

"Six months isn't a long time!" she'd commented.

I started the car and turned to Bernadette. "Are you sure you wouldn't rather have Sarah drive you to the hospital?"

"Please," she replied, "I want to get there. Sarah drives way too slow. You know that."

I didn't think she'd go for Sarah driving, but I thought I'd offer. Sarah was always so poky when driving. She rarely went faster than 35 mph. A couple days after she'd gotten her license the cops had pulled her over while on Highway 2. We had been nervous as we waited, and it seemed to take forever for the policeman to walk to the car. Sarah had been so scared that she'd kept her head down, even as she dug through her black umbrella purse for her driver's license, and again as the officer read it over. "Do you know why I'm stopping you?" he'd asked.

"Because of no muffler?" she'd asked shyly.

"I probably should be stopping you for that, too, but it's because you're holding up traffic. Cars can't get by you. You're going too slow!"

"That's dumb!" she'd said, lifting her head and looking right in the officer's face. "If they can't get by me when I'm going this slow, how the heck are they going to get past me if I go any faster?" My face had grown hot with embarrassment. I'd thought for sure he was going to give her a ticket because of the way she'd talked to him, but he'd laughed.

"Guess you have a point!" He'd taken a final look at all of us and then tipped his hat. "Have a nice day, ladies." We'd held our breath as he walked back to his car.

"Whew!" Sarah had said as he drove away. "That was a close call."

As she'd driven the hunk-of-junk home, Bernadette had been so happy that Sarah hadn't gotten a ticket that she'd shouted for joy. But she certainly wasn't shouting for joy now with me at the wheel. Gears were grinding as I tried to get the car into reverse. Backing out of the driveway, I suddenly wished we were little girls again, making mud cakes and pies, jumping from the limbs of trees, making angels in the snow or just playing a game of jacks at the kitchen table. "Dear Lord," I prayed, "Please watch over Bernadette. Don't let her die!" I put the car into first gear and started down the road, wondering if she, too, was as worried about her life as I was.

As I turned onto U.S. 2, I asked Bernadette how fast I should go. "Just get going!" she said. For the next few miles no words were spoken. Halfway to the hospital we met Mark and Sandy on their way to our house. Mark flashed his lights and pulled off onto the side of the road, so I pulled off too. He jumped out of the car and crossed the road. Bernadette was in constant pain and howling.

"I figured something must be wrong when I saw you driving," he said to me. "Do you want me to take over? I can have Sandy follow us in our car."

"No. It's okay," I said. A confidence was brewing within me. I fearlessly stepped on the gas to resume the journey. I tried to comfort Bernadette but at this point nothing eased her pain. "You'll be fine once we get you to the hospital. The doctors will help you," I reassured her as I stopped at the first light in Escanaba. A few miles later I pulled up to the emergency entrance at St. Francis Hospital. I was relieved. Mark pulled in behind me. A nurse saw us and came running through the doorway. "What do we have here?" she asked. I looked at Bernadette. Her tears had splattered her mascara that she'd insisted on applying before we left.

Two days later Bernadette came home empty handed. She went right to bed. Mark told us that she'd miscarried shortly after I'd left the hospital. The doctor had called him into Bernadette's room. He'd put the premature boy into Mark's hands. Mark had carried the little baby over to the bed to allow Bernadette to see her child. "She didn't cry," Mark said. "She didn't say a word." That's the way she remained, sleeping a lot, speaking little. It wasn't until her husband returned from boot camp that she started being herself again.

Donna Jean Pomeroy

Twenty-Six
CR

As I crawled into bed the night before our senior class trip to Chicago, I was afraid I'd miss the bus the next morning. It was leaving at 6 a.m. and we'd been told to be on time or they'd be forced to leave without us. Our life-long alarm clock was gone — Dad had left for Chicago to stand as godfather for John's second daughter's baptism. Without him at home I wasn't sure if I'd be able to get up in time, but the angels woke me at 5:30 the next morning. I could hardly contain my excitement as I got ready to leave that Saturday morning. Months earlier Dad had given me money to spend on my senior class pictures or clothes for the class trip. I opted to spend it on clothes because I wanted to look nice while in Chicago. After all, it was my home away from home. I'd already been to many of the places on our schedule. Some of them I'd visited every year, like the zoo, the Museum of Science and Industry, the Field Museum and the Planetarium.

Going on the class trip was going to be my chance to show others that I was intelligent. I was tired of feeling less than them. Since seventh grade my self-confidence had been plummeting downwards at a steady pace. My school grades had improved since dating Bryan, but they were still far from the A's I'd once received. No longer was I the brave one in the class, like in my earlier days of school, reciting poetry and playing the lead role in a play. In fact, during the recent talent show that our class had put on, I had been so afraid of getting up in front of people that I'd reluctantly given up the "My Boy Lollipop" skit to Debbie. I had showed her all the movements to the song and given her the huge lollipop I'd made to use for the act. I had been mad at myself for not having the courage to do it, and it was made even worse when Bryan's mother had said that it was the cutest act she'd ever seen performed in a talent show at school.

I slipped into my bell-bottom pants and crop top. After brushing my long hair I made a small braid on each side and connected them with a rubber band in the back. I ripped the scotch tape from my bangs, brushed them slightly, went to brush my teeth and then woke up Catherine. "Catherine, I need you to take me to catch the bus."

"Darn," she said, "Why did you have to wake me up? I was having a good dream."

"You can tell me about it on the way to the school, because we have to leave right now," I said as she swept the hair from her eyes.

Returning to my room, I slipped into my clogs and grabbed my Jackie O sunglasses (that I splurged on) from the top of the dresser.

"Do you have everything?" Catherine asked.

"Yes, I'm ready and raring to go!"

"What about the things Bryan's mother made for you?" My heart skipped a beat. I ran to the closet. I'd packed the loungers she'd made, but still hanging in the closet was my beautiful cotton dress, a yellow and white floral design on a black background. Quickly I grabbed it from the hanger and gently folded it as Catherine unzipped my suitcase. I slipped it on top of my other belongings. "Thanks," I said giving Catherine a half hug, "I can't believe I almost left my favorite piece of clothing behind. I'm going to save it to wear for our class's special night that Mr. B has planned for us. He hasn't even told the chaperones because he was afraid they'd blab it all over the place."

"You are so lucky! I can't wait to hear what the special night was," Catherine said as we got into Dad's car.

"By the way, what was the good dream you were having?"

"Ah… ah… darn! I can't remember. I wouldn't have had time to tell you about it anyway. It was a long one," she said as we pulled into the school parking lot. No sooner had I grabbed my things and closed the door of the old Pontiac when Catherine squealed out. "Have fun," she hollered as she waved her hand high out the window.

"Who the heck took you here?" Richard asked.

"Catherine, she always peels out," I told him as I wondered how she could be so much gutsier than me.

There were twenty-five students on the bus, boys outnumbering girls almost two to one. Wally, one of the school's bus drivers was the driver for the trip; his wife came to chaperone the eleven of us girls. Mr. B was head chaperone. The trip down on the bus was nice. Gary played guitar, while he and Rod sang songs of the sixties, like "Happy Together" by the Turtles. In the latter part of the afternoon we arrived in the Loop of the Windy City and parked in front of the Palmer House, the motel where we'd be staying.

I'd waited for this week to come since the class had first chosen Chicago as the destination for the senior trip. After getting checked in, it didn't take long to unpack, freshen up and be ready to see another side of the world. But what I wasn't ready to see was another side of Mr. B. Back home, breaking a school law usually got us more than a slap on the wrist, yet in Chicago, breaking the law of the land got us a pat on the back. Mr. B. not only knew that most of the class was drinking, he joined them in the process. He also knew that many of the guys' dresser drawers in their rooms were filled with booze that they'd taken from home. One night he snuck into their rooms and lathered the boys with shaving cream. Couples from our class, including Bryan and me, were left unsupervised, which was completely groovy to us. Everyone was coming and going as they pleased. And so went the week of the class trip.

When the last day arrived, which was the day of our special class outing, some of us girls decided to go shopping to waste some time before the big event. At one of the ritzy downtown shops, Anne, Fran, Cheryl and I bought some chocolate covered ants, just to be silly. At another store we tried on all kinds of hats and then treated ourselves to Baked Alaska at a fancy restaurant. When we returned to our rooms, I pressed my dress and then used Cheryl's hot rollers to curl my hair. As I slipped into my dress I felt like prom night was happening all over again. I was giddy and excited, yet sentimental, knowing it was the last night of our trip.

"The school bus will be in the front parking lot at 7 p.m.!" Mr. B.'s loud voice sounded throughout the hallway. We took the elevators to the first floor and boarded the bus. Twenty minutes later, Wally drove beneath the burgundy awnings in front of a nightclub.

"My, gosh, look at this classy joint," Anne said. It made me even more excited about what was awaiting us on the inside. Maybe Mr. B. was going to present us each with a $50.00 bill, extra money from our class fund. Whatever it was, we were minutes from knowing. As we entered the place, male waiters in special suits escorted us to one of the three long tables set up for our group. I noticed a stage about ten feet in front of where Bryan and I and some of our friends were sitting. The waiters soon came and took our orders. Following their departure, we were told to sit back, relax and enjoy the show.

I was shocked to see that the "special surprise" was nude dancers, 15 to 20 of them. I was only seventeen, and immediately I felt ashamed to be there. It was against my moral and religious upbringing to be in such a place. I was so embarrassed that I refused to watch any of the show. I had no desire to watch the girls prance around in front of us. Bryan held my hand and told me that if it made me uncomfortable we could leave. "It certainly isn't impressing me," he said, and then told me how mad his mother and aunts and uncles (several of his cousins were in our class and on the trip) would be if they were to find out Mr. B. had taken us to such a raunchy place.

Just as I was about to get up and go out to the bus, I heard some of the girls asking Mrs. Bennette if they could leave. She said she'd be more than happy to take anyone out of the club with her because she didn't feel comfortable being there either. She went over to Mr. B.'s table, I suspected to tell him her plans. I could tell there was some kind of confrontation as I watched the two of them conversing. Mrs. Bennett looked angry with him. Shortly afterwards she returned to her table and said quite loudly that Mr. B. *demanded* that everyone stay put.

When I heard that, I was really mad. From then on I stared at him. I watched as Mr. B laughed and seemingly enjoyed the evening. I kept my disgusted face on him, and to my shock he seemed as thrilled watching the reaction of the boys from our class as much, if not more, than he did the dancers. It sickened me. When our expensive meals came, I only picked at it. Knowing my dad was in Chicago didn't help. I kept thinking that he might *surprise* me, too. The thought that such a thing could happen frightened me. I knew Mr. B would be in serious trouble. In the past my dad had gone to a school board meeting because one of my brothers felt he'd been treated unfairly. Dad hadn't taken the injustice as lightly as the superintendent had. When the superintendent had told my dad that he didn't think the complaint was legitimate and then abruptly asked my dad to leave the meeting, Dad had said he would, but before he left he'd put his fist up to the superintendent's face.

"You wouldn't hit a guy with glasses, would you?" The superintendent had asked. Dad had responded with a blow to the man's face, breaking the guy's glasses and leaving him with a large gash above the nose.

"I hope my dad never finds out about this joint," I told Bryan when we were boarding the bus to go back to the motel.

The trip back home the next day was one of disbelief. I still was having a hard time trying to understand how a teacher, our principal, an authority figure and role model, could have justified taking our class to such a place. When we arrived back at the school Mr. B hollered at a couple of the students for running to the door of the bus. "Why are you always shouting?" I asked, standing in the aisle, looking him straight in the eyes for the first time in my life.

"Don't you have respect for your elders, Miss Jacques?" he asked sarcastically, in his usual loud, gruff voice.

"Not for you, I don't! Not anymore!" I somehow managed to say, and then continued off the bus.

More than ever, I was ready to be done with school. Graduation day for our class of 1970 was approaching. A new beginning of my life would follow. All the good and bad during my years of school would be behind me. I knew I'd miss my classmates but other things I'd *never* miss, like always having to find my own rides to and from events, not having money for hot lunch or for candy sales at school or snacks at ball games — not once in the four years of high school had I ever bought myself a pop. It was going to be great always having shampoo for washing my hair. I hated when we'd run out and have to use Breeze washing detergent. Soon I wouldn't have to cope with panic attacks, fearing that I might be asked to do a particular task, like reading out loud in class or going to the chalkboard when I was on my monthly. I'd no longer have to feel like an outcast for not having anyone to attend P.T.A. meetings on my behalf or not have a mother to attend mother-daughter banquets.

For the ceremony I wore a pastel pink polka-dotted dress. The night was cool but for a change I had a spring coat to wear. Jim had given me money to buy myself one, as a graduation gift from him. Although I'd written the Last Will and Testament, once again lacking the courage to read it myself, I gave it to Debbie and Cheryl to read. Minutes later, with my diploma in hand, all I could think of was that I'd soon be earning money and would never have to go without basic needs again. I was free at last!

Days after graduation Debbie got married. Bryan and I went to the reception, ate, then left to waste some time until the dance started. "I can show you my Uncle Floyd's hunting camp," he said. "It won't take long. It's only about ten miles up the road. We'll be back within an hour."

So off we went in his '68 Ford truck. As we turned onto the road leading to the camp, we got stuck. Bryan thought it was just water over the road, but we were in a humongous mud hole. We tried everything to get the truck out. We put branches and brush as far under the tires as possible, but when Bryan gave the truck some gas, it sank down further. So, one by one, Bryan jacked each tire up and we put more limbs and brush and small and big rocks, too, into the mud hole to make a bed of traction. But again when Bryan tried to move it the truck slid off the pile of debris and deeper into the mud and muck. We repeated the process four or five times throughout the evening without success.

The moon was bright in the sky when we started walking the ten-mile trip out to the highway. It happened to be a year of a plague of Green Bay flies — giant-looking mosquitoes. They'd taunted us as we tried to free the truck, getting in our hair and sticking to our clothes and now they were in our faces. Before we'd left the vehicle Bryan took his mother's cigarettes from the glove compartment. There were only three of them in the pack. He lit one at a time and held it out in front of us so the smoke would keep the mosquitoes away. As we continued our walk, the forest of tall pines looked spooky. At one point, I thought I'd seen something coming from them. "What was that?" I asked Bryan hoping to hear him say it was nothing.

"Where?" he asked in a concerned voice. I'd been quite brave until I heard his response. I was uptight until we arrived at a local restaurant at 5:30 a.m. Bryan was happy because he knew his mother would still be sleeping. He wanted to call her right away before she noticed that he hadn't come home. Sally, the owner of restaurant let him use her phone but there was no answer at his house, so she gave us a ride there. His mother, older sister and younger brother were all gone, and so was his mother's car.

"Where the heck can they be?" Bryan said in a disgusted voice. About a half hour later they pulled into the driveway. His mother was so happy to see us when she stepped out of the car, but soon her joy turned to questions.

"Where have you two been?" she scolded. "We've been up for hours searching all the back roads, even in Garden. I thought maybe you two had gone parking and had been overcome by carbon monoxide."

"Sorry," we said, and then told her what had happened. We then all agreed that I should get home before my dad came looking for me. When we got to my house Dad was surprised to see us walk in. Immediately he stood from his chair. "You're just getting home?"

"Yes, Dad!" I said, "But let me tell you what happened."

"It better be good," he said. Once again, I began to tell the whole story, knowing it wouldn't be the last time I'd have to tell it.

Twenty-Seven
CR

It was July 3, 1970. The temperature was nearly ninety degrees and it was only 11 a.m. Anna, Monica and I were sitting on the front porch planning our Fourth of July picnic when Jim sped into the driveway. He had a job working on the ore boats on the Great Lakes and this day, like other days when his boat docked at port, he spent time with our family. Getting out of his car, Jim reached into the back seat and took out a big watermelon. As he came walking toward us, he hollered at me to quit biting my finger nails. It was a pet peeve of his. I pulled my fingers from my mouth. "Speaking of bad habits, I thought you were going to ease up on the booze," I said, after getting a whiff of peppermint schnapps on his breath.

"Here, put this watermelon in the fridge." I took it and set it on the porch between my sisters and me.

"Won't you be coming on the picnic tomorrow?"

"No, I won't be around."

"Did you get called back to work early?" I asked.

"No, I'm just too restless to be sitting at a lake all day," he said as he took a place near me on the porch. I was eating a Popsicle that I'd made from Kool-Aid. I snuck it behind his back and then slid it down his tee shirt. "You little shit!" he said, grabbing it and chasing after me.

"Run, Donna Jean, run," Monica and Anna screamed. He caught up to me and smeared what was left of it over my face; then he ran into the house. A couple minutes later he came back out drying his hands on his pant legs.

"I better get going. You guys have a nice Fourth," he said as he brushed the top of Monica's head. Then he left. We heard his tires squealing for several seconds afterwards. Sadness filled my heart. I hated when he would drink and drive.

When we could no longer hear the squealing of tires, my sisters and I went into the house and finished planning our picnic for the following day. We were in the process of making lime Jell-O with chunks of cream cheese cut up into it (Dad's favorite), when Dad drove up. We were surprised because we didn't expect him home so soon. I went to the door to ask him why he was home so early. When he got out of the car, I instantly knew something was wrong. Dad was walking slowly, with slouched shoulders. He took his big red hanky from his back pocket, wiped his eyes, then blew his nose. "What's the matter, Dad?" I asked, walking quickly toward him.

Never in a million years was I expecting to hear the answer he gave. "Jim just got killed up the road. He met his Waterloo," he said, as he shook his head slowly from side to side, not believing it himself.

"No!" I screamed. "No, it can't be true!"

Had Dad not used the words "Met his Waterloo," I might have not believed what he was saying, but over the years Dad had used the expression, not for a natural death, but when someone was killed accidentally. What he was telling me I knew was fact. "Yes," Dad said. "Jim's dead! He got killed up the road, about an hour ago. He was driving too fast and hit a tree. He was thrown from the car and he must have died instantly."

Within minutes, as if sent by God, Mark and Sandy showed up unexpectedly. Soon afterwards, Bryan came. None of them knew Jim had been killed. Bryan stood by my side trying to comfort me. I wanted him to take away all my pain, as he so often had done in the past when things were bothering me; but there was nothing he could do to help my sorrow. Jim was gone; no one could bring him back.

"Why, Jim, Lord? Why him?" I cried out that night when I climbed into bed.

During the night I awoke, and at first I thought the accident had been a bad dream, but reality soon sunk in. I could hear Monica sniffling. I kept picturing Jim everywhere, sitting on the couch, eating at the table, buzzing wood with Dad, getting the watermelon out of his car, and seeing him walk away for the very last time, how he had smiled, cocked his neck, then given us a thumbs up before getting into his car and driving away.

"I should've taken his car keys," I said to Monica. "I knew he'd been drinking."

"We all knew. He would never have listened to us anyway if we'd told him not to leave," she said.

"We need to send some flowers to the funeral home," Anna told us from the other bedroom.

"Beautiful ones," Catherine added.

A couple days later we went to Jim's wake. At first I didn't have the courage to view his body, so I walked around looking at the plants and flowers throughout the funeral home. The Hawaiian plant we'd sent was sitting on a stand near the casket. Reluctantly, I stepped closer to his dead body. I looked at him. He didn't look as bad as I'd thought he might. I touched his hand, then brushed the back of my own against his cold face. I thought about what my dad had told us when he came home on the day of the accident, how there was such force during the accident that both of Jim's boots had come off. "That's because you never tied your boots," I said to myself before continuing on in thought about the day he died. "My dad said that when your body was thrown from the car, it slammed up against a tree and your nose was ripped off." For a few seconds I thought I was going to pass out. Gaining my composure, I looked closer at his face. I could tell that his nose had been repaired. "You always got your nose hurt, didn't you?" I said.

"What did you say?" Sarah asked as she stood next to me by the casket.

"Oh, nothing," I answered.

"The funeral director just said this is our last chance to view the body before he closes the casket," she said, putting her arm around me. "So, you better tell Jim good-bye." That's when I started crying and couldn't stop, as was the case at the funeral the next day and during the procession to the cemetery.

Weeks later, I was still having trouble eating and sleeping. One night I awoke crying, and although Monica was only twelve, she rubbed my leg and told me it'd be okay. "Watch and see," she said, "Tomorrow will be better." I certainly never thought she'd be right, but each day that passed did get easier. Instead of my days being totally consumed with grief, I'd get a few hours' reprieve. As the months went by, more hours of each day were happier than sad. At Christmas time my sorrow faded fast when Bryan asked me to marry him.

Thoughts of my wedding day continued to ease my grief. Between my job at Escanaba's first fast-food restaurant, Burger Chef, and making plans for our wedding day, my mind was occupied with things other than grief. Dad had given me one hundred dollars toward wedding expenses. I decided to use the money to buy my wedding gown and veil. At the Fair store, the most exclusive shop for wedding gowns at the time, I chose an empire style with a mantilla veil. A week later, my mother-in-law-to-be and I picked out a pattern and material for my bridesmaid dresses, which she planned to make. Catherine was going to be my maid-of-honor, Anna and Monica my bridesmaids, along with my friend Sandi, Bryan's cousin.

June 19, 1971 finally arrived. My sisters and I scurried to get ready after returning from getting our hair fixed. At 12:15 p.m. Dad said that he and Matthew were going early to the church so they'd be out of our way. "Besides," he said, "I don't think you're going to want to ride to the church in my ol' clunker." But at 12:30 p.m., when still none of my siblings had showed up at the house, I wondered if I'd get to my wedding on time. It wasn't until 12:50 p.m. when Luke drove up in his '56 Oldsmobile that my mind eased. On the way to the church, he kept asking me if I really wanted to go through with getting hitched. "Of course, I do," I said, smiling at him.

"But, are you sure? You still have time to make a run for it."

"Just get me to the church! I'm nervous enough without you asking silly questions."

"Okay," he said, "But don't say I didn't warn you."

We arrived five minutes before the service. My friend Sandi was anxiously awaiting my arrival. She handed me my bouquet of yellow roses, daisies and baby's breath and then helped my sisters pin their corsages on. I grabbed Dad's arm and lined up behind the bridal party. I only had a couple seconds before the service was to begin, but I closed my eyes anyway, to invite Mama to my special day. "Help me to be calm," I asked. Then I walked down the aisle of St. John's church, arm in arm with Dad.

Aunt Geraldine played the organ while Jude sang "On This Day Oh Beautiful Mother." I nearly cried. But I couldn't help but smile as my husband's aunts and uncles (also a part of the choir) played guitar and sang "Put Your Hand in the Hand of the Man Who Stilled the Waters" as Bryan and I proceeded out of the church. Our friends and relatives greeted us in the sunshine of the great outdoors. Many of my mother's family said that they couldn't believe how much I resembled my mother. Uncle Homer told me I looked as pretty as my mother had on her wedding day. Aunt Geretha said that every time she saw me while I was growing up it was like watching my mother grow up all over again. (My dad's family had been close neighbors of my mother's family.) Later on at the reception, I was talking with a group of people and when I left them, Aunt Geretha called me over to her table. "I could hear you talking and laughing with your friends and not only do you look like your mother, you talk and laugh just like her, too." I squeezed my aunt's hand. "Thanks for letting me know," I said. To me it was a sign from my mother, telling me that she was with me on my wedding day.

For the summer months, Bryan and I lived close to home. He worked construction. In August we moved to Wisconsin, where he was enrolled in the Industrial Arts Program at Green Bay's Wisconsin Technical Institute. Meanwhile, I'd been all over the city applying for just about any kind of job. Then one day I got a visit from a friend of mine. She'd heard on the radio that they fired all the janitors at the public schools because of labor disputes. They were replacing the workers on a first-come, first-serve basis. I hurried down to the unemployment office and was hired on the spot. My title was janitress. I was happy to finally be working because we were so broke. But even with the money I earned, it was barely enough to live on. One day my dad stopped by on his way to Chicago. The only thing I could offer him was a cup of instant coffee and our last crust of bread. I felt foolish. When he left I found two dollars under his coffee cup and a ten-dollar bill under his saucer. That night Bryan and I treated ourselves to a movie with pop and popcorn.

The following Friday it was snowing when I left for work. By the time I drove the eight miles to the school, I knew the trip back to our apartment after work would be difficult. My shift didn't end until

11 p.m. At four o'clock the snowy conditions had turned into a major blizzard. Many of the local businesses in the area were closing for the evening. Every now and then, a fellow worker would holler that the storm was getting worse. I'd panic, because I didn't want to spend the night at the school.

I looked at the big clock. Another hour and I'd be off work and on my way home. By now more than two feet of snow had fallen since I'd left for work. Along with the snow, the wind had increased. The new-fallen snow had drifted halfway up the entrance doors of the building. Our cars in the parking lot looked like they'd be there until spring. One of the men tried to push the doors open but was only able to open them a few inches. We were told to use the other entrances if we had to get out of the school in a hurry. I knew no one would be going any-where if a plow didn't come to our rescue.

My thoughts went to Bryan. I knew he'd be worried about me. Hearing the plows going by on the main road in front of the school gave me hope that I'd soon be with my husband, snuggled together in the warmth and safety of our small apartment. But soon my hopes were dashed when a radio report said that police were asking everyone who did not absolutely have to be on the roads to stay off of them. By now, many of the workers had decided to spend the night at the school; some were already enjoying the swimming pool, while others were shooting baskets in the gym.

A single mother of two had left her children with a sitter. She didn't have a phone at home to get in touch with them, so she was desperate to get home. Some of us who also wanted to leave took turns shoveling the driveway to the main road, but our efforts were fruitless because not only had the winds increased, the snow was now wet and heavy. "We have to call the police," the mother cried. "I have to get home!" With that plea, our boss called the authorities. At 2 a.m. a plow rescued us. I debated taking the same route that she was taking. It was a longer route, but more traveled. I concluded that I would follow the woman, but at the last second I turned left instead of right. My car began to fishtail. "Oh, dear Jesus, help me," I prayed. The street had been plowed but was already drifted across in many places. Soon my wipers were thick with ice and snow. I wanted to stop to clean them, but visibility was so bad I decided that I shouldn't pull off; I wasn't sure if I was even on the proper side of the road, so I kept going.

Between each gust of wind, I was able to see a red glow from a neon sign, which seem to beckon me onward. When I got closer, I realized the light was from a bar sign located about three miles from our apartment. I took a deep breath. "You're going to make it!" I said to myself as I continued to pray. Then, from out of the corner of my eye, I saw someone running. It looked like the person had waved their arms, as if trying to flag me down. I went a bit further before I was able to stop. Although I hadn't seen any other car lights, I suspected that someone had gone in the ditch further up the road. Finally bringing the car to a stop, I pushed the door against the wind and opened it. The snow stung against my face as I looked back for the person. I could see someone running toward me. I thought it was a mirage, but it really was *Bryan* who came into view. I thought I was imagining him there. But soon his arms were around me. "Oh, hon," he said, "I've been so worried about you. I thought that you might be in the ditch, and maybe even hurt."

"It's the blizzard of the decade, the weather man said. You could have been hit by a car."

"I haven't seen any other cars," he said as we held each other tight, right there on the wrong side of the road.

"Let's get out of this nasty stuff," he said. As we drove slowly away, with Bryan at the wheel, I knew we still might end up in the ditch or stuck in the middle of the road, but my cares were now over, knowing he was by my side.

Catherine came to live with us that spring. With my sister around, Bryan didn't feel as guilty about studying all the time. She got a job at the school where I worked. It was a blast having her with me. Sometimes we were both assigned to work on the same floor, but in different rooms. While she was washing the blackboards in a classroom on the third floor one night, I crept up on her and scared her something awful. The next night she got me back. She locked me in the little dark room — the photo developing room. Neither of us could relax at work after those two nights. We were always on guard. I missed her after Bryan graduated and we moved to Chicago and she went back home.

Bryan had been deferred from the draft to attend college. The Vietnam war was still in progress, and though we hoped and prayed that he'd never get called, he got his draft notice in September. He left for Fort Leonard Wood, Missouri in October of '72 for his basic training. I moved back to Michigan, alternating my stays between my mother-in-law's place and my dad's.

Following basic training, Bryan went to Fort Polk, Louisiana for advanced schooling. On his twentieth birthday he called to let me know that he'd soon be leaving for his permanent assignment in Germany. Although we both felt sad that he wasn't going to be stateside, we were relived that he wasn't going to 'Nam. Germany was a place where I'd be able to join him. We were excited about that and thrilled he'd be able to spend a couple weeks at home before going overseas.

Bryan looked stunning in his uniform when he walked off the plane in Escanaba. I ran to him. A million butterflies seemed to be doing cartwheels within my stomach. Unfortunately, the two weeks zoomed by. When he left for Germany, a zillion bees seemed to be attacking my heart. As he boarded the plane, my throat tightened. I felt my world was coming to an end. I was determined to stay focused on Bryan's last words.

"I'll be the first husband to send for his wife. You can count on that!"

Twenty-Eight
ल्ह

My heart and every artery running to it seemed thickened with mercury, my mind poisoned by my thoughts as I walked down the road that I'd walked down so many times as a youth. I'd been a lover of life, born with the gift of joy and love for people. Yet now, here I was on a mental precipice debating death over life. I didn't want to physically see, hear or touch another person again. Fear and worry had conquered me, and whether I liked it or not they were running my life without opposition. I was defenseless against their power. Like a killer virus they'd taken up host within me, creating an erosion of my life's dreams and visions. Fear and worry were dictating what I would or wouldn't do each and every minute of each and every day. They kept me from my responsibilities, the very responsibilities I'd once enjoyed. I was like a prisoner confined to four walls, spending most of my time in my bedroom. This day, I'd forced myself to go walking

225

despite the fact that the spring weather resembled early winter. With my "I don't care what happens to me" attitude, I walked more relaxed than I'd had in years, as the freezing rain stung against my face. "Why am I pregnant?" I scolded myself. "Wasn't I the one that was going to adopt my kids?"

With the confirmation that I was indeed pregnant, past conversations that I'd overheard as a young girl began cluttering my mind. By the time I left the doctor's office and made it to my car, facts of both my mother and my grandmother's early deaths came to the front of my mind, illuminating stories told by aunts, uncles, cousins, friends and acquaintances. There was no other way to interpret the conversations other than that giving birth could mean death for me, and maybe for my child, too. Did I want to risk my life? Did I want to risk leaving my baby to be raised without a mother like my siblings and I had been, and my mother before us? Besides, over the years, I'd heard women talk about having babies and none of them ever said delivering a child was easy. Most thought at one point during the process that they were dying.

With the genetic make-up that I'd inherited from my mother, death by pregnancy seemed probable. Of all my sisters, it was me who people thought resembled my mother most. Throughout the years they'd told me I smiled and laughed like my mother, and walked and talked like her, too. I'd heard it said time and time again, especially by my mother's siblings. Dad, too, had referred to me as being "all LaMarche," referring to my mother's family. It was obvious that my mother had contributed more to my gene pool than my father had. If her physical characteristics could be passed on to me, along with Benign Familiar Tremor (my shaking disease), I was certain I'd also inherited the gene for an early death.

Leaving my baby behind to be cradled in the arms of another after having grown up without my own mother was depressing. I still hadn't dealt with the emotional trauma from the separation and loss.

The more I thought about the idea of dying, the more the tears rolled down my face. Fear of dying was so frightening that the thought of having an abortion entered my mind. After all, the main story in the news each day was a woman's right to an abortion, which had just been put into law during the month of January.

"Oh my gosh, look how far I've walked!" I said to myself, noticing that I was in front of the Tarzalli home, which was nearly five miles from my dad's. Covered completely with sleet, I turned around. "Dad is probably wondering where I am." I picked up the pace as the sleet continued to sting against my face and stick to my eyelashes as I headed home. "I must be crazy to be out here in this freezing cold without a hat or gloves, wearing tennis shoes and constantly talking to myself." But the more I tried not to think about it, the more my mother's death invaded my thoughts.

Monica and Anna were getting off the school bus as I neared the driveway. Anna was now a senior in high school and Monica a sophomore, though they both looked more like junior high kids, since they were so petite. "You look so sad," Monica said as she and Anna came walking toward me.

"And you're frozen," Anna remarked grabbing my hand. The aroma of pumpkin pies greeted us as we entered the house. My sisters tossed their books onto the table and hurried to get themselves some. Normally I could've eaten two or three pieces, but even the smell of it was making me nauseated. As nighttime came, I figured I'd sleep better than I had been because of my long walk, but again like so many other nights, I was awakened by a nightmare. "Grenade!" I screamed, which brought Dad running.

"What the hell's going on in here?" he asked, turning on the light. "You dreaming? Waking a man during the night when he has to be to work in the morning."

"Sorry, Dad," I said, feeling foolish for having awakened him.

The dream had seemed so real. A grenade had hit Bryan while he was in his bunker. I was glad when morning arrived and the dream slowly faded from my mind. Later that morning, I left Dad's and went to the cemetery. I parked the car, and then trampled through the fresh new snow to my mother's grave. I stood there trying to tell her my troubles, like I'd done so many times in the past. But this day she didn't seem present. I couldn't trust that she was really listening to me and hearing what I needed to say. But I knew who would listen. I knew who did care. His concern for me was still fresh in my memory. So I made my way to Jim's grave. Yes, he was dead, but I could still visualize him, as if he still belonged to the earth. The memory of him was very much with me, his coming and going from our house with the laces of his big Sorrels untied, his brown eyes and curly black hair, his gruff voice and his unique facial expressions. It was *he* who I needed to talk to, not Mama. So there I stood at the foot of his grave.

"Hi... Jim... I still miss you... Dad does, too. He keeps playing the song 'Carroll County Accident.' He hasn't been the same since your accident. Last fall he starting painting the house, but he never finished it. This morning he told me that he's only planting a small garden this year. He quit working in the woods. He got a job at the Fayette State Park... Catherine said that you appeared to her... It freaked me out! Since then, I've been afraid that you're going to appear to me...

"Suppose you know I'm going to have a baby... I'm afraid I'm going to die having it... Oh, 'don't worry'... That's easy for you to say... I'm sure I'd be thinking like you, if I was where you're at... How dare you tell me to 'Have faith.' You couldn't even make it one day without drinking! You just had to have that liquor! You just had to drink and drive! Even my dad told you several times not to drink and drive, but did you listen? NO! You didn't care about anyone but yourself... That's right, just yourself... You didn't think for one second what it might be like for the rest of us if something were to happen to you. Did you?

"Oh, I'm sorry, Jim, I didn't mean to say all those things... I don't know what's gotten into me lately. It's just that I'm so depressed, and... "

Suddenly, I fell limp to the ground upon Jim's grave. There I lay, sobbing. I was searching through my coat pockets for more Kleenex when someone in a car going by beeped. The sound of the horn startled me. "Oh, my gosh. People are going to think I'm crazy lying on this snow-covered grave." I stood up, brushed off my pants and jacket, then headed to my car. I sat for a few minutes warming my fingers before driving away.

When I got to my mother-in-law's she handed me a letter from Bryan. He wrote to tell me that, though there wasn't any on-post housing available, he'd found us a small apartment located in the city of Goeppingen. Since he'd learned of me being pregnant he was desperate to find us a place. Our letters continued back and forth, both of us filled with excitement at our eventual reunion. Anna was soon to graduate from high school, so I decided I'd leave for Germany a couple days after her graduation in May.

Twenty-Nine
CR

Graduation day for Anna was approaching, so Monica and I went to town to buy graduation gifts for her. We were looking at some of the clothes in the Neisner's store when Bobbi Lou came walking up to us. "Are you girls lost?" she chuckled. We were happy to see her. She was a favorite cousin of ours, always friendly and upbeat. She'd always stayed in touch with us after our mother's death.

"How have you girls been?" she asked.

"Donna Jean is going to have a baby," Monica blurted. "But she's leaving for Germany, so I won't get to see the baby until it's almost a year old."

"You don't look too excited about it," she said lifting my chin in a motherly way. "It's your first one, so you're scared, right?" Before I had time to answer, she placed my hand on her stomach and said, "Guess what's going on in here?"

My eyes lit up. "You're having *another* baby?" I asked, surprised.
She laughed. "The good Lord continues to bless me."

Without thinking, I blurted, "But aren't you afraid of dying one of these times?"

"Oh my gosh! You're not excited about having a baby because you're afraid you'll die like your mother did." I nodded, as tears filled my eyes. She gave my hand a squeeze. "That was years ago. Doctors are smarter today and better equipped. Don't dwell on such a thing. Instead, think about the beautiful baby growing within you. Why, I bet you've been so worried that you haven't even started thinking about names."

"Actually I have," I chuckled.

"And?" she said, putting her hand behind her ear and bringing it forward. "I'm waiting."

"Jacques, if it's a boy and Onna Rose, for a girl."

She put a thumb and index finger across her chin. "Those are beautiful names." Then she smiled and said, "Maybe you'll be able to use them both."

I laughed. "I hope it's not twins. I'll die for sure," I said as we parted ways. An hour later as we were leaving the store, we noticed that Bobbi Lou was also just leaving.

"No more worrying now," she said. "God has us in the palm of His hands. So relax and enjoy Germany and be looking forward to that little bundle of joy."

On the way home Monica was mad because she had lost some of the money Matthew had given her to spend. She'd taken a tissue from her pants pocket and the twenty-dollar bill had evidently fallen out. I tried to listen to her complain, but Bobbi Lou's words about God having us in the palm of His hands kept running through my mind. They were comforting. I felt at peace for the first time since finding out that I was going to be a mother.

Following Anna's graduation ceremony at the school, she and

Monica left with friends to attend parties that some of the other gradu- ates were having at their homes. Dad, Bernadette, Terry and I went down to the local bar to eat. We had no sooner been served our drinks than someone came running over to our table to tell us that a car had just hit Anna. "It doesn't look good. It's just up the road a couple miles," the guy exclaimed. Within a couple minutes we were at the accident site. Anna was lying in the road in a semi-comatose state. She was moaning. One of her legs was twisted in a weird position. The village ambulance was already there. "Who did this to her?" Dad demanded. "Come on now, I want an answer." No one said a word.

"Let's get her to the hospital!" I shouted to Dad and the attendants. "We can find out that other stuff later."

I rode in the back of the ambulance with Anna and Francis, an at- tendant. As the driver took off to the hospital, Anna kept talking, but she wasn't making any sense; nor was she acting like her shy self. She kept hugging and kissing Francis throughout the thirty-mile journey. When we finally arrived at the hospital, the ambulance stalled, right at the emergency entrance. "That's what you call a close call," the driver said. After Anna had been taken out of the vehicle, the driver tried to restart the ambulance, but was unable to. When I walked into the emergency room doorway, I looked back and saw the two atten- dants lifting the hood of the ambulance. A nurse directed me to the waiting room. I was relieved to see Dad, Bernadette and Monica. All three were standing by the doorway waiting for me. "Where's Terry?" I asked.

"Terry?" Dad asked, seeming confused as to why I'd even men- tioned his name and not Anna's.

"The bathroom!" Bernadette said. "How's Anna? Is she going to make it?"

Monica's hand gripped onto mine. "She's not going to die, is she?"

"All I can say is that she was talking mumble-jumble on the way here. The nurse said that the doctor would let us know her condition as soon as possible." We all sat down and took a deep breath. I told them how it seemed to take forever to get to the hospital and how the ambulance had stalled just as we'd arrived.

"How are they going to get back home?" Dad asked.

"They're trying to get the ambulance started right now, but they said it's probably useless. Francis thinks that the battery is dead. They're going to come and check on Anna's condition before they leave."

No sooner had I said that, when they walked into the waiting room. "Any news?" Francis asked.

"Not a word," Dad said, and then he proceeded to ask if they'd gotten the ambulance started.

"It won't budge," the driver said. "It's the battery. She's dead."

"She's dead? Oh, no!" Terry said as he walked in on the tail-end of the conversation."

"Not Anna," Bernadette said, almost in a whisper, taking his arms from around her. "They're talking about the ambulance — the battery! It quit working just as they arrived." Terry fell into a chair. I could see the relief on his face. Within seconds the doctor came rushing into the lobby to tell us that Anna needed to be transferred immediately to Marquette General, a hospital about ninety miles away, equipped to handle serious injuries. The doctor told Dad to go out and get into the front seat of the Manistique ambulance. Dad asked me to go with him as he started to leave. "You aren't allowed to," a nurse said. So I ran and caught up to the doctor who was on a rush to his office. "Please let me go with my dad," I pleaded. "If he had a wife, she'd be going. He doesn't want to be alone."

"Run!" he said. "Catch the ambulance."

I sat in the middle, between Dad and the driver on that terribly foggy night. When we turned onto U.S. 41, the fog was so thick that visibility was only a few feet. Yet the driver continued at a high rate of speed, as if equipped with radar. Dad kept pinching my arm. "Are we going to be next?" he whispered, loudly. I looked at the speedometer. We were going 120 mph! I patted Dad's arm. Further up the road, a car with a camper was overturned and in the ditch. Again, Dad asked if we'd be next. Again, I patted his arm. Anna began cursing with words I'd never heard her say before. "Listen to that mouth on her," Dad said. "Where did she learn such language?"

"At least she's alive!" I told him as I turned slightly around to look at Anna through the little window. She was trying to get off the stretcher, slapping and scratching the two nurses in her attempt. Blood ran from their arms and faces as they fought to keep the IV in her arm. I was relieved when the ninety-mile ride came to an end and we arrived at the hospital. Attendants came running outside to meet us. One of them scolded the driver for not calling the hospital as we entered the city. They took Anna to one of the rooms. Dad was out of it when we arrived and couldn't talk with the nurses about Anna. He couldn't even register her. Instead, he went to the intensive care waiting room and patiently waited with other family members for news of Anna's condition while I took care of the paperwork and such things as granting permission for her clothes to be cut off. When I was leaving the emergency room to join my family in the waiting room, another doctor was arriving to treat the cuts and scratches that the nurses had endured while in route to the hospital.

It wasn't long before a couple doctors stepped in and told us that Anna had been seriously injured. She had a fractured skull, ruptured bladder, cracked pelvis and a broken femur, along with being bruised from head to toe. She needed blood transfusions, but the hospital didn't have a supply of type O on hand. So we patiently waited for donors, worrying that the blood she needed wouldn't arrive on time.

One by one, my siblings arrived and were given the latest news on Anna's condition. By mid morning I was beginning to feel hopeless because her condition was still critical. It was about this time when our hometown priest, Father Tim, walked into the ICU. I was so grateful that he had come to see Anna. He administered the sacrament of the Anointing of the Sick to her, and from that time on, I felt much more confident that she was going to be okay. In fact, at that point, I put Anna's healing into God's hands.

For the first two nights I remained at the hospital, occasionally sleeping on the carpeted floor behind a chair that Dad had claimed as his. On the morning of the third day the doctor reassured our family that Anna was out of danger, but would eventually need to be put in a body cast and go through a lot of physical therapy. After hearing the good news, Dad took me back home to get my belongings so that I could leave for Germany. Later that afternoon he and I left for Escanaba, where I planned to catch the Greyhound to Chicago. At the corner gas station, where we stopped to fill up, I noticed Janet in a car parked on the other side of the pump. "Oh, my gosh, Dad, that's Janet!" I said. "I'll be right back."

I knocked on her car window and felt a bit foolish for scaring her. She was sitting in the middle of the seat and reached over and rolled down the window. "Janet, how have you been? I haven't seen you in so long. How are your babies?"

"They're great," she said, without any of her usual giddiness and joy.

"Are you okay?" She ignored my question and asked me how Anna was doing

"The doctors said she's going to make it."

"That was a close call for her."

"Oh, Janet, I'm pregnant! And I'm so scared," I said, hoping she'd give me encouraging words, like Bobbi Lou had.

"You always said you were going to adopt your kids because of what happened to your mother."

"I know, but it just happened!"

"You know, I could never *truly* imagine what your family went through without a mother, but now that I have kids of my own, I cringe at times thinking about what it must have been like for your family without her. I hope my kids never have to grow up without me."

"How old is your baby now?"

"He's seven months and Robbie is two."

"Hey!" Dad hollered, "If you're going to catch your bus, we better get going!"

"Bus?" Janet asked, inquisitively.

"Oh, Janet," I said, reaching for her hand, "I'm leaving for Chicago for a couple days and then on to Germany where Bryan's stationed."

"Well, aren't you lucky. You're going to see the world. Have fun," she said as I turned and walked away.

"Was that the Bouchard girl you used to always stay with when you were younger?" Dad asked as we drove away.

"That's Janet," I said, "But she sure has changed. She wasn't her giddy and teasing self. But she's probably just tired. Her boys are just over a year apart."

"Quiet for a minute," he said, as he turned on the car radio. "I want to get the five o'clock news. They've been having updates about Anna's condition." I lay my head against the back of the seat and played through my brief conversation with Janet before falling asleep.

"Hey," Dad said, nudging my arm a few miles from Escanaba. "If you keep sleeping now, you're not going to be able to on that long bus ride." I opened my eyes. I heard Anne Murray singing her song "What About Me." It was as if Anna was saying the words. Tears filled my eyes. I tried to hold them back and was successful until we pulled into the bus station.

"I don't want to leave Anna behind," I said sniffling, as I took my suitcase from the car.

"She'll be fine," Dad said as he shook my hand good-bye and told me to hold my head high until he saw me again.

Thirty
℘

It was only by the grace of God that I managed to board the 747
Lufthansa Airline to Germany. So much had taken place back home
during my bus trip to Chicago that I contemplated not leaving the
country. Before leaving for O'Hare airport, I'd put on the television at
Luke's place. His wife Bonnie had gone outside for a couple minutes
to help her neighbor carry a bench into her house. To occupy myself,
I was flipping through the channels trying to find the Chicago news.
Suddenly I was jolted by what I was hearing. They were reporting how
a deputy sheriff from the village of Garden, in Michigan's Upper Peninsula, had killed his wife and their two young sons. Instantly, I knew
my kindred spirit friend Janet and her sons were dead. Her husband
was the Deputy Sheriff of Garden. Within minutes her picture came
over the air. Authorities already believed that the crime was premedi-
tated and that her husband, Dennis, was responsible. He had set fire to

their house, burning his family beyond recognition.

By the time Bonnie came back into the house, I was in shock. One look at me and she knew I'd found out what she'd been trying to keep from me until I arrived in Germany and was with Bryan. I realized then that had been the reason she'd played canasta with me all morning instead of doing her normal routine. Together we continued to get the details of the murders. After setting the house on fire, Janet's husband had driven to the fire hall. On a wall, using a tube of Janet's lipstick, he'd written, 'I WILL KILL YOU MURPHY BUT FIRST YOUR WIFE AND KIDS.' He'd also disconnected the distributor hoses of both fire trucks before handcuffing himself to a backhoe behind the building.

As the news continued, another anchorman told how members of the Garden fire department had freed Dennis, thinking he was also a victim. Before long, Janet's graduation picture came on the screen, along with their wedding picture. The newsman told how Janet's parents were devastated when learning of the crime, yet her father, not knowing at the time that it was Dennis who had murdered his daughter and grandsons, accompanied his son-in-law by ambulance to the hospital. When the reporter choked up for a second before he could continue on, I lost it! Especially when he said that Janet's father had no idea that the hands he held were the hands of the murderer. He'd been told the FBI's findings only a few hours after returning from the hospital.

As John and his wife, Annette, drove me to O'Hare airport, I felt a part of me was dying. I couldn't understand why Dennis would do such a thing. He had always been such a gentle and loving person. I felt I was carrying a million pound weight in my handbag as I went through customs and boarded the plane. I found my assigned seat, which was next to a man in an Army uniform. I managed a slight smile and sat down, buckled up and got ready for take-off. He looked out the window as we started down the runway. Although I sat silently throughout the take-off, to my surprise, I loved the excitement of the speed and the floating feeling as we ascended into the air. I peeked over the guy's shoulder and enjoyed the awesome sights. But my apparent thrill at take-off was soon overcome by the monotony of not seeming to move and that got me thinking again of Janet being murdered.

Though my calmness during take-off might have mislead the soldier for a while as to whether or not I'd flown before, I'm sure it didn't take long for him to know the truth. I had to observe the way others were doing things before I could do them myself, like the oxygen mask, finding the restroom, how to put the little tray in front of me down and the seat back. Then when the stewardess asked if I'd like to watch a movie, I replied, "Yes," but didn't give her the money needed for the headset rental. The soldier ordered a set for me and paid for them, too. I felt like a Class A idiot as I thanked him for his kindness. I was grateful that my flight to Frankfurt was nonstop. I was sure, after not being able to figure out the littlest of things, that I'd definitely get lost even in the smallest of airports if I ever had to switch planes.

All my thoughts and cares of Janet and her family and Anna and her condition, along with my lonesomeness for everyone back home disappeared when I spotted Bryan at the airport. I smiled and started running toward him. When he saw me he put his fist up in celebration and came running toward me, also. When we met I jumped up on him, hugging my legs around his waist. I was kissing his face all over, as he was mine, when I noticed two guys looking at us. "Oh, don't worry about them," Bryan said. "They're just my friends." He set me down and looked me over. "Man have I missed you!" he said as he grabbed me and embraced me once again. He turned me around, put his arm around my back, and then introduced me to his friends. The first one was Sgt. Merrelli, whom he'd paid to take him to the airport to pick me up. Chip, another friend, had just come along for the ride. We visited only briefly when Bryan said, "Let's go! I can't wait to get home."

As we got into the sergeant's sports car, I knew Bryan was unaware of my sister's accident or Janet and her son's murders. What I was unaware of was that there weren't any speed limits on the German highways. Already stressed to the max, I had no clue that I was about to go for the ride of my life. Thinking Sgt. Merrelli was showing off by going 100 mph, plus some, I got closer and closer to Bryan as if being nearer to him would safeguard me from injury if we were to collide with another crazy driver. The faster we went, the sicker I became. Bryan kept kissing my cheek, smiling and staring at me, and on and off he'd rub his hand over my stomach, which didn't look at all pregnant. I couldn't help but smile back despite feeling mentally, emotionally and physically exhausted. All I really wanted was his presence and a place to lie down after having been cramped up for so long. By the rate of speed we were going, I knew I'd soon be in my glory.

The four hours of travel flew by. Soon we came to the city of Goeppingen, where we'd be living for the next eighteen months. Sgt. Merrelli slowed as we entered the city. I was amazed to see things like a grocery store next to a goat barn, next to a house, next to a gas station. Every inch of the earth was in use, if not for a building, for crops or flowers. At the busiest intersection, Sgt. Merrelli peeled into a narrow driveway and hit the brakes. We jerked forward. "Here we are," he said. Bryan thanked Sgt. Merrelli for picking me up and getting us to our place, then we said good-bye and they took off.

Bryan took my hand and led me up the three flights of narrow stairs. My head was pounding by the time he unlocked our apartment door. We passed through a kitchenette and then into an L shaped area. I saw a settee (like a small narrow day bed) and lay upon it. Bryan lay next to me and put his arm around me. Fastened to the wall was a small half-lamp fixture with an attached string. I pulled the string on and off a dozen times or so, not saying a word. Finally I asked, "Was that a refrigerator I saw in the other room?"

"It's the biggest I've seen thus far," Bryan said, with a smirk on his face, as if he knew I was going to inquire about its three-foot height.

"What is the little tank over the old fashion sink for?"

"Oh, that! It's the hot water tank. It holds three gallons!"

"Why does it look like we're in an attic?"

"Because we are!" he laughed.

There were only a few feet of head clearance in our new home. The bathroom was down a flight of stairs. It was a very small room with only a sink and stool. "Isn't there a tub or shower?" I asked, hoping to soon take a hot bath.

"There's a tub in this room," he said, opening a door and grabbing out a small plastic container that I knew I'd barely fit into. "This is for us, only us," he explained, "But we have to share the bathroom with the two apartments on this floor." He then explained that a single man in his mid-thirties from Czechoslovakia, occupied one of the apartments, while another man from Hungary, also in his mid-thirties, lived in the other apartment. I couldn't help but notice all the cases of Heineken stacked next to their doors.

"How many apartments are on the first floor?" I asked.

"None. The bottom floor is where our landlady and landlord's business is. They sell dental equipment. Their home is about five miles away I guess."

"Are there any other wives here?" I asked, hoping to have someone to be around when Bryan was at work or had to leave the area on field maneuvers.

"So far, I'm the only private from Company A that found a place to live."

"So, I'm the only wife over here?"

"Yes, didn't I promise you'd be the first to cross the ocean?" he asked as he squeezed my hand with excitement. "You'll get to meet some of my buddies after we come back from field duty. And for the next ten days you're mine, all mine!"

Ten days later, Bryan left with Company A for two weeks. I knew no one. I was afraid of being alone because there was no one to turn to if something were to go wrong with the baby or me. Other than our landlady and landlord, I hadn't met anyone. I couldn't speak any German, so I didn't dare leave our apartment, worried that if I got lost I wouldn't be able to ask directions how to get back home.

The first three days I had no appetite, so I didn't eat a thing. The only times I got out of bed were to use the bathroom. Although I'd never been a sufferer of headaches, my head throbbed constantly. Finally, on the third day, unable to cope with the throbbing any longer and feeling terribly weak, I crawled to the refrigerator. Despite the nausea, I drank some juice and ate a slice of bread. I lay there on the floor, next to the refrigerator, until I began to feel better. For the remainder of my time alone I forced myself to eat on a regular basis so that I wouldn't harm my baby.

The only time I'd talked to my landlady was the day I'd arrived. But I ventured down the stairs to tell her that she didn't need to hire a cleaning woman to wash down the stairwell, as she had planned to do. I told her I was capable of doing the job for myself and that I'd be scrubbing them later that morning. Just as I was finishing, she came up the stairs and handed me a large salted pretzel and a beer she'd bought for me.

"Jus in time. You must eat ta keep yer energy up," she said, in broken English. She noticed my hesitation as I reached to take the beer and pretzel from her. "Don't vorry bout tis bier. All peoples in Deutchland drinks bier cause dis vater, it tis not goot. Dis bier ist fur vomem who are having a baby. It tis safe fer drinking."

Though it was hard to understand her, I was glad to finally be talking with someone. She was the first person I'd talked to in nearly a week. The only other contact came through letters from home. My mother-in-law sent me the newspaper articles to keep me posted regarding Janet and her children's murder. I'd glean the papers by day and fear what I'd read by night. I wanted to call home, but doing so was not an option; the cost was forty dollars every three minutes, nearly an eighth of our monthly income.

Without Bryan, both the days and the nights continued to tick by. I'd lie awake at night for hours before falling asleep. Only a handful of times had I ever slept alone in a bed. Even after Bryan left for the service I'd always managed to sleep with a sister or two. One morning at 4 a.m., I was frustrated because I hadn't slept a wink, so I went to the couch and grabbed Bryan's extra Army blanket. I rolled it up and placed it under the covers on my bed. I hugged it tightly and was finally able to drift off to sleep. Other nights I couldn't sleep because of being so petrified. One article reported that her husband had struck her on the head with a heavy object just prior to setting the house on fire. The windows of our attic apartment were in the ceiling, one right above my bed. I'd always enjoyed seeing the stars at night, but the only thing now I saw in the window was the face of Janet being struck by every object imaginable.

Knowing the men on the second floor were home when Bryan was gone brought little comfort. The smell of sauerkraut or other concoctions they cooked would usually rise up to our apartment. Being nauseous was a given on those days. But that wasn't the worse thing of them being home. I felt vulnerable. I feared one of them would find an excuse to come up to my apartment and do something to me. Other than the window, there was only one way in and out of our place, so if that were to happen, I didn't know what I'd do.

Thirty-One
CR

The weekend following field duty Bryan invited his friends from the base over for a party. The GIs brought in cases of booze, beer, mix and cartons of American cigarettes. (I would soon learn that they hated the tasteless German cigarettes.) They also took along an album by Susan Raye and played a song for Bryan and me called "Pitty Pitty Patter of the Little Bitty Feet," referring to our baby that was on the way. It made me excited about having a baby, knowing that they were all looking forward to "Pomeroy" (as they referred to my husband) having a kid. Though, when I first arrived, Bryan told me that the guys thought their fun with him would be over. But at our party, despite the small space, when I grabbed Bryan to do the polka with me, they were thrilled. Soon they were all getting their turn for a few seconds. None of them had had any contact with a woman in months, so they were also grateful when I cooked for them and listened to their stories from home. Our apartment soon became a haven on the weekends for the GIs, since there wasn't any other place off base for them to hang out.

Party after party took place, from Friday night until Sunday afternoon. Two things bothered me about the parties, my lack of privacy and that I was the only woman. A couple months later, Steve Maly's wife, Dusty, and son, Steven Lee, arrived. Steve sent for them even though he was unable to find an apartment. He knew once they arrived that the American Housing officials would be forced to put his name at the top of the list for a place to live. However, until an apartment became available, we invited them to stay with us. Our couch, which could also serve as a futon, became a bed by night for the three of them.

My Cat (its given name), had also accompanied Dusty and Steven Lee from Los Angeles. The cat was retarded and blind and would oftentimes run into walls or other objects. Bryan welcomed our California friends, but My Cat was another story. Day by day it did things to irritate Bryan. It occasionally mistook a rug or shirt, or some other piece of clothing for its' litter box. The stench it left was unbearable. No matter what we used to clean up the mess, the odor stayed. The only way we could get rid of the smell was by throwing out the items, which ticked Bryan off. The worst day, though, was the morning the guys were getting in their dress greens to take part in a military parade. Bryan threatened to throw the cat out the third story window after he found doo-doo in his dress shoes.

Needless to say, the day an apartment became available for the Maly family, we celebrated. Yet, we were glad they'd gotten a place only three miles away. They were part of our new family. We continued to spend time together, especially on the weekends. Either they'd come to stay overnight at our place or we'd spend it at theirs. Whenever the guys left the area for field duty, which was usually every couple months for a month at a time, I spent the entire time at Dusty's place. It made it easier for her little boy. During one of these times,

245

Steve was allowed to stay back at the base because of a back injury. I was glad since I was then seven and a half months pregnant and knew if I needed a man's help that he'd be available. Plus, he saved us the long walk each day to the base for mail call. On the day before Bryan was to return, Steve came in with a letter for me. It was from home, so I was anxious to read it. When I stood from the couch to take it, the baby kicked. I grabbed my stomach. "What's wrong?" Steve asked.

"Just another jab."

"Thank goodness," he exclaimed. "Don't be going into labor when Bryan isn't here." The weather was getting colder, which left their place a bit chilly. As I lay on the couch, Steve covered me with a quilt. "Let me tuck these covers under your feet, too," he offered, just as Dusty walked into the room.

"You big jerk," she said, with a cocked smile and giving him a slug in the arm. "You never do nice things like that for me, and I'm pregnant!"

"Well, Donna has the chills, plus she's almost eight months. You're only five," he said as he lay down on the other couch. I looked at the return address on the envelope. "Ah, from Monica," I said to myself. I always enjoyed letters from her and Anna. They were like a shot of penicillin when I was sick. Anna always gave me updates on her progress in physical therapy. Getting a letter from her was comforting in knowing that she was all right and doing better since her accident. On the other hand, Monica's letters were of fun stuff. She talked about school and how she loved being a Pom-Pom girl. One time it surprised me when she told me how she and a couple girlfriends had bought some Boone's Farm and they'd gotten all tipsy.

I got myself more comfortable on the couch and slowly opened my letter, savoring it, like my sisters and I had done with the unwrapping of Christmas presents. I was excited because I could tell by the thickness of the letter that it was nice and long; I hated getting one pagers. I unfolded the yellow lined papers, made one last maneuver of the pillows beneath my head and began to read.

> Dear Donna Jean,
>
> Hope all is okay with you. Do you have a name picked out for the baby yet? I think you're going to have a little girl... I hate to be the bearer of bad news but I have to tell you that Aunt Geraldine died of a heart attack a while back. So Jude is motherless now, too!

I couldn't believe what I'd read. The words were blunt and to the point. They stuck to my mind like feathers to honey. "How could this be?" I asked myself as my eyes welled with tears. My brother was only thirteen. The last thing I wanted for him was to be motherless like the rest of us. He still needed a mother very much. Disgusted, I quit reading the letter, quietly folded it, and then slipped it under my pillow.

"That bad, huh?" Steve asked, intuitively knowing it must contain bad news. I couldn't respond. I turned onto my other side and buried my head into the pillow. Realizing that I'd have to answer a bunch of curiosity questions if I didn't regain my composure, I quickly turned back toward him. I wasn't used to talking about my troubles. I'd learned as a child to throw my worries and cares into the cellar of my mind. So instead of answering him honestly, I asked if he was hoping for a girl or for another boy. He hadn't even answered before Dusty stepped back into the room to tell us supper was ready.

"Everything okay at home?" she asked as we sat around the table. I nodded, but didn't dare make eye contact.

"Something's wrong, I can tell. I'm getting to know you. You'd tell us if something were wrong, wouldn't you?" I forced a smile but a tear rolled down my cheek. Both of them became alarmed. I thought I was going to break down and tell them everything, but just then their friend Russ made a couple raps on their door and walked in. "Whatcha got cookin', good lookin'?" he asked Dusty.

"Tacos," she replied, without having to explain what they were, like she'd had to explain them to me.

In my eyes, his visit was perfect timing, a great distraction. But later that evening Dusty asked me if I was ready to talk about whatever it was bothering me. At that moment, since first arriving in Germany, I missed not having television to watch. Being able to turn on "Sonny and Cher," "Bonanza," "Mayberry RFD," or anything else would have been a great distraction. Since I couldn't, I told her some news from home had upset me, but once I'd had a chance to think it over, I was okay with it. In reality, I was not at all okay with my aunt dying so young, but I'd decided ahead of time that my pain would have to wait until bedtime, when I had the privacy to ponder it alone.

After everyone retired for the night, and I figured they were asleep, I turned on the little lamp next to the couch and grabbed the letter from beneath the couch. Quietly I unfolded it. Avoiding the first page with its' bad news, I turned to the next. "It'll be better if I wait until Bryan gets back before I reread that upsetting part," I said to myself, while fighting back the tears. Then, in the dim-lit room I began reading the second page.

> I wish I wouldn't have to tell you this because I know how afraid you are about having a baby, but Dad said we should have wrote and told you a long time ago, but I was afraid to tell you that there has been another tragedy. I sure hope Bryan is there with you right now as you read this letter. Our precious cousin, Bobbi Lou, died about ten days after Aunt Geraldine. Wayne Sr. and Wayne Jr. rushed her to the hospital during the night because she was having difficulty breathing. Sadly, she died before they got there. They'd stopped on the way to give her CPR, but unfortunately both she and the baby died. The baby was a little boy. Needless to say, her family is devastated. Our Dad, too, has taken the news hard. It brings back a lot of memories. He's been walking around here like a zombie.

I twisted the letter around and around in my hands until it ripped in half, then threw the pieces across the room. Without expecting it, a devastated wail came out of me, which caused Dusty and Steve to both come running.

"Oh shit," Steve said. "Not now, when Bryan's out in the field!"

"It's not the baby! Look at her. She's crying," Dusty said, spotting the torn paper and picking it up. Then she came over to me and sat down on the floor next to the couch and began putting the letter back together. Just then a knock came on the door. Steve opened it.

"Whadt da hell ya up ta in der. For God's sake, it's tree a.m. ya fools. Can't a person get some sleep 'round here?" It was Zieglenda, their German neighbor and friend who usually spoke her mind.

"Cool it," Steve said, opening the door crack.

"My, God, she's not havin da kid already, is she?"

"No, no, everything's groovy," he said and closed the door, then he returned to bed.

Tears streamed down my face as Dusty began reading the letter. I had zero courage or energy to hold my emotions back. I cried and shared, and cried and shared with them how my own mother had died while giving birth and that her mother had died shortly after the birth of my uncle Elmer. I told her that I feared having inherited the same genetic make-up as my mother because my dad and mother's relatives always thought I resembled my mother most of my five sisters and me.

After talking to Dusty, I felt relieved about my fear. Yet, the very next morning, the reality of Bobbi Lou's death sank in deeper and tightened the noose on my depression. If there was light at the end of my long dark tunnel, I certainly couldn't see it.

As I continued on in my pregnancy, I spent nearly every waking moment living with anxiety. The closer I got to my due date the more depressed I became. Fearing for my baby's life, and my own, too, I was rarely able to get a good night sleep. Many times I'd awaken in total panic, thinking the delivery time had arrived. My friend Sharon, who had arrived a few weeks after Dusty, suspected something was on my mind and had tried to get me to talk also, but I remained silent. Strangely enough, with all my fear of giving birth, Bryan and I had never *once* prepared for the big event. Never had we discussed what we'd do when the time came to leave for the hospital.

Despite cautioning from my friends, I went to Munich to tour the Olympic stadium only two weeks before my due date. Along with Sgt. Merrelli and his wife, Christina, we did the ten-hour round trip in a single day. Three days past my due date the four of us took off again. This time we went to France, to have a French dinner. The trip was eight hours one way. While in France we also visited with a cousin of Christina's who just so happened to be an OB doctor. Before we left for home, he insisted on checking me out. By then it was one in the morning. He was very concerned about the baby and made me promise to lie down on the back seat on the return trip home. So I rested my head on Bryan's lap. We got to our apartment around 10 a.m. the next morning.

The following Friday, Bryan was scheduled for guard duty. He was nervous about leaving our apartment that morning, knowing that I was now nine days overdue. "Can't you get out of it?" I asked in desperation, knowing the inevitable was soon to happen.

"No one, and I mean *no one* gets out of guard duty!" On the way out he told me that he wouldn't be home until well after midnight because his shift at guard duty was after the regular work day.

Around noon, my friends Patti and Sharon came over and the three of us played cards throughout the afternoon. They left for home around four. Shortly afterwards our oil furnace started smoking. I went downstairs to tell the landlord or landlady about it, but they'd already left. I climbed back up the stairs to our apartment and called my friends, but none of them were around either, so I tried messing with the knobs and levers on the oil furnace myself to see what I could do to fix it. The furnace continued to smoke so I hurried down to the second floor apartments to see if one of the men might be able to help, but both of them were also gone. When I returned, the place was filled with smoke. I didn't know what to do, so I turned the heater off.

Outside the temperature was close to zero on this fourteenth day of December. Fierce winds had blown throughout the day and it was beginning to snow. Without heat in the apartment I knew I'd soon be cold. Without other options left, I called Cooke Barracks to ask to speak with Bryan. The sergeant in charge flatly refused my request and actually chuckled as if I was stupid to have asked such a thing. I hung up and tried to think of some other alternative. My landlady and landlord had informed us that they'd be out of the area for the weekend, so again I tried to phone my friends. I was sure that Sharon's husband Don, being mechanically inclined, could fix it if I could get a hold of him. When again there wasn't an answer at any of their homes, I had no choice but to call the barracks again. This time the sergeant was so put off by my calling that he hung up. I was mad! Immediately I called back and asked to speak with the First Sergeant. He had obviously been informed about my previous call and was also annoyed that a *woman* would dare to call for her husband while he was pulling guard duty.

"It's standard military policy, ma'am, that every soldier complete his mission, be it big or be it small. Therefore your request is denied by me also."

"Please," I said, "I'm overdue for a baby and I'm cold and need him to come home and check our furnace. There's something wrong with it."

"Denied!" he shouted in my ear.

As I was hanging up the phone a voice from the past echoed in my mind. "Oh, no you don't, Mr. B," I said to myself as I picked up the phone and redialed the number. When the First Sergeant came back on the line he started giving me more static, so I interrupted him. "Then

I'll see you in a few minutes," I said. "I'll have to sit in your office where it's warm and free from smoke. And, by the way, if I go into labor, remember you won't be able to release Bryan from guard duty, so you'll have to take me to the hospital."

Within an hour Bryan was home and working on the heating system. It ended up being a minor malfunction and soon our apartment was warming up again and getting aired out. Bryan tucked blankets around me, trying to get me warmed up as I lay on the couch. He was so excited to be home that he said he would make us a snack. It was just after eight when I finished eating the banana pudding. As I stood to take the bowl to the sink, my water broke. "Oh, my God!" I screamed. Bryan came from the bedroom area. "It's time!" I hollered, already frantic. Quickly he grabbed the phone to call an ambulance from the base. Unfortunately, the attendants had no idea where we lived and suggested we call a German taxi to bring us to the base. Bryan hung up the phone and began looking through the German directory to find the number.

"Bryan," I yelled, getting up into his face. "If you don't find that number soon, our baby is going to die!"

"I'll find it," he said calmly. "Why don't you lie down until the taxi gets here?"

"You don't get it, do you? If you don't get me to the hospital *right this minute* our baby will die, and probably me, too!"

"You're going to be fine. Just let me find the number and… " WHAM! I'd slapped the book from his hands. In total panic, I shouted. "I can't believe you don't care if the baby and I die!"

Suddenly, Bryan had to do what he'd never done before, something very foreign to him, something he never believed in doing. "Enough!" he hollered as he swatted me gently across the face, startling me. Then he grabbed me and held me tight. "You have to settle down, hon, so I can call for a taxi. Okay?" He lifted my chin with his fingertips and looked me in the eyes and smiled slightly. I nodded and took a seat on the couch.

About a minute later, I heard Bryan ask the person on the other end of the line to send a taxi quickly to *Geislinger Strassa noomber funf*. I left him standing in his underwear and headed down the flights of stairs. By the time I reached ground level, the taxi was waiting and I climbed in. Bryan came out of the apartment buckling up his belt. "You should've waited for me," he scolded as he climbed into the taxi. I didn't say a word because the first contraction was beginning. I yelped out in pain. The taxi driver looked to the back seat. "*Knicks, knicks,*" he said. I knew that was German for, "No, no!" His complaints of me possibly bringing a baby into the world while in his taxi meant nothing. Frankly, at that moment, it didn't matter to me where I was at, in his taxi, eating lunch with the queen of England or touring the Lincoln bedroom at the White House, I was going to do whatever it took to keep my baby and me alive, whether that meant climbing aboard the historical Lincoln bed, forcing Queen Elizabeth to be midwife, or even having my baby on his luscious upholstered seats! Frankly, I didn't care!

As soon as the pain began, it was unbearable. After arriving at the base dispensary, Bryan helped me from the taxi into the dispensary. Dr. Orduba was waiting for me and after a quick exam, verified that the baby would be born within minutes. He told us he'd have to accompany us in the ambulance on the way to the hospital, which was thirty miles away. Two American medics came along and sat up front in the ambulance, one as driver, and the other to help should the baby be born before we could make it to the Stuttgart hospital.

We'd only gone a couple miles before we had to turn around and go back to the base. The blizzard conditions made it impossible for the ambulance to make it up a small incline so the driver said we'd have to go back and get the Red Cross vehicle. I laid on the stretcher in it, but the attendants couldn't get it to lock into place. It kept moving from side to side, so Bryan and the doctor tried to hold it stationary as we maneuvered over the cobblestone streets. My contractions became closer and closer and stronger and longer in duration. Bryan and Dr. Orduba took off my bottom clothes. I hadn't said a single word after leaving the dispensary. I wanted to save all my energy for the birthing process. The contractions kept coming until one was so severe that I thought for sure I was going to die. My mother's death flashed across my mind. I knew without a doubt that I was walking in the same footsteps as she had and her mother before her. I looked into my doctor's eyes and pleaded for him to save me. "You'll be okay," he conveyed in his Indian accent, then told me the hospital was just a minute or so away.

In the nick of time, the doors of the medical facility opened. Minutes later they placed our little bundle upon my stomach. I looked at my son in astonishment. Smiles plastered across Bryan's face and mine. I thought about the prophecy that I'd been carrying around with me since I was a young girl that I'd die if I ever gave birth. I'd die as my mother had died, and her mother before her. I could scarcely believe that I'd made it through the ordeal of bringing our child into the world. It was a miracle! I squeezed Bryan's hand. "Our baby's alive! I'm alive!" I cried. I couldn't keep from smiling. Looking upwards I said to Mama, "Thank you, Mama, oh thank you, for passing on to me faded genes!"

German Born

Dear Wellyn,

I thought it was the end.
Even God could not help
As I bounced along the cobblestone *straßen*
In the back of a Red Cross van.

My body felt like it was tearing at the seams,
My mind like the lid of an overloaded pressure cooker
I was afraid to talk, but afraid not to

Faded Genes

So I asked the doctor to save me.

My hopeless eyes secured themselves
On my beat-up brown shoes and
My past-the-knee polka-dotted socks
I was still wearing.

Another contraction came, with it constant pain
I took a breath, thinking it would be my last
I saw pain and helplessness in your dad's eyes
"We're almost there," the doctor assured.

Upon arrival, the doors opened
The pain vanished.
I counted: *eins, zwei, drei, vier, fümf, sechs, seiben, acht, nuen* and *zehn*.
You had ten fingers and ten toes!

**"Placing *people* before *things* makes the world
a better place to live." – Donna Jean Pomeroy**

Afterword

CR

Today I've come to tend to Mama and Dad's graves. Dad died from skin cancer on October 11, 2004. About two weeks before his death, I sat up with him until three in the morning at his fifth-floor apartment in Escanaba, where he'd been living for three years. Since he wasn't tired, he was busy reminiscing about his earlier years and I was enjoying every minute of it. It's one of my fondest final memories of him. Earlier that evening, Catherine, Anna, Monica and I had taken him to the hospital because his feet were very swollen. He didn't want to go, but when I told him he had no choice, he demanded we make sure that we had the keys to his apartment with us. Yet before we left he had to once again check it out. "Now, do you have apartment keys and the keys to the main door, too?"

"Yes," Monica answered, swinging the keys in front of him.

"I just want to be sure. It's already five o'clock, and the lobby door gets locked for the night at six. I don't want to get back here around midnight and find that we're locked out."

"Well, we have them," Monica assured again, "so let's get going."

Dad's prediction of getting back at midnight was accurate, and he was crabby — with a capital C. And as he also predicted we got locked out of the apartment after I misplaced the keys. Needless to say, when he found out he wasn't too happy. I think he would've given us up for adoption on the spot if he hadn't been so hungry. "I should never have expected anything but this," he complained. We had to buzz another apartment to get the main door open. During this time he continuously crabbed about being starved. "I'm so hungry, my bellybutton is touching my backbone," he said.

The minute we entered his apartment, Anna wheeled him up to the table and the rest of us hurried to his kitchenette. I grabbed some bread and cheese to make him a couple of grilled cheese sandwiches. I saw a small bowl with softened butter in it and spread it out quickly onto the bread while Monica covered it with the cheese. We already had the cast iron frying pan heating up so I placed the sandwiches on it. But as I tried cooking them they kept sticking to the pan and falling apart when I tried to flip them.

"Is that food coming?" Dad hollered.

"What's the problem?" Anna asked, approaching us.

"I don't know, maybe it's this butter," I said as I lifted the small bowl it was in.

"That's not butter!" she blurted out. "That's vanilla pudding I made Dad for lunch!"

We hurried and applied butter to the bread and the sandwiches began cooking.

"Are you going to get in here with that food before morning?" he hollered again.

"I'm coming with it!" I said. "Be patient!"

Once his stomach was filled, he settled down and my sisters left.

I had decided at the hospital that I'd stay the night with him, and I'm so thankful I did. Dad reminisced about his life as a kid, how he loved visiting with the Elliot sisters. These were three well-educated and wealthy maiden ladies who had lived near my dad's childhood home in Fayette. They were the first on the peninsula to own a car. He said that many times when they saw the sisters coming down the road in their car, all work came to a halt. He and his siblings would run to the road to watch them go by, marveling at the car as they went by.

Dad continued reminiscing into the earliest hours of the new day. He told about his journey to Kentucky to go see John when he'd learned about the accident John had been in. "It was cold in Kentucky. The family housing they put Gordon, Luke and me in was none too comfortable. I couldn't wait to be home and stoke the fire to get warm. But when John and I got home, the oil heater was out and the water lines were all frozen up. How terrible it must have been for John, being hurt and all, and then to come home to all that crap. It took over two days to get everything thawed and working. But, I did my best," he said.

"Yes, you did, Dad," I told him, and then I took the opportunity to say something that I'd always wanted to say to him. "It must have been so hard for you after Mom died, being left with all of us to take care of."

Dad raised his shoulders, lifted his hands, palms up, and said, "I just did what I had to do."

Eight days later Dad slipped into a semi-comatose state. Mark slept with him during this time, lying right next to Dad throughout the night to be there should he need something. On his final full day of life, my sisters and I all got up on his bed and sat around him. We sang "daddy" songs to him, like, "Oh My Papa" and Donna Fargo's "Daddy Dumpling." We were all holding our own until Mark stepped into the room and started singing "That Silver Haired Daddy of Mine." Immediately we broke down into tears.

The following day God took Dad home to be with Mama. He had a beautiful send off. Here is a song/poem that I'd written for my dad years earlier that I recited at his funeral.

He Ain't no Mother Teresa, but he is a Father John

He ain't no Mother Teresa
But he is a Father John.
Who raised eleven kids on a heartache
Still missing his heavenly love.
Death was all around him
From the tears to the dirty clothes
There were no apple pies to smell
And no more hugs from Rose.
As the years went by Father John tried
But found it hard to make ends meet.
Reluctantly he'd turned down the heat
While he stood in shame
Cause his kids had little to eat

The nights were cold
But Father John told them stories
To keep them warm
As he tucked them in
He reminded them to say their prayers
Unto the Lord

There were times he felt so consumed
By oh so many fears
So to hide the tears he'd head to town
To have a couple of beers
I was told that he would go
Right to the jukebox to play his song
Of the Seven Spanish Angels
The ones that would take him home.

No, he ain't no Mother Teresa
But he is my Father John.

Donna Jean Pomeroy

Siblings Today
ରଷ

Matthew James is sixty-eight and is still active in his auto salvage business and, in fact, he just put up a new sign today! He remained single and is the family joke teller.

Mark Harold and Sandy have six living children: Kim, Harold, Julie, Lisa, Jennifer and Joseph. Their son John died at birth. Mark adores his sixteen grandchildren and two great-grand children. Since retiring, he's been tinkering in woodcrafts.

Luke John has three sons, although Paul is in heaven. He was killed in a car accident when he was twenty-one. His oldest son John has given him his six grandchildren, who love doing things with their grandpa. Luke works with his youngest son Mark in the asphalt business.

John Joseph and wife Annette live in Lemont, Ill. They have two daughters, Theresa and April. John spends a lot of his time with his five grandchildren. He especially loves following their sports activities, as sports have always been a passion of his.

Sarah Connie has one son, Dennis. She spends as much time as possible with her three granddaughters and a grandson. They are blest to have her for a grandma.

Bernadette Jeanine and Terry have been married 37 years and have spent nearly the same amount of time in the food industry, mainly Subway franchises. They have three sons, Brad, Chad and Ryan. Bernadette, too, loves spending time with her five grandchildren.

Donna Jean — my hubby and I have four sons: Wellyn, Colin, Ashley and Levi. We both enjoy our two grandsons, Brendan and Aiden. Soon we'll be blest with two more grandchildren and hopefully many more, although I'm sure we'll never catch up to Grandma Jacques. When she died at age 97, she had 252 grandchildren! This count included her great-grandchildren and great-great-grandchildren.

Catherine Darla and husband Jack have two children. Their daughter Jessica made them proud when she graduated with high honors from Princeton. Their son Jason loves to play guitar.

Anna Jacqueline has worked for over twenty-five years at the local paper mill. Her daughter Janell has given Anna her only grandchild, whom she has nicknamed Chunky Monkey. Wyatt is a big boy now, but at birth only weighed 2 lb., 1 oz.

Monica Mary and husband Mike have two daughters, Mari and Miranda and a son Michael. Monica loves spending time with her two grandchildren Kali and Trenton. She works as a manager for Subway.

Jude Jacques like me, is an author. He writes mostly fiction. He is single and lives in beautiful Petoskey, Michigan. One of his favorite hobbies is traveling.

Donna Jean Pomeroy

(Clockwise top left) Catherine being held by Matthew, Mark, Luke, John, Bernadette (looking upward), Donna Jean and Sarah

Family home on Garden Peninsula

262

John holding Jude, Bernadette, Donna Jean holding Monica,
Anna, Catherine, Dad and Sarah at Jude's house

Donna Jean and Catherine at Prudential Building

Donna Jean Pomeroy

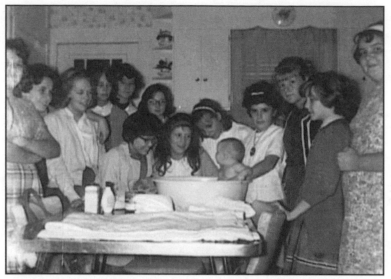

Home Economics class, Donna Jean center

Sarah, Terry, Bernadette, Donna Jean, Catherine, Anna and Monica

Faded Genes

Prom 1969

High school Graduation 1970

265

Luke taking Donna Jean to church on wedding day.

Wedding Day June 19, 1971

266

Catherine, Matthew, Anna, Mark, Monica, Luke, Dad, John, Sarah, Jude, Bernadette and Donna Jean in the dress I made, thanks to Aunt Celia's sewing lessons.

Dad loved when we called him "Father John"

From left to right my sons Ashley, Levi, Wellyn, Colin & my
wonderful husband at Levi's wedding

Grandchildren Brendan, 4 and a half and
Aiden, 18 months (Wellyn's sons)